Bodies of Peace

Bodies of Peace

Ecclesiology, Nonviolence, and Witness

Myles Werntz

Fortress Press
Minneapolis

BODIES OF PEACE

Ecclesiology, Nonviolence, and Witness

Cover design: Laurie Ingram

Cover image: Sloviansk, Donets Basin, Eastern Ukraine. © Sergei Grits/AP/Corbis

Library of Congress Cataloging-in-Publication Data is available

Print ISBN: 978-1-4514-8042-9

eBook ISBN: 978-1-4514-8946-0

The paper used in this publication meets the minimum requirements of American National Standard for Information Sciences — Permanence of Paper for Printed Library Materials, ANSI Z329.48-1984.

Manufactured in the U.S.A.

This book was produced using PressBooks.com, and PDF rendering was done by PrinceXML.

Contents

Acknowledgments

Writing a book of any kind is a solitary and sometimes mystical undertaking in which the author struggles to put intuitions into words and suspicions into cogent arguments. That said, the thinking and formation of these words and arguments cannot occur apart from what the book of Hebrews describes as a great cloud of witnesses. The book in hand began as a dissertation under the guidance of Barry Harvey at Baylor University; I thank him for his patience with endless drafts of chapters in search of theses and his encouragement to refine my arguments—answering some questions while widening the scope of others. In the fall of 2008, he suggested that I read William Stringfellow as a conversation partner for Yoder and Day, a suggestion for which I will always be grateful.

I wish to also thank other friends of this book for their formation and friendship along the way. On a trip to the archives of the Mennonite Church of America in Goshen, Indiana, with Paul Martens, the first intuitions of this dissertation came into view. Since that time—through hours of conversation on Yoder, nonviolence, and rock and roll—I have come to call him a mentor and a friend. Thanks to Jonathan Tran, who challenges me to read with charity and commitment, qualities I pray are manifest in this work and in future writings as well. Thanks are also due to Scott Moore and

Ralph Wood for their comments on the hopefully-never-retrieved dissertation version of this work and for their encouragement over the years.

This book was written in large part while teaching at George W. Truett Theological Seminary at Baylor University, under the leadership of David Garland and W. Dennis Tucker. I cannot possibly thank them enough for their attention to the formation of ministers of Jesus Christ and for the opportunity to teach seminarians, for whom the issues of this dissertation are fundamentally issues of Christian discipleship.

I am also grateful to Chris Moore, Chris Dodson, Will Williams, Claire Hein, Matt Porter, Brandon Frick, Jenny Howell, David Cramer, and countless others for the opportunity to wrestle with the matters in this book regarding both war and the church. Conversations, email exchanges, and critical readings by William T. Cavanaugh, Anthony Dancer, Daniel Bell, and Gerald Schlabach greatly strengthened my work. The 2010 Seminar in Christian Scholarship at Calvin College on war and religion in American history, directed by Harry Stout, provided time and space to think more deeply alongside historians about the claims of this book.

Our lives are hopefully more than the sum of our writing. Calvary Baptist Church of Waco, Texas, has been my home for ten years, during which time I have learned what it means to commit oneself to the body of Christ in times of joy, fidelity, and struggle. The love and support of my parents, David and Kathy Werntz, continues to be a source of joy and delight; their support remains constant. Without the friendship of Kevin Still these last fifteen years, life would be far less rich—less full of laughter, literature, and God. Thanks beyond words and measure go to my wife, Sarah Martin-Werntz, whom I met at the beginning of this work and married in 2009. She is the reason I continue writing on discouraging days and the reason I stop writing to come home on good ones. Just after this book was completed, we welcomed our son Eliot. The birth of a child, as any parent will attest, puts our vaunted ideas and commitments under scrutiny; as a theologian, I find myself thinking about these issues now more concretely than ever because of him. I dedicate this book to Eliot, not because I believe that war will cease in his lifetime, but in the hope that he will belong to a church that knows how to bear witness to Christ in the midst of wars and rumors of wars.

Introduction: Ecclesiology, Nonviolence, and the Claims of War

For many years, the relationship between war and Christianity was relatively invisible to me. In my hometown of Shreveport, Louisiana, the world's largest arsenal of B-52 bombers cast a large economic and political shadow over the region as one of its largest employers; bombers from the base have played significant roles in every major foreign conflict since World War I.[1] The relation between military force and church celebration was underscored by the familiar scene of military personnel in dress uniform and the singing of patriotic hymns in church worship on the Fourth of July and Memorial Day. I do not recount this to damn my upbringing or to call into question the devotion of members of the military, who are also members of my home church and my own family. If anything, I offer this observation as a description of this book: the relationship between churches and war—particularly for those churches who choose to witness against war—is complex and difficult; it must begin from the midst of the church's embeddedness within a culture linked to war.

1. "2D Bomb Wing Fact Sheet," Barksdale Air Force Base, posted April 10, 2014, http://www.barksdale.af.mil/library/factsheets/factsheet.asp?id=16244.

For me, as for many of my generation, this complicated relationship revealed itself on September 11, 2001, when an early morning seminary class was interrupted by an office administrator delivering news that would shape both the moral imagination and political life of America for the next decade. In the wake of national deliberations involving the use of force in Iraq and Afghanistan, it became painfully apparent to me that despite my theological training, war and military life were not pursuits that I had ever considered in relation to Christian witness. Waco, Texas, where I received my seminary training, is located less than an hour from Fort Hood, the largest military installation in North America. The Veteran's Administration building, which serves the central Texas area, employs a large number of people; L-3 Communications—an engineering firm and another of the area's largest employers—specializes in military vehicle modifications and surveillance.[2] As the smoke settled after 2001, these aspects of the city I had grown to love became visible to me in increasingly dissonant ways.

I present these anecdotal scenes to illustrate the foregrounding of this book: Christian arguments against participation in war originate in the midst of cultures deeply implicated by war. *How* churches bear witness against war, however, is a different question. For those living in Shreveport or Killeen, offering a witness takes a more direct form—in conversation and in relationship to military installations; for those in Waco, it means recognizing the more subtle ways in which the church remains connected to acts of war.

Churches that see themselves as free from complicity because of their non-participation in war suffer from myopia in this respect, viewing non-cooperation with the state to be a sufficient witness.

2. "L-3 Integrated Systems Background," L-3 Integrated Systems, http://www2.l-3com.com/is/isBackground.html.

The majority of Christian nonviolent responses to war continue to operate in this frame: witness to the state.[3] By viewing the state as the focus of witness, non-participation in the state's actions become the predominant mode of witness; this response—the refusal to go to war— while significant, neglects two important considerations. First, it neglects the ways in which churches are culturally bound to wars in ways that do not correspond to direct state participation, and second, it limits our vision of the plurality of ways in which the church might live out its witness against war.[4]

3. The ways in which advocacy against violence is articulated depend upon the framework that one sees as responsible for violence or most capable of ending violence. This assumption, however, will shape the kind of response that is possible in the future, often leaving those who challenge war with an impoverished imagination. See Judith Butler, *Frames of War: When Is Life Grievable?* (London: Verso, 2009). Modern documents emphasizing the value of nonviolence have, by and large, been framed with the sovereign authority of the state in view. See in particular, Vatican Council II, *Gaudium et Spes* [Dogmatic Constitution on the Church in the Modern World], July 12, 1965: sec. 77–78; United States Conference of Catholic Bishops, *The Challenge of Peace: God's Promise and Our Response, A Pastoral Letter on War and Peace by the National Conference of Catholic Bishops*, May 3, 1983, http://www.usccb.org/upload/challenge-peace-gods-promise-our-response-1983.pdf. Conversations about the national draft and conscientious objection have likewise assumed this form. See Charles C. Moskos and John Whiteclay Chambers, ed., *The New Conscientious Objection: From Sacred to Secular Resistance* (Oxford: Oxford University Press, 1993).

   Anthony Lang, "Authority and the Problem of Non-State Actors," in Eric Heinze and Brent Steele, *Ethics, Authority, and War: Non-State Actors and the Just War Tradition* (New York: Palgrave-Macmillan, 2009): 47–72. Rightly, the ways in which traditional categories of thinking about war will continue to be upended. The emergence of categories such as "cyberwar" alongside non-state actors as increasingly capable perpetrators of political violence continue to stretch the framework of traditional categories of war, built largely upon the assumption that state sovereigns alone have the authority to declare wars. As Stephen L. Carter, *The Violence of Peace* (New York: Beast Books, 2011) observes, one of the fundamental questions for the Obama Adminstration is how to name and deal with violence perpetrated not by sovereign nations but by these non-state actors. As Carter argues, the language of terrorism arises in the vacuum created by non-state political violence (78ff). This issue has caused tangible effects on war; in a recent report, the much vaunted B-52s from Shreveport (which contributed substantially to the Persian Gulf War in the 1990s) have seen their flight times reduced in scope, in part, to reflect the changing nature of war). In an age when an increasing number of military activities occur in insurgency situations, the aggressive appearance of the B-52 is no longer a priority. See "A New Tomorrow," Barksdale Air Force Base, posted May 23, 2013, http://www.barksdale.af.mil/news/story.asp?id=123349882.

4. This trend is not limited to pacifists such as Hauerwas; in Nigel Biggar's recent book, *In Defence of War* (Oxford: Oxford University Press, 2013), the chapter titled "Against Christian Pacifism" is devoted solely to the work of Stanley Hauerwas, John Howard Yoder, and Richard

The proliferation of war in various and new forms provides a providential opening for Christians who desire to think about the possibilities of nonviolent resistance in a significant way. Contemporary ambiguity about both the actors and the means of war offers Christians an opportunity to reclaim a way of thinking about nonviolent witness against war that proceeds first from ecclesiological logic; the way in which Christians engage their neighbors—particularly their international neighbors—need not be driven fundamentally by making their witness known to the state, particularly in an age when wars are conducted in an increasingly irregular fashion.[5] For Christians to have something to say, they must consider who they have been most fundamentally called to be: a people joined together in Christ. The claim that Christians begin their witness against war from an ecclesiological center is nothing new; in recent years, this claim has been repeated most frequently by John Howard Yoder and Stanley Hauerwas in a variety of ways. I want to build upon this claim here, to show that the connection between ecclesiology and nonviolent witness against war exists in more than one way. Through an examination of Mennonite, Roman Catholic, Episcopalian, and Presbyterian ecclesiological traditions, I hope to make known the ways in which Christians who understand themselves as the body of Christ can be involved in shaping nonviolent responses to war.

Hays—who for all intents and purposes represent one mode of how churches bear witness against war. I have argued elsewhere that Yoder and Hauerwas's vision of the relation between church and nonviolence needs to be distinguished in a way that Biggar tends to conflate, but this is a conversation for another day. See Matthew Porter and Myles Werntz, "On 'Seeing' Nonviolence in 1983: Nonviolence and Ecclesiology in Hauerwas and Yoder," *Conrad Grebel Review* (2011): 32–45.

5. "Irregular" wars designate wars that occur between state entities and non-state actors. See Robert M. Cassidy, "Counterinsurgency and Military Culture: State Regulars Versus Non-State Irregulars," *Baltic Security & Defense Review* 10 (2008): 53–85; George R. Lucas, Jr., "'New Rules for New Wars' in International Law and Just War Doctrine for Irregular War," *Case Western Reserve Journal of International Law* 43 (2011): 677–705.

In part, the burden of my argument lies in stating why I believe these are not necessarily competitive forms but the work of the same Spirit for the benefit of the church's unity and the good of the world. War's plurality occasions a new opportunity for the church to consider the ways in which resistance to war can flourish in new and surprising possibilities. I intend to work out the logic of these positions as clearly as possible in order that a fuller picture of the ecclesial possibilities for nonviolent witness against war might appear.

The Scope of the Argument

In this book, I will not attempt to analytically defend the virtues of nonviolence, as a variety of other books have taken up such a task.[6] While worthwhile, this debate tends to function as if war or nonviolence were things independent of time and space. I will also not provide an analytic account concerning nonviolence in an abstract sense, insofar as nonviolence—defined as a practice that refuses to resort to violence to oppose war, issuing forth from a people gathered before God—does not exist apart from enactment by those people in particular times and place.[7] Throughout this book, I

6. For example, see the recently published *The Ethics of Nonviolence: Essays by Robert L. Holmes*, ed. Predrag Cicovacki (London: Bloomsbury Academic, 2013) and Dustin Ells Howes, *Toward a Credible Pacifism: Violence and the Possibilities of Politics* (Albany: State University of New York Press, 2009). Howes, for example, ultimately concludes that pacifism "offers a reaffirmation, and a realistic view of human freedom that does not depend upon institutions for its preservation," (180) meaning that pacifism is ultimately affirmed by thinking clearly about our natural interactions with others apart from an a prioripresumption, which would need an account of humanity created by God to be coherent. Within theology, examples of this include David L. Clough and Brian Siltner, *Faith and Force: A Christian Debate about War* (Washington D.C.: Georgetown University Press, 2007).

7. In Oliver O'Donovan, *The Just War Revisited* (Cambridge: Cambridge University Press, 2003), for example, nonviolence is described as prevented from speaking in public, belonging to the "philosophy of transcendence, the *via negative*," which "circumscribe the possibility of action in the world" (10). By this, he means that nonviolence names a negative stance regarding war, though not one that permits constructive engagement. In doing so, O'Donovan describes nonviolence as a singularity, ignoring the varieties of theologically motivated pacifism, which are not all derived from this atemporal, eschatological premise.

will be describing Christian nonviolent resistance to war as a form of witness to the reconciling work of God in Christ born out in public life; insofar as one cannot witness except by enacting that testimony, nonviolence (as a form of witness) cannot be described as an ahistorical concept without diminishing its theological status as an act of obedience performed by Christians operating out of particular ecclesial frameworks.[8]

Traditionally, pacifism encompasses the concept of nonviolent war resistance, but I will not be using the term *pacifism* here for three reasons. First, in common usage, pacifism most often refers to a principled objection to war resulting in a withdrawal or refusal to participate in war.[9] Second, *pacifism*, as defined by Richard Miller and others, is an absolutist position that refuses involvement in any and all wars.[10] While this description may be appropriate for Yoder and Day, it is problematic for Stringfellow and McAfee Brown. Early in his life, Stringfellow counseled youths to join the army and (while embracing nonviolence later in life) refused to rule out the possibility of Christian involvement in acts of violence.[11] Likewise, as a proponent of liberation theology, Brown supported the use of violence in certain limited circumstances but increasingly considered

8. For works that treat *nonviolence* as a transhistorical concept, see Mark Kurlansky, *Nonviolence: The History of a Dangerous Idea* (Modern Library: New York, 2006); David Cortright, *Peace: A History of Movements and Ideas* (Cambridge: Cambridge University Press, 2008).
9. See John Howard Yoder, *Nevertheless: Varieties of Religious Pacifism* (Scottdale, PA: Herald, 1971); Peter Brock, *Liberty and Conscience: A Documentary History of the Experiences of Conscientious Objectors in America through the Civil War* (Oxford: Oxford University Press, 2002); with Nigel Young, *Pacifism in the Twentieth Century* (Syracuse, NY: Syracuse University Press, 1999). Manifold varieties of pacifism certainly proceed in ways other than simple withdrawal, though the absolutist refusal characterizes the majority trajectory. Cf., Richard B. Miller, *Interpretations of Conflict: Ethics, Pacifism, and the Just-War Tradition* (Chicago: The University of Chicago Press, 1991).
10. Ibid., 12. Miller's definition of pacifism includes "building harmonious relations, reducing tensions," and "developing pacifist virtues," but these are built on "the moral prohibition of war."
11. William Stringfellow, *An Ethic for Christians and Other Aliens in a Strange Land* (Waco, TX: Word Books, 1973), 130–33.

participation in war to be incompatible with Christian witness.[12] Third, though the term *pacifism* is appropriate for Yoder and Day, this designation—as Richard Miller's definition suggests—easily obscures the nuances of their work by reducing their opposition to war to an ideological position abstracted from issues of political judgment and temporal enactment. In sum, whereas *pacifism* tends to more popularly describe an abstraction, I will use *nonviolence* or *nonviolent resistance* to name a posture of discipleship, a response to God by witnesses of the church.

Specifically, I will use the term *nonviolent resistance* and *nonviolence* interchangeably to refer to an opposition to war that does not seek bodily harm or loss of life in its tactics and that seeks, by its actions, to offer a positive vision of creaturely life. Specifically, I will describe what nonviolent resistance to war might comprise if—as I suggested above—ecclesiology shapes this act of discipleship. If Christians act in witness as members of the church, then moral action by Christians cannot ultimately be described apart from the way in which belonging to the church colors and shapes these actions. To do this, I will examine four practitioners during the Vietnam War who not only wrote against resisting war via nonviolent practices and tactics but who also saw this action, in various ways, as a way of bearing witness to the reconciling work of Jesus Christ, understood proleptically through the worship, doctrine, and practice of the gathered church of Jesus Christ. During the era of the Vietnam War, many well-documented resisters came to prominence as the anti-war movement gained traction—a phenomenon that had not occurred previously in the history of the United States.[13] I argue that

12. Robert McAfee Brown, *Liberation Theology: An Introductory Guide* (Louisville: Westminster John Knox, 1993).
13. For histories of the popular resistance of Vietnam and analysis of the manifold forms that protest took during this era, see Joel P. Rhodes, *The Voice of Violence: Performative Violence as Protest in the Vietnam Era* (Westport, CN: Praeger, 2001); Stephen A. Kent, *From Slogans to Mantras:*

what makes the work of these four unique is the inextricability of nonviolent resistance to war from ecclesiology, of peace in the world from the life of the church.

Christian theology offers a variety of responses to war, though nonviolent resistance constitutes a minority position within the broader theological spectrum.[14] In this book, I have chosen to examine nonviolent responses to war for two reasons. First, while personally persuaded by the arguments for nonviolence, I find that discussions of Christian nonviolence suffer from a great deal of conceptual clarity. Often, writings on nonviolence either rely upon tired rhetorical tropes or emotive appeals, which evaporate upon examination or collapse a number of theological practitioners into a singular position. Second, a number of philosophical and political accounts of nonviolence exist that are perfectly coherent apart from Christian faith; the lack of clarity among much contemporary writing on Christian nonviolence is partly to blame here, I think. It is my hope that a more thorough account concerning the ways in which Christian nonviolent resistance to war can become an embodied practice, inseparable from the context and contours of ecclesial life, might help remedy this situation.

Social Protest and Religious Conversion in the Late Vietnam War Era (Syracuse, NY: Syracuse University Press, 2001); Michael S. Foley, *Confronting the War Machine: Draft Resistance during the Vietnam War* (Chapel Hill: University of North Carolina Press, 2003); Walter L. Hixson, ed., *The Vietnam Antiwar Movement* (New York: Garland, 2000); Robert Buzzanco, *Masters of War: Military Dissent and Politics in the Vietnam Era* (New York: Cambridge University Press, 1996); George Q. Flynn, *The Draft, 1940–1973* (Lawrence: University of Kansas Press, 1993); Charles M. Bedenedetti, *An American Ordeal: The Antiwar Movement of the Vietnam Era* (Syracuse, NY: Syracuse University Press, 1990); Lawrence M. Baskir, *Chance and Circumstance: The Draft, the War, and the Vietnam Generation* (New York: Knopf, 1978).

14. For surveys of the various Christian understandings of war and peace, see Roland H. Bainton, *Christian Attitudes toward War and Peace: A Historical Survey and Critical Re-Evaluation* (Nashville: Abingdon, 1979). Bainton's survey has been modified and updated by a number of works, including John Howard Yoder, *Christian Attitudes to War, Peace, and Revolution* (Elkhart, IN: Mennonite Co-op Bookstore, 1983); Lisa S. Cahill, *Love Your Enemies* (Minneapolis: Fortress Press, 1994); Arthur F. Holmes, *War and Christian Ethics: Classic and Contemporary Readings on the Morality of War* (Grand Rapids: Baker Academic, 2005).

For the figures under consideration here, nonviolent resistance to war was inseparable from how this witness was shaped by ecclesial traditions and the ways in which nonviolence pushed back against certain aspects of those traditions. *Ecclesiology*, as I will be referring to it, consists of the structures, practices, and presuppositions that facilitate the gathering of the body of people joined together in Christ—the church. For the subjects of this book, nonviolent resistance to war is one practice that bears witness to the new social life, which Christ makes possible. This relationship does not form a one-way street. As I will show, the practices and structures of the church can provide resources for thinking about nonviolent resistance to war, though the practice of nonviolent resistance sometimes comes into conflict with certain ecclesiological presuppositions.

As Luke Bretherton points out, ecclesiology consists not only of the ways in which the churches negotiate their relationship to the world for the sake of witness but also how these churches serve as the context for responding to events that affect both them and their neighbors in various times and places; not surprisingly, the relation between the church's structures and its modes of witness do not always harmonize well.[15] Likewise, for the figures of this book, the practice of nonviolent resistance to war works both *in concert with* the practices of the church, being formed and shaped by churchly life, and *in tension with* them. I do not take the latter movement—pitting a theologically articulated act of nonviolence against forms of ecclesial life—to negate the connection between nonviolence and

15. Luke Bretherton's recent work, *Christianity and Contemporary Politics* (Malden, MA: Wiley-Blackwell, 2010), 21, makes this point most potently when he writes that "any attempt to arrive at a definitive classification not only ignores changes in historical context but also the dynamic relationship between the prior actions of Christ and different dimensions of society whereby Christ's Lordship comes to be exercised in different degrees over different aspect of society at different times. Accordingly, Christians need to develop the ability to improvise faithfully in response to Christ within a variety of different political environments."

ecclesiology. When the practice of nonviolence exceeded the current imagination of church practices, these figures did not view this as a reason to abandon ecclesial life; rather, the disconnect between the practice and confession provided them with an opportunity to spur the body of Christ on to more faithful theological reflection.

In the background of these ecclesiological considerations, I will discuss how the church figures into God's sustaining of human life—in other words, how to think of the church within the larger divine economy. For these figures, describing the nature of the church vis-à-vis the question of war necessarily involves reflecting upon the place of the church in a shared world; insofar as these figures understood the church to provide a vision of social life counter to the agonistic practices of war, an examination of the church's nature as a body of witness within a larger theological economy in which God upholds and sustains creation will be integral to these discussions.[16]

Connecting Nonviolence and Ecclesiology

This historical connection between nonviolent resistance to war and ecclesiology has been described in histories of both Mennonites and Roman Catholics, but the theological rationale for the union between ecclesiology and nonviolent resistance to war is often underexplored in these works.[17] Interestingly, the contemporary revival of constructive thinking about war in relation to ecclesial practices and presuppositions originated with the "just war" proponents.[18] Oliver

16. I am aware that, in highlighting this, I am stepping into a larger body of literature concerning social ontology, which I see as important but not the direct concern of this work. The debates concerning the social ontology of the church, therefore, will be adjunct concerns for this work and emphasized only as needed.
17. Cf. Ronald G. Musto, *The Catholic Peace Tradition*, (Maryknoll, NY: Orbis Books, 1986); Perry Bush, *Two Kingdoms, Two Loyalties: Mennonite Pacifism in Modern America* (Baltimore: Johns Hopkins University Press, 1998).
18. This ecclesial recovery can be seen most specifically through the work of Daniel M. Bell, *Just War as Christian Discipleship: Recentering the Tradition in the Church rather than the State* (Grand Rapids: Brazos, 2009). Other works that seek to critically interrogate the just war tradition

O'Donovan's argument concerning Christian approval of war, for example, rests upon the church's place within the larger economy of God's providence; according to this model, political judgments on war are considered the rightful domain of the nation, and the church serves as a witness to the nation's agents of judgment.[19] In a different way, recent work by Daniel M. Bell has sought to resituate just war as an ecclesial discipline rather than a deliberation abdicated to the state.

But with regards to nonviolence, a number of recent writings have in fact argued for the separation of nonviolence and contemporary ecclesiology. For example, Nigel Biggar's recent critique of Richard Hays's work argues that a public/private divide in Paul's writings allows for Christian involvement in war without compromising the church's witness.[20] Other arguments for distance between nonviolence and ecclesiology argue that even if a rejection of participation in war was normative in patristic writings, such a prohibition cannot be absolutely normative for contemporary churches.[21] More fundamentally, others contend that because the

theologically, though not necessarily through the lens of ecclesiology, are Mark Allman, *Who Would Jesus Kill?: War, Peace, and the Christian Tradition* (Winon, MN: St. Mary's Press, 2008); Daniel C. Maguire, *The Horrors We Bless: Rethinking the Just-War Legacy* (Minneapolis: Fortress Press, 2007); Gary M. Simpson, *War, Peace, and God* (Minneapolis: Fortress Press, 2007); and, preeminently, Oliver O'Donovan, *The Just War Revisited* (Cambridge University Press, 2003). Other recent and significant modern analysis of the just war theory or just war tradition through the lens of Christian theology include James Turner Johnson, *Just War Tradition and the Restraint of War* (Princeton: Princeton University Press, 1981); Paul Ramsey, *The Just War* (New York: Scribner's, 1969).

19. Oliver O'Donovan, *The Desire of Nations: Recovering the Roots of Political Theology* (Cambridge: Cambridge University Press, 1995), 132–44. Cf. Bell, *Just War*, for a more fulsome analysis of the connection between ecclesiology and just war.
20. Nigel Biggar, "Specify and Distinguish! Interpreting the New Testament on 'Non-Violence,'" *Studies in Christian Ethics* 22, no. 2 (January 2009): 164–84. Richard Hays's response appears as "Narrate and Embody: A Response to Nigel Biggar 'Specify and Distinguish,'" *Studies in Christian Ethics* 22, no. 2 (January 2009): 185–98. Cf. Richard Hays, *The Moral Vision of the New Testament* (New York: HarperOne, 1996), 317–46.
21. Bell, *Just War*, 29. Bell seeks to put the onus of reviving the just war back on the churches but disagrees that nonviolence is always normative for Christians. Concerning this continuing debate about the roots of Christian participation in war, see George Kalantzis, *Ceasar and the Lamb: Early Christian Attitudes on War and Military Service* (Eugene, OR: Cascade Books,

church is caught in an ambiguity between total rejection and total affirmation of power, Christians must exercise power in ways that are often not commensurate with the Gospel.[22]

In contrast to those who maintain that nonviolence need not be intrinsic to ecclesiology, a corresponding ecclesiological trend can be found that, while recognizing peaceability as a prime characteristic of ecclesiology, does not draw the connection between this characteristic of the church and the church's response to war. In these works, emphasis is placed upon the peaceable ontology intrinsic to the Christian *ecclesia*, focusing on the reconciliation that has been accomplished by God for humanity.[23] Broadly, these proposals are concerned with articulating the internal life of the church as a body of peace but accomplish this independently of what it might mean to bear witness to peace in the the great violence of war.

Finally, a number of accounts contend that Christian nonviolence does not require a consideration of ecclesiology.[24] In the last twenty

2012), which continues the debates begun by Adolf von Harnack, *Militia Christi: The Christian Religion and the Military in the First Three Centuries,* trans. David M. Gracie (Philadelphia: Fortress Press, 1981) and Louis J. Swift, *The Early Fathers on War and Military Service* (Wilmington, DE: Michael Glazier, 1983), among others.

22. Stephen Sykes, *Power and Christian Theology* (London: Continuum, 2006), 116–17: "Christians have a particular way of living in the world of powers, to which the key concept is that of sacrifice. That by no means resolves the ambivalence of power. The ambivalence remains because, on the contrary, the essential resource for speaking of the sacrifice of Christ is the particular collection of narratives we possess in the New Testament . . . moreover, both the doctrine of sacrifice and ritual of Eucharistic sacrifice lend themselves to abuse; because they participate in the world of power they share its ambivalence." As Oliver O'Donovan, frames it, nonviolence tends to import an eschatological conflict in history and, in doing so, "shortchanges the ethical task of describing a witness that takes form within the conditions of the world" (*Just War Revisited*, 11).

23. While this has been articulated in a variety of ways, the most notable modern figure advocating "ontological peace" of the church is John Milbank, *Theology and Social Theory* (Malden, MA: Wiley-Blackwell, 1993). Milbank, in particular, has been criticized for not drawing the connection between his "original peace" ontology and acts of nonviolence. Cf., Paul G. Doerksen, "For and Against Milbank: A Critical Discussion of John Milbank's Construal of Ontological Peace," *Conrad Grebel Review* 18 (Winter 2000): 48-59; Gerald W. Schlabach, "Is Milbank Niebuhrian Despite Himself?," *Conrad Grebel Review* 23 (Spring 2005): 33–40; Chris K. Huebner, "What Should Mennonites and Milbank Learn from Each Other?," *Conrad Grebel Review* 23 (Spring 2005): 9–18.

years, a great deal of literature has emerged that refers to the "spirituality" of nonviolence, arguing (with some variance) that nonviolence is a matter of personal spiritual disposition.[25] The most common approach here attempts to speak of a "spirituality of nonviolence" based on the divine life; such arguments depend upon the character of God as a nonviolent reconciler of humanity but often do not extend this argument to include the ways and means by which this witness is incorporated in the life of the church. This approach, seen most prominently in the work of Walter Wink and J. Denny Weaver, rests upon identifying the inner life of God as nonviolent but does not sufficiently address the role of the church in this witness.[26]

Among those who *do* connect nonviolence to ecclesiology, it is not always evident that theology gives nonviolence much more than a set of practices or moral justifications, pragmatic justifications that could be easily sought elsewhere. Such proposals emphasize nonviolence as an effective ethical act that does not require a theological economy or the church as a tactical resource that can be leveraged for political purposes.[27] The recent Just Peacemaking movement, which

24. In particular, see Paul Valliere, "The Spirituality of War," *Union Seminary Quarterly Review* 38 (1983): 5–14; John Macquarrie, *The Concept of Peace* (New York: Harper and Row, 1973).

25. Grady Scott Davis, *Warcraft and the Fragility of Virtue* (Moscow, ID: University of Idaho Press, 1992), 27–51, describes pacifism in this fashion. One of the most promising examples of this approach—Michael Battle's *Blessed Are the Peacemakers* (Macon, GA: Mercer University Press, 2004)—assumes the framework of ecclesiology for articulating a spirituality of nonviolence. For Battle, cultivating the "spirituality of nonviolence" means witnessing to the overflowing abundance of the Trinitarian life, but he does not discuss this in regard to nonviolent resistance at any great length.

26. See Weaver, "Violence in Christian Theology," *Crosscurrents* 51 (Summer 2001): 150–76 and "Forgiveness and (Non)Violence: The Atonement Connections," *Mennonite Quarterly Review* 83 (April 2009): 319–47. Walter Wink makes a similar argument for nonviolence on the basis of intra-Trinitarian life in *Engaging the Powers: Discernment and Resistance in a World of Domination* (Philadelphia: Fortress Press, 1992), 210–65. This approach is also seen in John Dear, *The God of Peace: Toward a Theology of Nonviolence* (Maryknoll, NY: Orbis Books, 1994).

27. Classic works in this vein include Richard Gregg, *The Power of Nonviolence* (Philadelphia: J.B. Lippincott, 1934), a work that introduced the English-speaking world to the work of Mohandas Gandhi and was influential for Martin Luther King, Jr. Also important for this approach are the

emphasizes practices that have been empirically shown to reduce warfare, is a good example.[28] This approach "bases its ethics instead on what practices are actually proving to decrease the number of wars in real history" and seeks to be "realistic in the sense that it focuses on what in fact works to prevent wars in real history, based on empirical reality."[29] While practical nonviolence retains a long history, describing Christian nonviolence in this fashion renders the theological roots of the movement—Christian or otherwise—irrelevant to the ways in which nonviolence relates to a larger theological vision of God's work. By focusing on the practicality of this practice apart from the context that makes it intelligible, the origins of the practice are made secondary concerns. Additionally, it is unclear whether justifying nonviolence as a universally "practical" way to end wars is an empirically justifiable claim.[30]

works of Gene Sharp, including *The Politics of Nonviolent Action* (Boston: Porter Sargent, 1974) and *Nonviolent Action: A Research Guide* (New York: Garland, 1997).

More recent Christian works in this vein emphasize nonviolence as a practice of *imitatio Christi,* including John Dear, *Put Your Sword Down: Answering the Gospel Call to Nonviolence* (Grand Rapids: Eerdmans, 2008) and Robert Brimlow, *What about Hitler? Wrestling With Jesus' Call to Nonviolence in an Evil World* (Grand Rapids: Brazos, 2006). Materially, the difference between the former and the latter writings is not significant, with the exception that Christ remains the exemplar of ethical action in the latter.

28. Glen Stassen, ed., *Just Peacemaking: Ten Practices for Abolishing War* (Cleveland: Pilgrim, 1998). The subtitle, as Stassen clarifies in subsequent writings, was intended to be "a new paradigm" rather than the optimistic title attributed to it in "The Unity, Realism and Obligatoriness of Just Peacemaking," *Journal of the Society of Christian Ethics* 23, no. 1 (Spring–Summer 2003): 171–94. See my criticism of this paradigm in "War in Christ's World: Bonhoeffer and Just Peacemaking on War and Christology," *Dialog: A Journal of Theology* 50, no. 1 (2011): 90–96.
29. Stassen, *Just Peacemaking*, 11.
30. As Joseph Kosek notes in *Acts of Conscience: Christian Nonviolence and Modern American Democracy* (New York: Columbia University Press, 2009), nonviolent movements in protest to war (with the exception of the Vietnam Conflict) are small-scale and, in terms of democratic process, have very little impact upon the decision of nations to go to war. As Martin L. Cook argues in "Just Peacemaking: Challenges of Humanitarian Intervention," *Journal of the Society of Christian Ethics* 23, no. 1 (Spring–Summer 2003): 241–53, the Just Peacemaking movement would do better to view nonviolence as a tactic to be exercised aftermilitary acts rather than before.

The most common criticism levied against practical nonviolence, however, centers on the

While consideration must certainly be given to the practical aspects of nonviolence, I take Richard Hays's argument that "the *ekklesia* is a community set apart for a special vocation in the world" to be fundamentally correct in terms of how to view the church in regard to war: for the Christian, nonviolence is based not on its probability of success but on its nature as a means of witness to the work of God in Christ through the life of the church.[31] Considering nonviolence as bearing witness to a particular form of social existence lifts the burden of nonviolence to be "practical" or "effective"; the heart of nonviolence consists not in ending conflicts at any cost but in bearing witness to the coming kingdom of God.

In asserting this position, I am not retreating again into a theoretical account of nonviolence or arguing that those who refuse to participate in war are excused from the burden of accounting for the successes of violence or the failures of nonviolence. Rather, I contend that all four of the figures I will discuss bear witness to a social possibility that begins as a theological reality, to the extent that the act of nonviolence—as a social strategy—is derivative of and is a witness to the work of God. In theological terms, nonviolence is "effective" insofar as it bears witness to a social reality of which nonviolent resistance to war is the logical outworking.

fact that nonviolence depends upon the presence of violence (to make space for nonviolent practice). Reinhold Niebuhr powerfully argues this point in his essay, "Why the Christian Church Is Not Pacifist," in *The Essential Reinhold Niebuhr: Selected Essays and Addresses*, ed. Robert McAfee Brown (New Haven: Yale University, 1986). Cf. Ward Churchill, *Pacifism as Pathology* (Oakland: AK Press, 2007); Peter Gelderloos, *How Nonviolence Protects the State* (London: South End, 2007). Also see Jean Bethke Elshtain, *Just War against Terror: The Burden of American Power in a Violent World* (New York: Basic Books, 2003), 99–124; Davis, *Warcraft and the Fragility of Virtue*, 53–61.

31. Hays, "Narrate and Embody," 195. Hays goes on to say that Biggar's distinction between public and private commands for the Christian is rooted in a "moral discernment [that] takes place chiefly with reference to the realm of public political order rather than with reference to the *politeuma* of the people of God (Phil. 3:20)" (ibid.,198).

Moving Forward

In the first chapter, I will answer two important ground-clearing questions before proceeding to describe the plurality with which this ecclesially-informed witness occurred during the Vietnam Era. Specifically, I will address the larger questions concerning 1) how to think of the relationship between a church that desires to resist war and the war-sustained culture in which it exists, and 2) whether the diversityof nonviolent responses offered by churches in response to war inhibits their witness. To address these issues, I will argue that Augustine of Hippo's *City of God* portrays war not only as the drumbeat of creaturely life but also as a practice that permeates the temporal ground upon which churches live and breathe.[32] As Augustine rightly argues, churches cannot escape some form of response with regards to war because they benefit from the wars perpetuated by their countries; thus, no church (at least in the American context) is excused from thinking about this issue. As I will suggest, this is particularly true for churches who are persuaded by nonviolence, insofar as non-participation in war does not mean that there is nothing left to say or do.

Having called churches to honestly acknowledge their connection to cultures that sustain and are sustained by war, I will turn to the question of the church's divided witness in this area. Not all churches who bear witness against war will do so in the same way or out of the same theological and ecclesiological commitments. As Gerald Schlabach acutely observes, the persistent problem of war has become a church-dividing issue, even among pacifists.[33] For Schlabach, the

32. See also Michel Foucault's comment that war—far from being a rational activity that is separate from normal political life—is "the military procedure itself, in its ordinary durability . . . in short, the dissolution of the state of war and the military's infiltration into the movements of daily life," in Michel Foucault, *Security, Territory, and Population: Lectures at the College de France 1977–1978* (New York: Piacador, 2009), 35.

ecclesially-rooted nonviolent witness of the "historic peace churches" must be brought into conversation with other churches who do not hold this view so that the churches, as a whole, can speak with a single voice.[34]

I agree with Schlabach that war unnecessarily divides the church, and will offer a different way forward from Schlabach.[35] Drawing on the work of Dietrich Bonhoeffer, I will present an account of how diverse ecclesial approaches might be seen not as competitive options but as a common work of the Holy Spirit. For Bonhoeffer, the renewing work of the Spirit—who binds individuals together, unites churches, and contextualizes the work of Christ—does not gloss over the broken state of creation or the disunity of the churches

33. Schlabach has articulated Just Policing most clearly in "Just Policing: How War Could Cease to Be a Church-Dividing Issue," *Journal of Ecumenical Studies* 41, no. 3–4 (Summer–Fall 2004): 409–30. See also Schlabach, "Just Policing and the Reevalution of War in a Less Divided Church," in *Just Policing, Not War: An Alternative Response to World Violence*, ed. Gerald Schlabach (Collegeville, MN: Liturgical, 2007); cf. Stanley Hauerwas and Samuel Wells, "Breaking Bread: Peace and War," *Blackwell Companion to Christian Ethics*, ed. Stanley Hauerwas and Samuel Wells (Malden, MA: Blackwell, 2004), 360–75. The ecumenical impulse central to Just Policing has been expanded in other volumes, particularly *The Fragmentation of the Church and Its Unity in Peacemaking*, ed. Jeffrey Gros and John D. Rempel (Grand Rapids: Eerdmans, 2001) and Fernando Enns, *The Peace Church and the Ecumenical Community: Ecclesiology and the Ethics of Nonviolence* (Kitchener, ON: Pandora, 2007). This approach has not been without its critics. See Matthew John Paul Tan, *Justice, Unity and the Hidden Christ: The Theopolitical Complex of the Social Justice Approach to Ecumenism in Vatican II* (Eugene, OR: Cascade Books, 2013).

34. In various Roman Catholic documents—most notably the Second Vatican Council's *Gaudium et Spes* and the National Conference of Catholic Bishops's *The Challenge of Peace*—both nonviolence and just war are described as defensible options for Catholics. For an affirmation of both options, see Tobias Winright, "The Liturgy as a Basis for Catholic Identity, Just War Theory, and the Presumption Against War," *Catholic Identity and the Laity*, ed. Tim Muldoon, Annual Publication of the College Theology Society 54.(Maryknoll, NY: Orbis Books, 2009), 134–51.

35. Schlabach argues that, at some level, certain church bodies must be willing to modify their absolute commitment against participation in war ("Just Policing and the Reevaluation of War," 3–19). In an age in which no single Christian voice emerges in the midst of a divided church, Schlabach's assumption that a single voice can give validity to both nonviolence and the possibility of violence remains problematic, insofar as the unity Schlabach proposes would involve placing denominations that cannot abide just war thought in a subsidiary place to those traditions that consider both options viable. See Thomas R. Neufeld Yoder, "Ecclesiology and Policing: Who Calls the Shots?," *Conrad Grebel Review* 26, no. 2 (Spring 2008): 91–101.

in their politics and witness. I argue that Bonhoeffer sees the common work of the Spirit in the churches as *proleptic* to the church's visible unity; as such, he is not threatened by the plurality of witness in these various traditions. In short, the Spirit's work in and through these bodies offers a common witness that can be read as a starting point for the recognition of theological unity and discussion concerning other doctrinal and ecclesiological divisions rather than an occasion for further ethical division.

Having sketched the place of churches within the world—bodies of witness (bound together by the Spirit) who must reckon with war's corrupting and sustaining presence in creation—I will begin to explore how ecclesially-informed witness might proceed in a variety of ways. In chapter 2, I begin the task by addressing one of the most well-known proponents of nonviolence from the twentieth century: John Howard Yoder. Here, I will argue that Yoder offers a vision of the church *as* a socially embodied alternative to war. For Yoder, God's life—made known to us through the acts of Jesus—narrates God's presence among us. I will argue that, for Yoder, nonviolence is Jesus' preeminent act because it relates both God's presence and the intended structure of the world. Following in the way of Jesus, the church engages in these Christologically authorized practices, which find their analogy in the larger society. As the church bears witness through its practice of nonviolence, it bears witness to the world of Christ's alternative to war: the church.

In chapter 3, I turn to the work of Dorothy Day, who, like Yoder, presents nonviolence as intrinsic to the logic of Roman Catholic ecclesiology. Unlike Yoder, however, Day emphasizes the way in which the church forms nonviolence, that nonviolence requires being formed by a charity which refuses to validate social divisions among persons. Arguing that all people are united through the "Mystical Body of Christ," Day sees Christ as the peaceable form, unity, and telos of all human life—a form made visible in and through the Roman Catholic communion. In other words, Christ's mystical body—which necessitates a rejection of violence—is known most fully in the Catholic Church, the visible telos of human social existence. While the practice of nonviolence is non-negotiable for Day, it is only one act among a nexus of practices by which a person's loves are formed and directed toward this end. Whereas Yoder's work emphasizes the church as the alternative to war, which necessitates that the church embody nonviolence, Day's work posits that the church is the telos of moral formation; nonviolence is one way among many by which people are formed in the love of God, moved toward the unity of Christ, and directed away from the disunity perpetuated by war.

In chapter 4, I introduce a lesser-known voice, powerful in his own day: William Stringfellow. Operating out of an Episcopal context, Stringfellow argues that Christ's work is effecting a renewal of all human existence, which Stringfellow names the "community of the resurrection". As Christ creates this community of redemption, the institutional church is drawn into the world, and the world is drawn into the church. This "community of the resurrection," known primarily by its resistance to the powers and principalities of death, leads Stringfellow to name nonviolent resistance to war as a practice that witnesses to what both church and world should be. Because Stringfellow relates the world and church through the work of the Word, the church is called into conversation with the Word's work in the world, participating in the resistance to death (i.e. resistance to war) that occurs outside of the church. For Stringfellow, the church helps name nonviolence as the act of the Word of God; the church is called not to lead in this work but simply to name what the Word is doing and participate in it.

In chapter 5, I approach the work of Robert McAfee Brown and CALCAV (Clergy and Laity Concerned about Vietnam). CALCAV emerged as a para-ecclesial body that advocated for the end of the Vietnam War on behalf of various denominations and faiths. As a public theologian and key member of the group, Brown connected the ecumenical impulse of unity found among the churches to the quest for unity on a sociopolitical level. In Brown, we find a different form of nonviolence that is neglected by the previous three thinkers: the relationship between ecclesially-rooted nonviolence and public policy. For Brown and CALCAV, nonviolence proceeds as an ecumenical consensus that brings the weight of the united churches together toward issues of common concern for both church and world. In sum, Brown's work offers an account of how the church can support nonviolence in public policy and arenas beyond the church. Rather than offering up the church as the nonviolent witness, Brown and CALCAV believe the church possesses material resources and theological wisdom—resources that led to wise policy initiatives designed to bring the Vietnam War to a close as expeditiously as possible.

In the conclusion, I will return to my initial claim that the various forms of nonviolent witness seen in these diverse figures does not present a set of mutually exclusive options but rather gesture in the direction of an ecumenical witness. Insofar as the Holy Spirit is the singular life of the church, the plurality of witness performed by these bodies of Christ does not constitute distinct options as much as they constitute facets of a singular witness. It is my hope that this work, in addition to clarifying the diverse Christian approaches of resistance to war, will articulate this ecumenical dimension of a Christian nonviolent witness: a witness to the One who is bringing the church into being not for its own sake but for the sake of witness to the reconciling work of Christ. As part of this work, the shared act of nonviolence across ecclesial borders becomes a foretaste of a more full ecumenical communion.

To provide a common context for reading these various witnesses together, I have chosen to examine their responses to the Vietnam War, though the work of Yoder, Day, and Brown extends far beyond Vietnam in both directions. In choosing these particular witnesses, I am not suggesting that they represent the only possibilities; the era of the Vietnam War was filled with voices whose work simply could not be related in this book without making it several hundred pages longer. Were I to expand this book, I would look most immediately to the work of Dr. Martin Luther King, Jr.—whose advocacy for the common good, including nonviolent opposition to war, was inextricable from the life of the local church—to Clarence Jordan (founder of the Koininia Farm in Americus, Georgia), or to the writings of Thomas Merton. I hope, in light of the method and framework presented here, that others might recover the work of these witnesses.

1

War, Church, and the Plurality of Witness

To begin our exploration on the ways in which ecclesiology sets the tone for nonviolent resistance to war, we must first deal with a direct and potentially problematic supposition: that churches doin fact live with war and benefit from societies that make war, regardless of their stance on the matter.[1] This supposition, I will argue, is a theological one, insofar as it claims the church—as Christ's body in the world—involves acknowledging the church's unity with the world as a part of creation, for the sake of the world. Prior to discussing how churches witness against war, we must first acknowledge the ways in which the lives of churches in the American

1. No single source exhaustively explores the relationship between American churches and American wars. Recent literature that surveys this dynamic includes Harry Stout, *Upon the Altar of the Nation: A Moral History of the American Civil War* (New York: Penguin Books, 2007); Jonathan H. Ebel, *Faith in the Fight: Religion and the American Soldier in the Great War* (Princeton: Princeton University Press, 2010); James P. Byrd, *Sacred Scripture, Sacred War: The Bible and the American Revolution* (New York: Oxford University Press, 2013); Andrew Peterson, *Sword of the Spirit, Shield of Faith: Religion in American War and Diplomacy* (New York: Random House, 2012); and Patricia Applebaum, *Kingdom to Commune: Protestant Pacifist Culture between World War I and the Vietnam Era* (Chapel Hill: University of North Carolina Press, 2009).

context are intertwined with the wars of their country as both material and cultural inheritors of these wars. As I will suggest, coming to terms with this reality is therapeutic for churches who see nonviolence as the church's vocation, insofar as acknowledging this interaction with the world allows them to recognize the ways in which witness is already possible.

In his provocative work, *The Complex*, Nick Turse highlights the ways in which the "military-industrial-complex" that President Eisenhower warned of has come to pass in ways that wildly exceed Eisenhower's expectations. As Turse points out, distancing oneself from involvement with or support of military ventures in America is nearly impossible because the suppliers who provide support and aid to military forces are now the same vendors who supply the vast majority of American groceries, fuel, housing, and entertainment.[2] What Turse details on the economic front also applies to the socio-political front due to the fact that American churches benefit from war, insofar as internal American political freedoms are enabled by what Andrew Bacevich describes as war's external projection of power.[3]

Avoiding purchases as well as cultural and material forms of support that directly aid the military does not release American Christians from acknowledging that all persons—regardless of direct agency—live within a society framed by its wars. Furthermore, the material benefits we now enjoy are due in part to past wars.[4] In

2. Nick Turse, *The Complex: How the Military Invades Our Everyday Life* (New York: Metropolitan Books, 2008), 1–47.

3. Andrew Bacevich, *Washington Rules: The Permanent Path to War* (New York: Metropolitan Books, 2010), 21–27.

4. Framing the question of Christian participation in war in this way directly addresses what we owe to our culture. Because our choices about engaging a culture must begin with our inheritance from that same culture, the ways in which we form questions are irrevocably framed and enabled. In the words of Abraham Joshua Heschel, "Some are guilty, but all are responsible"—a statement that distinguishes between active and passive guilt while acknowledging that the sins of some persons are bound up and contribute to the well-being

noting this, I am suggesting that America's social and economic development and its present geopolitical position are attributable to America's wars, which presents a datum that American Christians cannot avoid. War's ubiquity and inescapable heritage might cause Christians to despair if they believe that no alternative to complicity exists. However, I suggest that only when we come to terms with the inescapability of a church benefiting materially from the military activities of its country can we begin to see how this situation provides, ironically, an opportunity for witness.

By beginning in this manner, I want to defer a common practice in Christian accounts of nonviolence, namely, that of offering Christianity as a counter-narrative to the mythos of war. For example, Stanley Hauerwas rightly points out that Christians are given a grammar and a narrative that helps them avoid the conclusion that war is inescapably coterminous with natural life.[5] However, offering an alternative way of thinking and behaving with regards to war (i.e. that war is "unnatural") must also account for Christians being unable to "untangle ourselves from the logic of war and the imperatives of the war system."[6] If, as I will argue shortly, disentangling is impossible, a Christian response to war cannot begin with a "counter-narrative" (though this work is both important and indispensible for the reformation of the Christian moral imagination).

Instead, we must begin with an account of how Christians are embedded in a society implicated by its wars.[7] As Kathryn Tanner

of others. See Heschel, "Toward a Just Society," in *Moral Grandeur and Spiritual Audacity* (New York: Noonday, 1996), 220ff. Theologically, this is one way to understand the Pauline claim that "there is no one righteous, not even one" (Rom. 3:10, NIV).

5. Stanley Hauerwas, *War and the American Difference: Theological Reflections on Violence and National Identity* (Grand Rapids: Baker Academic, 2011), 43ff. Hauerwas defines "war" as only those events that could claim justice and does not include ubiquitous phenomenon that designate any collective action of violence in that definition. See in particular 44–47.

6. Ibid., 51.

7. As Rowan Williams points out, Christ's life (and by extension, Christian existence) works from within the contours of creaturely life to rework it from the inside out rather than denying

points out, the Christian culture and narrative emerge only through a continual sharing, borrowing, and remaking of that which is common—an insight that becomes increasingly problematic when we recognize that what is shared between church and the world is not simply language and cultural forms but also moral culpability, resources, and political procedures that allow for war.[8] Only when Christians come to terms with this reality can we see that the Spirit's work within creation—to form churches capable of witness to Christ's work—creatively "makes use" of the elements and situations at hand for witness. While Christian witness certainly involves the discipline of cultural assumptions and a witness to another way of life, we must be careful that these undertakings occur within a prior acknowledgment that Christians are creatures who share creaturely things with their neighbors. I will argue that operating from a position "inside" war provides churches with the basis for bearing witness to their societies, as one creature to another. I will then explore how churches, in the multiplicity of their witness against war, might view this common witness from within society as a sign of their pneumatic unity—in contrast to the society in which they live, which is marked by division.

War, Creation, and Creaturely Life

One of the primary temptations facing Christians in thinking about war is that churches are absolved of involvement in war if they are not directly involved. As I have previously stated, this position is not a sustainable claim on economic and political grounds. Theologically, the relationship between war and churches must be addressed. Does

its commonality with that life. See Williams, *On Christian Theology* (Malden, MA: Blackwell, 2000), 230–31.

8. Kathryn Tanner, *Theories of Culture: A New Agenda for Theology* (Minneapolis: Fortress Press, 1997), 147ff.

war fall within the purview of all Christians, or does it concern only those whose congregations, relations, or societies are directly affected by war?

By way of Augustine of Hippo, I will argue that in societies such as America—which have benefited materially and politically from the use of military force—churches cannot avoid being implicated by war, regardless of their position on the matter. In Augustine's *City of God*, we find a description of the temporal life of the City of God (seen in the church) as nourished and benefited by the wars of the City of Man. According to Augustine, this reality should not occasion despair; it simply acknowledges the conditions of temporal life: a place of retreat does not exist outside of war, insofar as one's life is bound up with one's neighbors, for better or worse. Far from cheapening Augustine's vision of the church as bearing witness to the work of God in Christ, the intimacy of the two makes the difference between the sustaining work of God in Christ and the sustaining practice of war all the more acute.[9]

9. Recent debates between proponents of "Augustinian liberalism" and Radical Orthodoxy highlight this Augustinian question of the relationship between church and extra-ecclesial life. Proponents of a form of political liberalism rooted in Augustine's thought—such as Charles Mathewes—argue that because all persons participate in the *imago Dei* in creation, the love that they share from God provides the basis for communion between Christians and non-Christians. See Mathewes, *A Theology of Public Life* (Cambridge: Cambridge University Press, 2007), 84. Mathewes's argument does not intend to blur church into "world" but to acknowledge that "during the world" (as Augustine puts it), the common love of and from God, which all creation participates in as creaturely beings, provides the basis for distinction of Christian and non-Christian as well as the productive possibilities for uniting them. See also Eric Gregory, *Politics and the Order of Love* (Chicago: University of Chicago Press, 2008), 27ff, who roots this union in the giving and receiving of reasons made possible by a common ontology.

By contrast, see John Milbank's Radical Orthodox reading of Augustine, which emphasizes civic life as a parody of ecclesial existence to the extent that questionable allegiances can be made between church and world as bearers of two different social ontologies, in John Milbank, *Theology and Social Theory* (Oxford: Blackwell, 1990), 390ff. For an analogous position, see Gregory W. Lee, "Republics and Their Loves: Rereading *City of God* 19, *Modern Theology* 27 (2011): 553–81. This is not to say that Milbank proposes a sectarian vision of Augustine in which the church withdraws from liberal society but rather that the overlap between church and society cannot be as uncomplicated as envisioned by Gregory and Mathewes. Milbank's view of Augustinianism has been criticized for overreading Augustine through *The City of God*

In the *City of God*, we find an account of human sociality that paradoxically depicts the City of Man alongside the proleptic City of God (the church), with war playing a key part in Augustine's narration of this creaturely drama.[10] The two cities—the city of God and the city of Man, or "the city of the world"—are distinguished by the objects of their love: the love of God and the love of temporal goods.[11] Though the objects of their love divide them, a number of striking similarities can be found between the two cities. Both cities

in numerous places, including Mathewes, *Theology of Public Life*, 125–27, and Gregory, *Politics and the Order of Love,* 125–48. In later writings, Milbank modifies his position in *Theology and Social Theory*. In *The Word Made Strange: Theory, Language, Culture* (Oxford: Blackwell, 1997), 268–92, he argues for a kind of complex space that would at least forestall the emergence of a secularized sphere that seeks to remove any theological voice from the public sphere.

In my view, the distinction between the cities drawn by Milbank and Lee is properly made, but this distinction is carried out within a larger context of union borne by creation (Mathewes and Gregory). This union is not for the sake of building a common life or sustaining temporal order but for the sake of a witness that makes use of a common life in love and that occasionally stands in stark opposition to the City of Man. In short, this witness is accomplished only insofar as the church shares the temporal burdens of creation, acknowledging its share in a society nurtured and sustained by war.

10. It should be noted that I am working from Augustine's conception of war in *City of God* and not from other texts, such as *Against Faustus*, 22:74–75, 78, in *Augustine: Political Writings,* ed. Ernest Fortin and Douglas Kries (Indianapolis: Hackett, 1993), 222–26, which is central to formulating a just war concept in Augustine's thought. R. A. Markus argues that between the authorship of *Faustum* and *City of God*, Augustine became more pessimistic about the prospects of war and society. Cf., "St. Augustine's Views on the 'Just War,'" in *The Church and War,* ed. W.J. Shields,Studies in Church History20 (London: Basil Blackwell, 1983), 1–13.

11. Identifying the two cities within Augustine's work is a matter of debate among scholars. Most problematic is that the "cities" are not static, temporal locales but socialities that are formed by that which is loved corporately, creating "cities" which are temporally fluid. It is my contention that Augustine points us toward the church as that sociality which can be most clearly, though not absolutely, identified with the City of God. Cf., William R. Stevenson, Jr., *Christian Love and Just War: Moral Paradox and Political Life in St. Augustine and His Modern Interpreters* (Macon, GA: Mercer University Press, 1987), 13. William Cavanaugh, "From One City to Two: Christian Reimagining of Political Space," *Political Theology* 7 (July 2006): 299–321 furthers this reading by depicting the cities in terms of their temporally coherent performances. Cf. Robert Dodaro, "Between the Two Cities: Political Action in Augustine of Hippo," in *Augustine and Politics*, ed. John Doody, Kevin L. Hughes, and Kim Paffenroth, (Lanham, MD: Lexington Books, 2005), 99–115, which describes Augustine's own political activities. Following Cavanaugh, I suggest that—though the temporal loci of the love of God and the love of self are mixed—we should provisionally identify the City of God with the church as Augustine does, while acknowledging that the church does not fully exhibit the eschatological fullness of the life of the City of God.

are characterized as dwelling in time and circumscribed by space;[12] both cities are characterized by their pursuit of peace.[13] Likewise, both cities are characterized as social entities on pilgrimage seeking permanent habitation.

However, war figures most prominently among those practices that distinguish the cities most clearly. The church—as the proleptic sign of the City of God—is bound up in time and space with the Roman imperium, which directly benefits from war even though the church does not directly undertake war. For Augustine, the City of God remains secure in the love of God; whereas the city of Man, in its love for itself, is characterized by a constant search for security, which results in innumerable wars to maintain its existence in time and space.[14] Even before the much-discussed passages of books 18 and 19, Augustine characterizes the Roman Empire as belligerent and dependent upon war for her survival.[15] As Augustine puts it, "the Roman Empire could not have been increased so far and wide, and Roman glory could not have been spread, except by continual wars following one upon another."[16] These wars, Augustine says, are

12. Augustine, *City of God*, trans. Henry Bettenson (London: Penguin Books, 1984), 881.

13. Ibid., 866: "Even when men choose war, their only wish is for victory; which shows that their desire in fighting is for peace with glory . . . and when this is achieved there will be peace. Even wars, then, are waged with peace as their object, even when they are waged by those who are concerned to exercise their warlike prowess, either in command or in the actual fighting. Hence it is an established fact that peace is the desired end of war."

14. Ibid., 599: "The earthly city will not be everlasting; for when it is condemned to the final punishment it will no longer be a city . . . And since this is not the kind of good that causes no frustrations to those enamoured of it, the earthly city is generally divided against itself by litigation, by wars, by battles, by the pursuit of victories that bring death with them or at best are doomed to death . . . that city desires an earthly peace, for the sake of the lowest goods; and it is that peace which it longs to attain by making war."

15. Ibid., 154: "So *if* it was by waging wars that were just, not impious and unjust, that the Romans were able to acquire so vast an empire, surely they should worship the Injustice of others as a kind of goddess? For we observe how much help 'she' has given towards the extension of the Empire by making others wrong-doers, so that the Romans should have enemies to fight in a just cause and so increase Rome's power . . . With the support of these two Goddesses—'Foreign Injustice' and Victory, the empire grew, even when Jupiter took a holiday. Injustice stirred up the causes of war; Victory brought the war to its happy conclusion."

16. Ibid., 98.

waged for the sake of a peace that consists of "none surviving to resist"—a peace founded on annihilation rather than coexistence.[17]

Stemming back to the prototype of Cain, Rome's behavior constitutes only the latest iteration of a much larger pattern of social existence.[18] Cain—killing his brother "because his power would be more restricted if both wielded the sovereignty"—establishes a pattern that is carried forth by Romulus and Remus and all "earthly cities" since: the cities of Man destroy those who would seek to share in goods rather than recognizing that goodness "is a possession enjoyed more widely by the united affection of partners in that possession in proportion to the harmony that exists among them."[19] In this way, the name of Rome is a substitute for human society, which perpetuates its existence by violent means; war is the epitome of this violence.

Augustine enables us to see that in addition to Rome, all of the Cities of Man prior to Rome depended on the function of war to flourish. War is the vehicle by which goods are acquired for the earthly city of Cain,[20] but rather than solving the crisis of scarcity, war reaps "fresh misery and an increase of the wretchedness already there."[21] In other words, war secures temporal space for the City of Man—but at the cost of amplifying the very conditions that it desires to eradicate. In the same way that Cain's violence was an effort to overcome a distance between himself and God, war (on the social level) leads to the perpetuation of war in its attempt to alleviate the original causes of social disunity.[22]

17. Ibid., 599.
18. Ibid., 600.
19. Ibid., 601.
20. Ibid., 599: "That city desires an earthly peace, for the sake of the lowest goods; and it is that peace which is longs to attain by making war."
21. Ibid., 600.
22. Augustine's mention of the name of Seth (Cain's new counterpart in the Genesis story following Abel's death) is not accidental. Seth means "resurrection"—the hope of the City of God—while Cain's name means "possession." Cain's descendants are known for various

Beginning with Cain's descendent, Nimrod, the theological dimensions of war in *City of God* comes more fully into view.[23] Augustine takes Nimrod's nickname of "hunter" to be less than innocuous, suggesting that it "can only suggest a deceiver, oppressor and destroyer of earth-born creatures"—a description fully in line with the violence attributed to the progenitor of his line, Cain.[24] Even more significantly, this destroyer of creation is named as the founder of an empire centered in Babel, a city whose ultimate goal (according to the book of Genesis) was ascension to God.

In his retelling of the lineage that runs from Cain to Babel, Augustine curiously passes over the wandering of Cain, moving him immediately from violence against Abel to the founding of another city; whereas in Genesis, Cain's punishment is to be without a home.[25] Sublating Cain's wandering into the structure of the lineage of the City of Man proves to be strategic, as it reveals the narrative of the earthly cities sustained by war to be the story of socialities endlessly travelling—unstable entities in constant search of their Edenic home. Within this paradigm, war always promises but never delivers peace. Not only is Babel the culmination of Cain's genealogy, but it is also the full expression of what a war-sustained civilization has sought since Cain: a restoration of Edenic peace with God. In both Babel and Rome, we are given a picture of societies seeking to overcome social discord—between people as well

economic and material skills, and the city of Cain, populated by those skilled in temporal *technes*, "has its beginning and end on this earth, where there is no hope of anything beyond what can be seen in this world" (ibid., 626–27).

23. Ibid., 652–53. Augustine makes no attempt to explain how the line of Cain reemerges through Noah's line after the flood, choosing to interpret Noah's children as "prophetic symbolism" of the world's condition. For example, Ham's name ("hot") is interpreted to represent those who are "hot, because they are on fire not with the spirit of wisdom, but with the spirit of impatience" (ibid., 650). As such, Nimrod's name becomes indicative not only of his character but of the city he founds.
24. Ibid., 658ff.
25. Gen. 4:12b-16.

as between creation and God—by recourse to violence. Whereas the City of God is united to God in its love for God, the bellicose city of Babel seeks to bridge this divide by possession of God and all opposing social bodies. Building a tower to "symbolize his impious pride," Nimrod sees his city suffer an appropriate punishment: division and the scattering of the city across the earth.[26] In other words, the frustration of war's claim to produce social unity.

Though the church in *City of God* is bound up in this society, it refuses this story—as Michael Hanby argues—by celebrating Christ, whose death "denies tragedy and death any ontological purchase"; in celebrating Christ's death as a self-donation of God on behalf of humanity and not a "necessary" feature of human social existence, the church's proclamation subverts the imperial violence from within.[27] The society created by war is cast in stark relief against the gathered community of Christ. In addition to the necessity of death and violence for sustaining life, war also produces new socialities out of this violence (as Augustine describes it), which will, in turn, use war as the means by which social unity is achieved, creating an endless spiral of human misery; violence will beget violence.

Despite the stark distinction between the cities, God grants them unity in creation, which war—though simulating—cannot ultimately replicate.[28] As Augustine argues in *The Good of Marriage*, human social life constitutes a good that speaks of its original Adamic unity and points toward God,[29] an affirmation that Augustine repeats in

26. Gen. 11:5-7.

27. Michael Hanby, "Democracy and Its Demons," in *Augustine and Politics*, ed. John Doody, Kevin L. Hughes, and Kim Paffenroth, (Lanham, MD: Lexington Books, 2005), 117–45 (126).

28. In *City of God*, 15:1-6, Augustine argues that beginning with Abel, a division takes place among humanity concerning damnation or salvation. In Adam, however, a fundamental unity exists between the two cities, to the extent that "the two cities are mingled together from the beginning, down to the end" (18:54). Though the focus of their loves divides them, it does not, for Augustine, negate the sharing of temporal goods, which is a vestige of their original unity in Adam.

City of God, citing the creation of Adam as central to a theological vision all human unity.[30] Within this vision of creation as good, war appears as a perverse attempt to fulfill the human vocation of peaceability—to restore unity through violence rather than through Christ's mediation.[31]

In summary, in *City of God*, Augustine depicts a society that is founded and perpetuated in acts of war and populated by those whose lives mirror these commitments. The City of Man, founded in a primal act of defiance, maintains its coherence in war and corresponding belligerent activities. Within this economy, war operates as an imitation of God in two respects. First, war mimics God's constitution of persons as social beings. By perpetuating deficient forms of social existence—as seen in the Cain narrative—war is the power underlying corrupted social life. In the case of Nimrod, it unifies social division, and in doing so, functions as an anti-Christ, an alternate source of social unity.[32] Second, war mimics God's sustenance of social community. The grace of God produces a just order of the City of God; by contrast, the city that is founded in war is one that attempts to secure its locus through competition and

29. "Because each man is a part of the human race, and human nature is itself a social thing, he has, as a great and natural good, the power of friendship also. For this reason, God willed to create all men out of one, so that they might be bound together in their society not only by similiarity of race, but also by the bond of kinship," in R. W. Dyson, *The Pilgrim City: Social and Political Ideas in the Writings of St. Augustine of Hippo* (Woodbridge, UK: Boydell Press, 2001), 62.

30. Augustine, *City of God*, 502: "God created man as one individual; but that did not mean that he was to remain alone, bereft of human society. God's intention was that in this way the unity of human society and bonds of human sympathy be more emphatically brought home to man, if men were bound together not merely by likeness in nature but also by the feeling of kinship."

31. Ibid., 503: "God was well aware that man would sin and so becoming liable to death, would then produce a progeny destined to die. He knew also that mortals would reach such a pitch of boundless iniquity, that brute beasts, deprived of rational will, would live in greater security among their own kind . . . than men . . . Yet not even lions or serpents have ever carried on among themselves the kind of warfare in which men engage."

32. For the modern development of this point, see William Cavanaugh, "The City: Beyond Secular Parodies," in *Radical Orthodoxy: A New Theology*, ed. John Milbank, Catharine Pickstock, and Graham Ward (London: Routledge, 1998), 182–200.

coercion rather than self-giving, denying God's grace and with it, its true being.

The distinctions that I have traced between the church (founded in the peace of Christ) and the City of Man (founded and sustained by war) should not lead us to conclude that churchly life is utterly distinct from war; in anticipation of one objection, churches have certainly played a role in perpetuating war.[33] While we can debate whether or not the visible church and its institutions as such are the font of conflict, I will note that, with Augustine, church doctrines, officials, and institutions are among those material resources that wars mobilize for ends alien to the social existence of churches. Given Augustine's other writings, it is difficult to argue that religious formation and institutions cannot or have not contributed materially to war. For churches in a society characterized by war, a paradox exists: mixed in with society, the City of God makes use of the goods of society while recognizing that the church should not be characterized by the ways and means through which society makes peace.

Three consequences follow, in regard to our thinking about the relationship between war and churches, particularly those who see the church as having a vocation of nonviolent witness against war. First, no space outside creaturely life exists wherein the church can live out its witness. However, this is not to say that the church exists to support society—which constitutes a perverse form of Justin Martyr's argument for Christians as the best members of society.[34] Rather, the affirmation that creaturely life is the space for the church's

33. Any number of historical examples illustrate the manner in which Christian churches have either supported or directly mobilized its members for engagement in American wars. See Gerald Sittser, *A Cautious Patriotism: The American Churches and the Second World War* (Chapel Hill: University of North Carolina Press, 2010).

34. Justin Martyr, *First Apology*, in *St. Justin Martyr: The First and Second Apologies*, trans. Leslie William Barnard (Mahwah, NJ: Paulist, 1997), 28–29.

witness enables the church to acknowledge that no space exists outside of the effects and gains of war in which they might offer witness.

Second, the goods that are sought by the City of Man are not entirely different from those sought by the City of God. According to Augustine, positing a stark divide between the two involves a flirtation with Manichaeism. Though war is an attempt to claim the peace of God rather than receive it, war can still be characterized as a pursuit of peace. I do not wish to equivocate between these desires but rather to say that, by virtue of their common origin in Adam, the church and the world bear certain analogical facets that should be affirmed and built upon. By this, I mean that the witness of Christians for the peace of God does not need to manufacture bridges between church and society; rather, churches can affirm—in fidelity to their own confessions and resources—those aspects of society that do not openly contradict Christian witness while simultaneously identifying the perversion of God's gifts. As Karl Barth puts it, to say that Jesus Christ is the light of life means being able to affirm other words in the midst of the Word of Christ, recognizing the pluriformity of creation as the context of God's providence, to which the church bears witness.[35]

Third, Augustine reminds us that the two cities exist together during the time of the world, persisting as wheat with tares. Theologically, this is one of the socially provocative implications that Augustine's vision gives us. Insofar as escape from the ubiquity of Adam's sin is impossible, American churches—as co-sharers of the benefits of war—must proceed from a posture of repentance in their witness; in the words of Paul, Christians are first among sinners.[36] As

35. This point has been made most cogently by Jessica DeCou, "Relocating Barth's Theology of Culture: Beyond the 'True Words' Approach of *Church Dogmatics* IV/3," *International Journal of Systematic Theology* 15 (2013): 154–71.

Jennifer McBride argues, Christian witness can never extricate itself from its entanglements with the world, so witness must begin and end with repentance for both its own sins and the sins of the world. Following Bonhoeffer, McBride contends that "confessing sin . . . is not simply an acknowledgment of what the church has failed to do."[37] If the church is the body of Christ in the world, confession means that the church must accept responsibility for its sins and for the sins of the world.

In short, standing outside of the effects of war is not a tenable position for American churches, but this need not cause Christian communities to despair about the church's complicity regarding war (despite protests to the contrary). Rather, this should encourage churches to come to terms with their creaturely status and intertwined relationships. The church's embeddedness within creation—the City of God among the City of Man—promises to restore a proper beginning point for witness, not lead us to despair. The desire for a place to stand apart from the world in order to theologically assess its difficulties is, in many ways, the desire for that which Augustine cannot conceive: a non-creaturely mode of discipleship predicated upon a refusal of the church's status of living (while *in via*) "during the world." In naming the tactic of retreat from social engagement with war in this way, I am advancing a fairly uncontroversial claim: the Christian life is not a release from creation but a right orientation within it. According to Augustine,

36. Concerning the procession of Christian witness through repentance, see Jennifer McBride, *The Church for the World: A Theology of Public Witness* (Oxford: Oxford University Press, 2012); Jeremy M. Bergen, *Ecclesial Repentance: The Churches Confront Their Sinful Pasts* (Edinburgh: T&T Clark, 2011), 243–84. Both McBride and Bergen imply, in different ways, that the nature of the church's holiness necessitates its admission of guilt—or as McBride puts it more forcefully, accepting guilt on behalf of others (*Church for the World,* 129–34).

37. McBride, *Church for the World,* 131. McBride builds this claim on a reading of the work of Dietrich Bonhoeffer, who advocates that the church's vocation as the body of Christ is to repent before the world both for its own sins and—as Christ's presence in the world—to accept guilt on behalf of the world that Christ came to redeem.

our standing as bodily creatures is not a predicament but rather the means by which we seek our proper end—the worship of God.[38] Unfortunately, within discussions of war and peace, this acknowledgment of intimate connection between the church and the world is often minimized in favor of positing a distance from the world that also minimizes the church's opportunity for witness.

Any ecclesiologically informed response to war must first confess its entanglement with the causes of war, insofar as it participates in a providentially sustained creation that consists both of church and non-church. The moral formation of a congregation—while enabling Christians to make use of political allegiances in ways that usurp the intention of those allegiances, creatively turning sources of antagonism into resources for peace—does not negate the fact that churches contribute to and benefit from the wars of their societies. Therefore, the way forward does not entail distancing churches from creaturely life but rather embracing the creaturely condition of the church, which joins churches to the world and offers the avenues, opportunities, and means for repentance and witness.

Though my own sensibilities lie with non-participation in war, I am not suggesting that Augustine is a crypto-pacifist or that he is inconsistent with regards to his broader thinking on war.[39] Such readings are beyond the scope of my intentions, not to mention historically untenable.[40] Rather, I am suggesting that Augustine's

38. On bodily life and the value of creaturely life in Augustine, see David Dawson, "Transcendence as Embodiment: Augustine's Domestication of Gnosis," *Modern Theology* 10 (1994): 1–26.

39. Augustine is no pacifist. Cf. Robert Dodaro, "Augustine's Use of Parallel Dialogues in his Preaching on Nonviolence," in *Ministerium Sermonis,* ed. Anthony Dupont, Mathijs Lamberigts, and Gert Partoens (Turnhout, Bel.: Brepols, 2009): 327–44; Peter Burnell, "Justice in War in and before Augustine," *Studia Patristica* 49 (2010): 107–10. This is not to say, however, that Augustine's thought on war does not change. As suggested by R.A. Markus ("Saint Augustine's Views on the 'Just War,'" 1–13), Augustine's views appear to shift over time. See Kevin Carnahan's treatment of this change in "Perturbations of the Soul and Pains of the Body: Augustine on Evil Suffered and Done in War," *Journal of Religious Ethics* 36 (2008): 269–94.

descriptions of the just person who undertakes war (which can be found throughout *The City of God*) do not mitigate Augustine's rendering of war as the perpetuation of a social existence counter to what can be found in the life of the church.[41] Adopting the analysis provided by the *City of God* in regard to war does not mean we must adopt Augustine's solution of tragic participation in war or participate in war on behalf of our neighbors.[42] If the church participates in a new social life made possible by Christ—a social existence constitutive of all human social life—and bears witness to

40. In *St. Augustine: The Retractions,* trans. Sister M. Inez Bogan, RSM (Washington D.C.: Catholic University of America Press, 1999), 79ff, Augustine makes clear that the peace Jesus speaks about in the Sermon on the Mount cannot be fully present within life; accordingly, temporal force cannot exclude the possibility of violent force. This has not prevented promoters of nonviolence from attempting such conversations with Augustine on violence. See Alain Epp Weaver, "Unjust Lies, Just Wars? A Christian Pacifist Conversation with Augustine," *Journal of Religious Ethics* 29, no. 1 (Spring 2001): 51–78. Weaver's contends that Augustine's absolution prohibition concerning lying begs the question as to whether he has simply been inconsistent in his reflections on war. Cf. James Turner Johnson, "Can a Pacifist Have a Conversation with Augustine? A Response to Alain Epp Weaver," *Journal of Religious Ethics* 29, no.1 (Spring 2001): 87–93.
41. For Augustine's comments on the just man and war in *City of God*, see 4.15, in which Augustine explains that the wars of Rome have produced such unjust neighbors that any war against the borders of the Roman empire can only be seen by Rome as "just." As Augustine argues, the "just" nature of these wars can only be attributed to Rome's unjust behavior; in this way, "just war" is a solution to the problem created by Rome itself, the bearer of a deprived form of social life. To be certain, God is described as the One who has given Rome its position within the world (5.21), and Augustine allows certain kinds of war for the sake of temporal peace (1.21). However, Augustine's description of God's gift of empire does not validate the violence of Rome. Rather, Augustine sees the emergence of violence when God is forgotten as the one who gives empire—for example, the murder of Julian (5.21). In sum, the presence and participation by the "just man" (judging war to be just when measured by a privation) does not diminish the distinction Augustine seeks to draw between the two cities—one that is perpetuated in war and one that is witnessed to by the church.
42. For introductions to Augustine on the just war, see J. Warren Smith, "Augustine and the Limits of Preemptive and Preventive War," *Journal of Religious Ethics* 35 (March 2007): 141–62; John Mark Mattox, *Saint Augustine and the Theory of Just War* (London: Continuum, 2006). Historically, appropriations of Augustine on war have centered on his "just war" reflections, overlooking the manner in which the nature of war in *City of God* is intrinsic to the perpetuation of the City of Man. While recent works on Augustine's political thought by Mathewes and Gregory have elegantly explored possibilities for how Augustine's thought contributes to a sustainable civic life, neither author addresses war directly as a problem for civic existence; whereas in *City of God*, war appears as an intrinsic feature of civic life's sustainability and perpetuity.

this life in times of war, it must be open to rejecting the necessity of war in favor of nonviolence in order to offer faithful witness to the work of God in Christ. In describing the misery of war and the embedded nature of the church, *The City of God* reveals the promises of war to be ultimately bankrupt.

The irony of war, as Augustine indicates, is that it promises peace but purchases it only as a temporary salve, yielding the seeds of the next war while wreaking moral and physical harm on all of its participants.[43] While the shared heritage of American war involves expansion, global positioning, and defense of interest, Augustine points out that the "misery upon misery" of war remains with us in untold and occluded ways. The rise in post-traumatic stress disorders among returning veterans, the rise in suicide rates among active military, and the toll (both financial and psychological) on the families at home are well documented in popular works and Congressional hearings.[44] The human toll of war, in addition to decreased recruiting numbers, has led to increased interest in forms of war that reduce the risk to soldiers (such as drones and cyberwarfare), but these forms do not avoid the fundamental issues as Augustine names them: the perpetuation of social division and the compounding of human misery. These techniques may be more effective in reducing personnel casualties, but for Christians, the loss of life experienced by members of one's own country represents only

43. On the phenomenon of the ironic ending of American wars, see Gideon Rose, *How Wars End: Why We Always Fight the Last Battle* (New York: Simon and Schuster, 2010). On the moral harm of war, see Jonathan Shay, *Achilles in Vietnam: Combat Trauma and the Undoing of Character* (New York: Simon & Schuster, 1995).

44. Concerning the financial and psychological costs of trauma to soldiers, see Warren Kinghorn, "Combat Trauma and Moral Fragmentation: A Theological Account of Moral Injury," *Journal of the Society of Christian Ethics* 32 (2012): 57–74; Rita Nakashima Brock and Gabriella Lettini, *Soul Repair: Recovering from Moral Injury after War* (Boston: Beacon, 2012); *Invisible Casualties: The Incidence and Treatment of Mental Health Problems by the U.S. Military, Hearing Before the Committee on Oversight and Government Reform*, 110th Cong. (May 24, 2007), available at http://www.gpo.gov/fdsys/pkg/CHRG-110hhrg46429/content-detail.html

part of the issue. Concern for the lives of one's own combatants to the exclusion of concern for the lives of others cements war's deepest problem—human disunity—at the level of policy.

Church Division, Violence, and the Problem of the Holy Spirit

While recognizing that the embeddness of the church within societies is a valuable starting point for Christian witness, how do we address the complicated matter of division within the universal church? Asking for a Christian witness immediately begs the question: "*Which* witness?" In the era of the Vietnam War (which I will use as the backdrop for this book) as well as our own, Christian resistance to war has taken a variety of directions that, at first glance, seem politically and theologically incommensurate; resistance emerges from all corners of the ecumenical spectrum. One solution involves describing each tradition's witness as belonging to its own communion—Dorothy Day provides a theologically coherent witness for Roman Catholics, John Howard Yoder for the Mennonites, and so forth. This solution, however, does not account for the reality of their practice (which freely adopts tactics from other Christian traditions) and, more significantly, does not take seriously the problem of Christian division in witness.

If each of the ecclesiological trajectories represented in this book are, as Scripture attests, grounded in the mediating work of the Spirit—who presents Christ to us, binds the church together in its worship and witness, and gifts the churches for witness and ministry—these witnesses cannot be viewed as significant only in their own tradition, since the Spirit is the Spirit of all the churches. Neither can these witnesses be assessed only according to their practices, for this would mean dividing the person and work of the Spirit from the diversity of practices that are borne and empowered by the Spirit. If we take seriously the claim that the Spirit animates and makes possible our witness to Christ, then this implies (among other things) that witness is an ecumenical venture leading divided churches toward one another and offering witness to the world of a different kind of unity than that promised by war. Put differently: for a resistance to war to have true ecclesial form, it must bear out a unity among churches in addition to a unity between warring parties.

In the previous section, I ended by suggesting that the witness of churches against war begins with the acceptance of its embeddedness within creation, which theologically provides an opportunity for both witness and evaluation of the ways in which churches benefit from war. This acknowledgment brings us to the question of the divided church, insofar as the witness against war is undertaken by a plurality of churches from a plurality of traditions, linking together questions of ecumenism and war.[45] Though the historiographic question of what the church's original position vis-à-vis war may have been is important, we cannot, in the words of John Howard Yoder, go back to scratch.[46] We can only begin where we stand—confessing that Christ is at work in the midst of the churches, calling them to be as one. The plurality in this witness against war cannot be resolved either by a pragmatic appeal to nonviolence independent of theological commitments or by the reduction of these approaches to mutually exclusive options that ignore other ecclesial divisions.[47] In what follows, I will argue that a variety of ecclesially-

45. For notable work on the question of ecumenicity and war, see Fernando Enns, *The Peace Church and the Ecumenical Community: Ecclesiology and the Ethics of Nonviolence* (Kitchener, ON: Pandora, 2008); Anwar M. Barkat, ed., *Conflict, Violence, and Peace: A Report of a Consultation on "Alternatives to Conflict in the Quest of Peace" in the Ecmenical Institute in Bossey in Summer, 1969* (Geneva: World Council of Churches, 1970). On the Vietnam era in particular, see Jill K. Gill, *Embattled Ecumenism: The National Council of Churches, The Vietnam War, and the Trials of the Protestant Left* (Dekalb, IL: Northern Illinois University, 2011).

46. John Howard Yoder, *The Jewish Christian Schism Revisited* (Grand Rapids: Eerdmans, 2003), 138.

47. Charles DeBenedetti and Charles Chatfield, *An American Ordeal: The Antiwar Movement of the Vietnam Era* (Syracuse, NY: Syracuse University Press, 1990) describes the inability of various

informed responses to war can be understood as non-competitive and mutually-informing, as an act of witness to both the divided church and society.

This argument—that the sociological division of the church does not pose an immediate challenge to a theological unity of churches—is not without its problems. Most notably, it may appear as though I am seeking a kind of cheap unity—an indiscernible unification that exists in name only. On the contrary, I suggest that unity of witness must take place in tangible, difficult, and informed ways—and that participants must be fully aware of differences as well as commonalities, with the common practice of resistance to war as a witness to ecclesial unity. While this act alone is not sufficient to achieve ecumenism, insofar as it is undertaken via the work of the Spirit, the common act of witness can be a starting point for further ecumenical recognition, discourse, and unity.

This argument for the pneumatic unity of the church in witness as foreshadowed in its common witness finds a potent challenge in the work of Ephraim Radner, most preeminently in his landmark volume *The End of the Church*. In that book, Radner presents a powerful case for considering the disunity of Christian witness to be indicative of its pneumatic reality; the disunity of the church is not simply sociological but reflective of the Spirit's abandonment.[48] Radner's case rests upon a figural understanding of the church in which he reads the history of the church not as a series of causalities but as a narration of God's ongoing work. Taking Scripture's story of the people of God as paradigmatic, Radner makes the breathtaking claim that ecclesial plurality—cast by many as evidence of the plural gifts of the Spirit—is indicative of God's judgment upon the church. In the same way that

peace movements to cooperate during Vietnam, which fragmented their effectiveness and ultimately led to the demise of many branches of the movement.

48. Ephraim Radner, *The End of the Church: A Pneumatology of Christian Division in the West* (Grand Rapids: Eerdmans, 1998).

Israel experienced division and an absence of the Spirit's presence as a result of its sins, so the modern church (as it persists in disunity) continues to reap the judgment of God in the form of persistent disunity.[49] According to Radner, the plurality of the church exists in the world not as a witness to the splendor of the Spirit but as a broken and disfigured body—a negative witness akin to Israel's public disfigurement in the Old Testament.

For Radner, reading ecclesiology in figurative terms means describing church division as the Spirit-abandoned, crucified body of Christ rather than the new life of the Spirit.[50] In making this case, he is not asserting that the Holy Spirit—the one who draws persons to Christ, represents Christ, and binds Christians into one body—is absent from the world; on the contrary, the Holy Spirit is present in the world in a way that figuratively renders judgment upon the disunity of the churches by displaying the body of Christ as broken. In Radner's words:

> It is rather a question of the historical experience of this grace, which "appears" to rob the object of the Spirit's indwelling of an open apprehension of such presence, love forming itself, as it were, through its own consistent self-questioning. The appearance however, is not an illusion in this case, because the Spirit's intimate work is accomplished—again, in figural conjunction with Jesus' own life—through the phenomenal assertion of its own distance.[51]

In other words, the Spirit's indwelling presence in the life of a Christian is simultaneously one of corporate estrangement, which results in divided practices, holiness, witness, ministry, and liturgy.[52]

49. Ibid., 3–10.
50. Ibid., 48–56.
51. Ibid., 343.
52. This is not to say that Radner, in more recent works, has abandoned hope for the church. In the mutual reading of Scripture, prayer, and baptismal recognition, Radner discerns signs of hope that historic divisions among various branches of the Christian churches might be healing after centuries of disunity. See Ephraim Radner, *Hope among the Fragments: The Broken Church and*

The disunity of the churches produces results that are disastrous for Christian life as well as the life of the world since the disunity of the church is accompanied by a fracturing of human life outside of the church.[53] As Radner explains, the division of the church emerged alongside the rise of the modern nation state, a development that created manifold bloodshed for both the church and the world.[54] In Rwanda, for example, church division created a competitive framework in which Rwandans were deemed either friends or enemies, to the extent that the churches were complicit in the Rwandan genocide as an extension of their exclusionary makeup.[55]

Radner's thesis poses a serious question to any project that draws from a diversity of ecclesial traditions in order to bear witness against corporate violence. Following Radner's thought, could it not be said that drawing out the many church-based traditions of nonviolent resistance to war only manifests further the problem of disunity? As Radner rightly points out, the disunity of the church has not only caused political divisions but has also contributed to certain political conflicts. While Radner views nationalism as a providential phenomenon that has preserved churches institutionally, he also points to the ways in which nationalism has co-opted the labor of the churches for its own end, putting them at odds with one another both in terms of internal struggles and external issues related to war.

Its Engagement of Scripture (Grand Rapids: Brazos, 2004). This healing, Radner argues, occurs not when Christians abandon their historic communions but when they work for reunion and recognition within them.

53. In the same way that nations existed in an uneasy relationship with Israel but are eventually incorporated into the body of Christ, Radner reads the goodwill of the nations as being providentially related to the life of the church. Ibid., 219ff.
54. Ibid. 220–22.
55. Ephraim Radner, *A Brutal Unity: The Spiritual Politics of the Christian Church* (Waco, TX: Baylor University Press, 2012), 68–73. The implication of churches in war is not limited to the modern age but can be seen, Radner argues, in the sixteenth and seventeenth century violence committed by Protestants and Catholics against one another (ibid., 41ff). His primary target in these arguments is William Cavanaugh, *The Myth of Religious Violence* (Oxford: Oxford University, 2009).

For Radner, the datum of a plural ecclesial witness boils down to a pneumatological problem: the divided church exists because of a Holy Spirit who lives at a distance from the church's social life; therefore, any mitigation of social division (such as a common social witness) prior to true repentance and ecumenism is irrelevant since the social violence churches attempt to overcome are, at some level, the consequence of church division.[56] Ecclesially-rooted acts of discipleship, such as resistance to war, seem only to offer a redoubling of church division, not a lessening of it. As a theological explication of church division, Radner's picture of the Spirit's presence-as-absence and of the church as the corporate body of the Spirit's absence is both breathtaking and disconcerting. However, Radner's proposal suffers from a kind of pneumatological bifurcation. While he maintains that the Spirit is absent from the corporate life of the church as evinced by the broken status of the body, he is unwilling to say that the Spirit is no longer operative in the lives of believers or that Christians no longer know, experience, or exercise the gifts of the Spirit.[57] In sum, Radner appears to divide the Spirit's work as the presenter of Christ from the Spirit's work as the giver of gifts for the church's benefit.

If Radner is willing to concede that individuals do, in fact, receive the gifts of the Spirit and that believers are joined to Christ by the Spirit, then it would follow that universal unity of the church should not be expected *in toto* but received as an eschatological gift—a gift that is present *in part*, that bears fruit in season, and that Christians eagerly anticipate but cannot demand. Here, it seems that Radner's figural approach to church history is not necessarily wrong but backwards. A figural rendering of the church that seeks

56. Radner, *A Brutal Unity*, 345–47. Radner places this proposal in explicit contract to other proposals that emphasize the churches have "always" been divided, with these divisions expressing pneumatically-given diversity and plurality.

57. Radner, *End of the Church*, 343.

to account for the gifts and signs of the Spirit would not be achieved by telling a story of the church at large—reading individual signs of life in light of the corporate failure—but by reading these signs in the reverse fashion: by looking at the Spirit's work, which is manifested ad hoc among individual believers as signs of a body being raised to the newness of life by the Spirit, despite the fact that portions of the church suffer from decay. While ecclesial plurality may be problematic, it does not impede a witness against war that seeks to acknowledge and work within multiple lines of the Christian tradition. Using Radner's figural template, a plural witness that is recognized across liturgical borders can be read as a sign of the Spirit breathing new life into the church catholic. Such a witness can lead the church to recognize its complicity and repent, which, in turn, will bring about moral renewal within churches and a desire to seek communion with other bodies of Christ.[58]

Drawing on the work of Dietrich Bonhoeffer, I will briefly sketch a counter-proposal of pneumatology and ecclesial plurality. Rooted in Bonhoeffer's first dissertation, *Sanctorum Communio*, my proposal suggests that the work of the Holy Spirit renews the fragmented church and that acts of witness to Christ's work (such as resistance to war) are pivotal in this ecumenical labor. Insofar as church plurality exists in and through the Spirit for Bonhoeffer, any witness that emerges from the Church should be, I will argue, a form of witness to the world of the unity of Christ as well as a witness against the disunity that persists within the Church. The resistance to war that emerges from multiple Christian traditions is, perhaps, not a sign of

58. It is worth remembering that the modern ecumenical movement began out of the modern missions movement insofar as the divided church posed a barrier to a unified witness in the world. In the same way that a plural witness called the divided church to reconsider its broken status, my proposal here can be read in a similar vein. See Brian Stanley, *The World Missionary Conference, Edinburgh 1910* (Grand Rapids: Eerdmans, 2009).

the Spirit's absence but rather a proleptic sign of the Spirit's renewing work.

The Holy Spirit, Ecclesial Unity, and the Witness of Discipleship

Though Bonhoeffer's pneumatology is regularly unacknowledged in his writings, it remains a pivotal aspect of his ecclesiology.[59] In *Sanctorum Communio,* Bonhoeffer writes that in the church, "God reveals God's own self as *Holy Spirit*" who "gathers individuals together to be the church-community, maintains it, and is at work only within it."[60] This work of the Sprit is nothing less than "the reality of revelation in Christ." Churches do not exist when they come into empirical form (in structure or institution), but rather, churches exist "when the Holy Spirit does God's work"—namely, actualizing the reconciliation of Christ between persons.[61] Whereas the "old humanity consists of countless isolated units . . . the new humanity is entirely concentrated in the one single historical point, Jesus Christ," who is present to us in the work of the Spirit, creating a church-community in solidarity with God.[62] Using "[humanity's]

59. See Eberhard Bethge, *Bonhoeffer: Exile and Martyr* (New York: Seabury, 1975), 62ff. While acknowledging that "in *Sanctorum Communio,* Bonhoeffer laid the basis for his ecclesiology" and "never retracted any of its important points," the Holy Spirit is not mentioned within Bonhoeffer's ecclesiology, either in Bethge's discussion of *Sanctorum Communio* or in later ecclesiological writings. By contrast, Green rightly exposits the Holy Spirit within *Sanctorum Communio* but mentions the Spirit only in passing with regards to later work, not mentioning the Holy Spirit as a facet of Bonhoeffer's writings past 1933. Charles Marsh, *Reclaiming Dietrich Bonhoeffer: The Promise of His Theology* (New York: Oxford University Press, 1994), 73–74 stands apart from much scholarship in its explication of the Holy Spirit's role in actualizing the objective work of Christ. Similarly, Joel Lawrence concludes his *Bonhoeffer: A Guide for the Perplexed* (London: T&T Clark, 2011) by naming the Holy Spirit as central to Bonhoeffer's ecclesiology, though he also does not discuss the Holy Spirit as a feature of Bonhoeffer's theology beyond the 1933 Christology lectures. Space permitting, I would trace the continued significance of the Holy Spirit within Bonhoeffer's ecclesiology, which persists all the way through Bonhoeffer's last works.
60. Dietrich Bonhoeffer, *Sanctorum Communio: A Theological Study of the Sociology of the Church,* DBWE 1 (Minneapolis: Fortress Press, 2009), 143.
61. Ibid., 144.
62. Ibid., 146.

social bonds and their social will," the Holy Spirit establishes a church that corresponds to the work of Christ.[63] For Bonhoeffer, the Spirit operates distinctly from Christ in that "the Holy Spirit's work applies to the social life of human beings and uses their social bonds and their social wills whereas the Spirit of Christ aims at the historical nature of human life as a whole."[64] In other words, the Spirit makes actual the work of Christ in time and space, appropriate to its setting.

In this early writing of the German martyr, the Holy Spirit accomplishes two pivotal works in the church that are relevant here. First, the Holy Spirit enables the church to be a church *in via.* With Christ as the objective form of the church, the Holy Spirit draws individual persons together into this community within history. As Bonhoeffer puts it, "what [the Spirit of Christ] is for the church as a whole, [the Holy Spirit] is for the individual"; the Holy Spirit is the actualizer in time and space of the objective person of Christ. For Bonhoeffer, the church "in Christ" never ceases to be "in Adam," remaining *simul justus et peccator*, for the persons constituting the church remain as such until the work of the Holy Spirit is eschatologically fulfilled. The completed act of salvation in Christ does not negate the historical activity of Christ's work through the actualizing work of the Holy Spirit; "the Christ in whom church-community is already completed seeks to win the heart by his Spirit in order to incorporate it into the actualized community of Christ."[65]

This actualization of Christ is formed over time and marked in its pre-eschatological life by "repentance and faith," a community that contains both weeds and wheat.[66] Because the church in history is nota cleanly demarcated body (i.e. only "in Christ" to the exclusion of it being sinful, or "in Adam"), the Holy Spirit sustains and continually

63. Ibid., 136 n29.
64. Ibid.
65. Ibid., 158.
66. Ibid., 289

actualizes a church that, prior to the eschaton, shares features of its life and organization with all other communities that exist purely "in Adam."[67] Put differently, the temporal brokenness (including intra-church divisions) is not because the Holy Spirit is absent from the church but because churches share in the broken state of creation. For Bonhoeffer, the Holy Spirit does not negate this aspect of creatureliness but rather renews the church *in* and *through* it. As we saw with Augustine, the creaturely nature and mixed composition of the church is not a reason to doubt God's presence but the occasion by which we recognize the connection of the church to all creation.

In Bonhoeffer's work, the union of persons *in via* by the Holy Spirit occurs in multiple actualizations of "Christ-in-community"—which has been rightly called the "polyphony" of Bonhoeffer's ecclesiology.[68] Bonhoeffer's ecclesiology pushes toward a certain kind of discipline and catholicity in which the church gathers together for the celebration of the Eucharist and in disciplined teaching. As Bonhoeffer argues, "the concrete function of the empirical church is worship that consists of preaching and celebrating the sacraments."[69] Because the visible church—Christ existing as community by the Spirit—makes use of the bonds of human relationships, it creates a range of interpersonal gatherings that constitute, according to Bonhoeffer's reading, pneumatic actualizations of Christ's body.[70]

67. Ibid., 107: "[I]t is not as if Adam were completely overcome; rather, the humanity of Adam lives on in the humanity of Christ. This is why the problem of sin is indispensible for understanding the sanctorum communion."

68. Barry Harvey, "The Body Politic of Christ: Theology, Social Analysis, and Bonhoeffer's Arcane Discipline," *Modern Theology* 13 (1997), 319–46 (330ff). See also Barry Harvey, "Accounting for Difference: Dietrich Bonhoeffer's Contribution to a Theological Critique of Culture," *Mysteries in the Theology of Dietrich Bonhoeffer: A Copenhagen Bonhoeffer Symposium*, ed. Kirsten Busch Nielsen, Ulrik Nissen, and Christiane Tietz (Copenhagen: Vandenhoeck & Ruprecht, 2007), 106–7.

69. Bonhoeffer, *Sanctorum Communio*, 226.

70. Ibid., 235. As Bonhoeffer refers to human relationships, they are "the channel for two powers, namely the objective spirit of the church community and that of the Holy Spirit."

Thus, as the One who joins persons together into the singular body of Christ, the Holy Spirit joins people to the objective celebrations and sacraments of the church in ways that do not diminish the historical circumstance of the ones through whom the Spirit works. creating a multiplicity of celebrations where the Spirit of Christ is at work. As Bonhoeffer argues, to be of the church is to have been moved by the Spirit; likewise, to be of the Spirit is to participate in the celebration of the church-community, creating a diversity of church expressions in accord with one another through the common fount of God's work.[71]

In Bonhoeffer's words, "when Christ comes 'into' us through the Holy Spirit, the church comes 'into' us"; the pneumatic gathering of persons and catholicity do not exist in opposition since the Spirit who actualizes the church catholic is the Spirit who sustains individuals.[72] Because the work of the Spirit operates upon natural bonds, actualizing communities of will and love, "wherever one of its members is there too is the church-community in its power, which means in the power of Christ and the Holy Spirit."[73] In other words, the church—as the work of the Holy Spirit upon creation—is a pneumatic renewal of human life in ways appropriate to time and place that necessarily differ from place to place, though borne by the same catholicizing Spirit.

Bonhoeffer contends that one of the corrosive influences on churches comes in the form of nationalism which, as Augustine notes, is perpetuated in war. Naming nationalism as "a sin against the Holy Spirit," Bonhoeffer understands the contrast between the pneumatic

71. Ibid., 158–59: "The Holy Spirit is at work only in the church as the communion of saints; thus every person who is really moved by the Spirit has to be within the church-community already; but on the other hand, no one is in the church-community who has not already been moved by the Spirit."
72. Ibid., 165.
73. Ibid., 178.

unity of the churches in plurality (which preserves individuals in God's own life without sublating them) to be no greater than war (which sublates individuals in death toward a corporate purpose).[74] Bonhoeffer's description of war as a nationally sacral event that celebrates an alternate unity to that of the church resonates with Augustine's account, including the admission that churches cannot escape this situation insofar as the church exists within creation as the proclaimer of God's preservation and Gospel.

If the problem of disorder and disunion is common to all those who are "in Adam," then the church is not exempt from disunion or immune from moral failure, which includes division between churches and the support of wars that draw false lines of allegiance or conceal certain moral failures for the sake of safety. Bonhoeffer does not read the disunion of the churches as the Spirit's absence (as suggested in Radner) but rather as the creaturely condition through which the Spirit works to heal via the church. Instead of seeing the plurality of ecclesial witness as a furthering of church disunion, it is possible to recognize the fruits of these various churches (made possible by the work of the Spirit) as instances of witness to other churches and the world. To put it plainly, Radner asks more of the Church as a creaturely body than the Spirit does; for Bonhoeffer, the unity of the church in the fullness of creaturely life is a gift to which the Spirit attests but that awaits the eschaton.[75]

74. Dietrich Bonhoeffer, *Ecumenical, Academic, and Pastoral Work: 1931–1932*, DBWE 11 (Minneapolis: Fortress Press, 2012), 262. As Bonhoeffer argues in *Creation and Fall: A Theological Exposition of Genesis 1–3,* DBWE 3(Minneapolis: Fortress Press, 1997), 84ff, creaturely life always contains certain limits—even in the Garden of Eden—such that humans know their creaturely limits not as external impositions but as internal regulations of existence. To attempt to overcome this creatureliness is to succumb to the temptation of the Serpent.

75. Bonhoeffer, *Sanctorum Communio,* 288–89: "It is beyond what we are able to conceive now as to how it will come to pass that all become one and yet each keeps their own identity. . . . All are united with each other and yet distinct. . . . At every moment we shall be aware of God's will to rule and implement it within the realm of the church-community. Here the realm of Christ has become the realm of God. The *ministerium Christi,* of the Holy Spirit, and of the

As I have suggested, with the help of Bonhoeffer, the diversity (and sometimes disunion) of churches constitutes part of what churches share with creation's brokenness, yet the Spirit moves among the churches for their reunion in ways that are appropriate to various historical moments. The church's existence as a pneumatologically animated reality (for all its fractured earthly life) is one of witness in which we follow the risen Christ into the world.[76] Bonhoeffer wrote that in the church we find a body where "God's Word [is] personally addressed to the human being, calling him to responsibility."[77]

According to Bonhoeffer, this concrete group of people, gathered together in the renewing work of God, constitutes the very presence of Christ today. To refuse the church's creaturely nature means repeating the heresy of Docetism, which reduces the concrete Jesus to "the embodiment of a religious idea."[78] Saying that Christ is present in a concrete situation does not negate the pre-eschatological status of creation in which the ongoing work of the Spirit and discipleship continues—a work that Bonhoeffer does not see as complete. If the divine economy operates within the church, the work of the Holy Spirit will not cease before the eschaton.[79]

As the church follows Christ into the world through the renewing work of the Spirit, two acts of witness are made possible, according to Bonhoeffer. First, congregations bear witness to each other

word have ceased. Christ himself hands over his church-community to the Father, in order that God may be all in all."

76. See Brian Gregor, "Following-After and Becoming Human: A Study of Bonhoeffer and Kierkegaard," in *Being Human, Becoming Human: Dietrich Bonhoeffer and Social Thought*, ed. Jens Zimmerman and Brian Gregor (Eugene, OR: Wipf & Stock, 2010), 152–75.

77. Bonhoeffer, "Lectures on Christology," in *Berlin: 1932–1933*, DBWE 12 (Minneapolis: Fortress Press, 2009), 317.

78. Ibid., 336.

79. Ibid., 360: "With the humiliated Christ, his church must also be humiliated. It cannot seek any visible authentication of its nature, as long as Christ has renounced doing so for himself. . . . There is no law here, and the humiliation of Christ is not a principle for the church to follow but rather a fact. . . . Even the church, as the presence of Jesus Christ . . . must receive the will of God every day anew from Christ."

concerning the work of God in their midst. As we have seen already, the Spirit draws congregations that are contextually different together into communion as members of the same body. This first movement of mutual witness occurs in tandem with the second movement: these congregations —alongside other congregations— offer witness to the world. As the Holy Spirit continues to actualize the work of Christ among the churches in their creaturely condition, churches are formed in unity in the image of Christ to bear witness to other churches and the fractured world.

In this way, the witness against war in one ecclesial setting need not be seen as mutually exclusive to other settings, nor does one ecclesial witness against war require conformity to another ecclesial context for a unified witness to exist. According to Bonhoeffer, the renewing work of the Spirit draws the churches into the life of Christ and calls them forth into discipleship and witness to one another and the world. Because of the creaturely condition of the church, the plurality of witness is not at odds with the unity of the Spirit but rather intrinsic to a unified witness. As Kevin Hector persuasively argues, confessional plurality does not obstruct the unity of the Spirit (if the Spirit is the norm of our confessions in judgment and conformity to Christ) to the extent that we allow for mutually-informing performances of this conformity to Christ to exist.[80]

With Radner, however, Bonhoeffer agrees that violence presents a tremendous problem for the church, insofar as violence—particularly violence perpetuated by religious bodies—is an indication that these

80. Kevin Hector, *Theology without Metaphysics: God, Language, and the Spirit of Recognition* (Cambridge: Cambridge University Press, 2011), 231: "The relevant conformity to Jesus, therefore, would be a matter not only of holding true beliefs about God, but of internalizing the norms by which Jesus judged what counts as following him . . . one becomes God's child by being conformed to Christ's image, one is conformed to this image as one internalizes Christ's normative Spirit, and one internalizes this Spirit as the norms implicit in Christ's own recognition of certain persons and performances are transmitted to one through a chain of intersubjective recognition stretching back to Christ himself."

bodies are at odds with their animus: the Holy Spirit. Writing in the early days of the Nazi party, Bonhoeffer argues that "the church knows nothing of the sanctity of war" and that, in war, the church sees "the struggle for existence is fought with dehumanized means."[81] The Spirit, who "exists in service and not in domination," remains the basis for the church, which "should be *one*"—a unity of the Spirit for all Christians.[82] Various configurations of witness against war need not be understood as mutually exclusive forms of witness but as mutually interpretative works of the Holy Spirit. The work of the Holy Spirit, as Bonhoeffer describes it, does not only involve the creation of communities of witness but also the unity of the these churches as they are confronted with the discipleship of other churches.

Life of the Church and Life in the World

Having established that the varied witness of the churches (assuming that ecclesiology exists in and through the Spirit) is not necessarily competitive and that a church's complicity in war constitutes part of its creaturely status for the sake of witness, one question still remains: How does the internal logic of churches communicate with the world external to the church? Describing how nonviolent resistance to war functions as Christian witness will be teased out in various ways by the four theologians under investigation here since each of them possess a different sense of how ecclesially-informed resistance relates to their non-ecclesial analogs. Following the thought of both Augustine and Bonhoeffer, I will offer a loose framework, which I believe is assumed by all of the figures, though this framework may be negotiated in various ways.

81. Bonhoeffer, *Ecumenical, Academic and Pastoral Work*, 262
82. Ibid., 265.

First, each of these figures assumes a divinely authored commonality exists between church and world prior to witness, a commonality that renders intelligible the Christian concerns of war and peace to the world. As Charles Mathewes argues, because humanity shares in a common (yet divided) originating love of God (central to our anthropology), we can reasonably believe that the church/world duality is an evasive posture taken to avoid the consequences of our ontology;[83] because all persons (in both church and world) share love as the root of the soul, the question for Mathewes is not whether church and world share something in common but how to name that which is held in common by all persons.[84] Whether one is persuaded by Mathewes's argument or not, he rightly identifies that for Augustine, creaturely life is a condition shared by church and non-church—that the sustained life of creation provides reason to assume that what Christians mean when they speak of "peace" is not entirely dissimilar to that which is meant in the discourses of the world. For Bonhoeffer, Augustine's interior movement of God manifests itself to us via the externals of human community. As Bonhoeffer argues, the call of God comes to the collective person; the Holy Spirit uses the natural bonds that exist between humans to reform human life through encounters with others.[85] Whether we understand the unity of human life to approach us via an internal animus of love or an external sociality, both Augustine and Bonhoeffer acknowledge that human unity is Trinitarian; the relation between the church (as the body of persons undergoing Triune restoration of human life) and the world is

83. Mathewes, *Theology of Public Life,* 81, 314ff.

84. Ibid., 82ff. For a clear rendering of this theme, see Oliver O'Donovan, *Objects of Common Love: Moral Reflection and the Shaping of Community* (Grand Rapids: Eerdmans, 2002).

85. Bonhoeffer, *Sanctorum Communio,* 118. The idea of the collective person does not negate the individual's knowledge of God or sublate individuals before the collective in the divine economy; rather, it means that individuals are given their specificity through social bonds, which the Holy Spirit uses (136).

already present because of the work of God, which makes the opportunity for witness possible.[86]

Second, the figures described in the chapters to come all believe that, though witness is performed in and through ecclesial resources, the church is not the end of witness. Rather, the church bears witness to the renewing work of God in Christ, who forms the body, structures, institutions, and practices of the church; however, the church is not identical to these things. This distinction-in-unity of Christ and the church allows the figures discussed here to practice a nonviolent resistance to war that is deeply framed by ecclesiological practices, doctrines, and institutions and that also pushes back against ecclesiology, insofar as nonviolent resistance is ultimately a practice of witness to the reconciling person and work of Christ to both the world and the church. As I have already suggested, acts of discipleship such as nonviolent resistance to war bear witness to the unity of Christ's work through diverse bodies.

As John Flett puts it, viewing the church as the terminus of witness is problematic in that witness can easily become propaganda for the church's doctrines, rather than witness to the ongoing work of Christ.[87] Viewing the Scriptures, church practices, and institutions as witnesses to Christ's person and work rather than the object of witness itself directs attention to Christ's person, in which the church participates by means of its institutions, doctrines, and practices but does not circumscribe. If God's creation—including human unity—is

86. Both Bonhoeffer and Augustine emphasize the way in which human unity is a datum of creation, though they differ on how this unity is witnessed to. For Bonhoeffer, the datum of howhuman life might have been unified in a prelapsarian world is lost to us, meaning that we can only speak of human unity insofar as we speak of its reunification in Christ. See *Creation and Fall*, 22–23. For Augustine, however, the datum of human unity exists in the soul of all created persons as an analogy of God's unity, which is also explicated in the doctrine of creation. See Jean-Luc Marion, "Resting, Moving, Loving: The Access to the Self according to Saint Augustine," *Journal of Religion* 91 (2011), 24–42.

87. John Flett, "Communion as Propaganda: Reinhard Hutter and the Missionary Witness of the 'Church as Public,'" *Scottish Journal of Theology* 62 (2009), 457–76.

torn apart as a result of war, as Augustine understood it to be, then bearing witness to Christ's work must emphasize the ways in which the church is the foretaste of human unity but not its creator.[88]

Third, in addition to witness assuming human commonality and bearing witness to Christ and not the church, the figures I will discuss understand nonviolent witness to proceed through the use of the goods at hand in the form of available discourses, tactics, movements, and allies. If war is a theological problem common to a creaturely life created by God—with the church embedded as the witness to Christ within the world—it is not surprising that ecclesially-born resistance to war resonates from within creation. As Augustine and Bonhoeffer both attest (in different ways), the church exists in commonality with the world; whether named by the common features of sociality (Bonhoeffer) or love (Augustine), the church exists as a creaturely body *in via*,witnessing to its neighbors by means of faculties, words, and practices common to the church and the church's neighbors.

Thus, the sharing of a common creaturely life by the church and the world does not preclude the use of alternate discourses, habits, and practices that do not have an explicitly ecclesial origin for the task of witness, insofar as the church exists in the world as the firstfruits of Christ's work. Sharing an origin and telos, however, does not mean that all tools, discourses, and cultural produces are equally available to both the church and world; as the figures of this book will attest, the church reconfigures creation by the Spirit to bear witness toward creation's true nature in Christ. As I will show, this shared creaturehood does mean that drawing from the wells of other

88. Cf. Leslie Newbigin, *The Gospel in a Pluralist Society* (Grand Rapids: Eerdmans, 1989), 232–33: "If the gospel is to challenge the public life of our society . . . it will not be by forming a Christian political party, or by aggressive propaganda campaigns. It will only be by movements which begin with the local congregation in which the reality of the new creation is present, known and experienced, and from which men and women will go into every sector of public life to claim it for Christ. . . . as sign, instrument and foretaste of God's redeeming grace for the whole life of society."

resistance movements—such as Marxism, international law, and Latin American politics—is permissible, insofar as these discourses also seek peace and can be appropriated critically by Christians in that light. With this in mind, let us turn to these four witnesses who, in their plurality, offer an ecumenical witness by the Spirit to the work of God in Christ through the church.

2

The Church *as* Nonviolent: John Howard Yoder, Dialogical Nonviolence, and the Church's Performance

In this chapter, I will examine one of the best known Christian proponents of ecclesially-rooted nonviolence from the last century: John Howard Yoder. The last decade has seen a flurry of interest in Yoder, with the emergence of various unpublished or neglected works.[1] Without question, Yoder's work has been an inspiration to

1. These new primary works include, but are not limited to: *A Theology of Mission: A Believers Church Perspective*, ed. Gayle Gerber Koontz and Andy Alexis-Baker (Downers Grove, IL: IVP Academic, 2014); *Revolutionary Christianity: The 1966 South American Lectures*, ed. Paul Martens, Mark Thiessen Nation, Matthew Porter, and Myles Werntz (Eugene, OR: Cascade, 2012); *The War of the Lamb: The Ethics of Nonviolence and Peacemaking*, ed. Glenn Stassen, Mark Theissen Nation, and Matt Hamsher(Grand Rapids: Brazos, 2009); and *Nonviolence: A Brief History*, ed. Paul Martens, Matthew Porter, and Myles Werntz (Waco, TX: Baylor University Press, 2009.

I would be remiss not to note the manner in which Yoder's personal shortcomings have become an issue of much discussion, particularly with regards to inappropriate relationships with women throughout his career. Though worth attending to, these issues do not fall within the direct purview of this chapter. Recent attention has been called to the interrelationship

many in the last twenty-five years, with his major contributions to theology and ethics coming in the form of his work on war and peace. Though he was resistant to being known only for his contributions to these subjects, the persistent theme of Christian witness in war pervades his work on biblical studies, ecumenism, church polity, and systematic theology. However, it would be wrong to reduce Yoder's work only to war and peace; as I will argue, his writings on war are embedded in a deeper logic of ecclesiology.

For Yoder, Christianity's best and truest witness against the challenge of war is the church itself. As he writes on more than one occasion, Christianity presents not an idea of peace but an embodiment of peace; Christianity offers a different way of existence as an alternative to war that is made possible by the person of Jesus Christ.[2] Far from being an isolationist proposal—wherein the logic of the church is unintelligible to society—Yoder's understanding both of the church and the church's witness trades on a dialogical relation with the world. According to Yoder, the church exists "as an anticipation of that consummation" of the world—"the absolute norm which is valid for both and in contradiction to which the world will never succeed in building even a stable temporal order."[3] Throughout his life, Yoder identified a number of practices that aid this witness, but, as I will argue, nonviolent resistance to war becomes the most significant of these practices for identifying the theological character

between these abuses and his theology by Ruth Krall, whose documentary work is available at http://ruthkrall.com/wordpress/downloadable-books/volume-three-the-mennonite-church-and-john-howard-yoder-collected-essays/. I have engaged these issues at length in my essay "The Body and the Body of Christ: Coakley, Yoder, and the Imitation of Christ," in *Sarah Coakley and the Future of Systematic Theology*, ed. Ben Myers and Janice Rees (Minneapolis: Fortress Press, forthcoming).

2. See, for example, John Howard Yoder, *Christian Witness to the State* (Scottdale, PA: Herald, 1992), 17: "The church is herself a society. Her very existence, the fraternal relations of her members, their ways of dealing with their differences and their needs are, or rather should be, a demonstration of what love means in social relations."
3. Ibid.

of the church and describing how the church is identified as Christ's witness to the world.

In this chapter, I will unpack how the church, as a dialogical body, bears witness to the world by displaying the church's practice, teaching, and worship as the embodied, nonviolent alternative to war. After briefly locating Yoder within the larger currents of Mennonite thought during the latter half of the twentieth century, I will describe Yoder's ecclesiology, emphasizing the manner in which Christ's work establishes the conditions proper to the church. Continuing in Christ's way, the church bears witness to a new way of social existence, to a world still suffering the violent effects of sin.

If Christ makes possible the "idea" of redemption as well as a new social reality, then the church becomes God's embodied alternative to war. While not a foundational practice of the church, nonviolent resistance to war is—for Yoder—an indispensible practice because the refusal to wage war bears witness to the kind of community the church inhabits and the nature of the God they serve. In this chapter (and in each subsequent chapter), I will limit my examination of Yoder's work to the years leading up to and involving Vietnam. Questions remain concerning the ways in which Yoder's theology changes after this point, though I maintain that my presentation of his thought here is largely consistent with his later writings, or at least provides a proper framework for reading his later work.[4]

4. Debate over how to read the overall shape of Yoder's corpus has been recently reignited by Paul Martens's *The Heterodox Yoder* (Eugene, OR: Cascade, 2011) and the subsequent responses to the book, most notably Branson Parler, *The Forest and the Trees: Engaging Paul Martens's* The Heterodox Yoder (http://erb.kingdomnow.org/wp-content/uploads/2012/03/BParler-Forest.pdf). Though I will not be directly engaging this debate, I maintain that Martens's thesis regarding the shape and direction of Yoder's work is by and large an accurate assessment.

Ecclesiology and Witness: Yoder's Theological Inheritance

Before describing Yoder's ecclesiology and its relationship to nonviolence within his writings, context is needed for understanding Yoder's concerns. For those unfamiliar with his work, Yoder can easily be misunderstood as a "sectarian" because of his abiding concern for the church's integrity over against the corrupting influences of "Constantinianism"—Yoder's shorthand for what he sees as the church's exchange of Christological peculiarity for worldly power and prestige.[5] However, Yoder's own theology attempts to overcome what he saw as a divide between the church and the world, which was perpetuated by prior generations of Mennonites.[6] Prior to the Second World War, most American Mennonites held a position known as "nonresistance," which implies not only a non-cooperative stance vis-à-vis the government and war but also a relationship between the church and the world that entails separation from the world.[7] Put differently, "nonresistance" implies a "two-kingdom"

5. In his use of the word *Constantinian*, Yoder names a shift away from Christ's particularity to a more generalized ethic, which entails compromises in the church's relationship to society, its eschatology, and its understanding of the temporal nature of salvation. See "The Constantinian Sources of Western Social Ethics," in *The Priestly Kingdom: Social Ethics as Gospel* (Notre Dame: University of Notre Dame Press, 1984), 135–50, as well as "The Otherness of the Church," in *The Royal Priesthood: Essays Ecclesiological and Ecumenical*, ed. Michael G. Cartwright (Grand Rapids: Eerdmans, 1994), 53–64.
6. Assessments of Yoder's theology and ethics suffer from a surprising neglect of historical context, which pay ill attention to the development of his work over time. Recent intellectual biographies on Yoder have begun to remedy this problem. See Earl Zimmerman, *Practicing the Politics of Jesus: The Origin and Significance of John Howard Yoder's Social Ethics* (Telford, PA: Cascadia, 2007); Mark Theissen Nation, *John Howard Yoder: Mennonite Patience, Evangelical Witness, Catholic Convictions* (Grand Rapids: Eerdmans Publishing Co., 2005). Nation comes to the conclusion that "John Howard Yoder was a remarkably consistent thinker, both over a period of more than four decades and across several sub-disciplines within theology," (189). While certain features may remain consistent, I have found that tensions within Yoder's work concerning the relationship of the church and the world become more strained over time.
7. The use of "nonresistance" and "non-resistance" will be used interchangeably, depending on the author's preference. For a pre-First World War Mennonite stance on war, see Gerlof D. Homan, *American Mennonites and the Great War, 1914–1918* (Scottdale, PA: Herald, 1994), 29–43. The theology of nonresistance is best summarized by Guy Hershberger, *War, Peace, and Nonresistance* (Scottdale, PA: Herald, 1946), 188, in which he states, "The New Testament

theology, which demarcates two areas of life within temporal existence—one Christocentric and one sinful.[8] The kingdom of Christ, governed by the teachings of Jesus (particularly the Sermon on the Mount), is accompanied by practices implied in these teachings, such as avoiding government involvement and the violence that often accompanies involvement in certain aspects of government life.[9]

During the Second World War (the era of Yoder's childhood), American Mennonite congregations underwent significant changes with respect to their relation to the broader American culture as well as to government structures and war.[10] As earlier "island

is concerned with redemption through Jesus and Christ and with the manner of life which Christians should live. All other matters are incidental to this . . . Jesus and Paul do not suggest what type of state is most desirable, nor how it should be conducted. It is not suggested that Christians should play any role in the affairs of state. The Sermon on the Mount is not a piece of legislation for a secular state in a sinful society; it is a set of principles to govern the conduct of members of the kingdom of God; and Jesus said this kingdom is not of this world, and that its members do not fight." This statement is dependent in many ways upon the much older Mennonite confession known as the Schleitheim Confession. See *The Schleitheim Confession*, trans. John Howard Yoder (Scottdale, PA: Herald, 1977).

8. This vein of nonresistance thought is not to be confused with Lutheran "two-kingdoms" thought, which is rooted in a vision of jurisprudence. The Mennonite vision is best characterized by Menno Simons, who wrote, "If you are rightly baptized according to the Scriptures, then you are incorporated into the holy inviolable body of Christ, which is the church . . . If you are one of these, why do you live in pride, whoredom, avarice, adultery, hate, envy, treachery, murder, idolatry, and all forms of ungodliness after the fashion of those not born of God and heaven but of a prince of hell? You surely know that Christ Jesus is not a leader nor a prince of unrighteousness, ferocious, and bloody men, and he will not have them in his body, the church, city, and kingdom," in *"Confession" and "The New Birth,"* trans. and ed. Irvin B. Horst (Lancaster, PA: Lancaster Mennonite Historical Society, 1996), 47.
9. Within Anabaptist historiography, many have challenged this description of Anabaptists. John Howard Yoder's dissertation, published in English as *Anabaptism and Reformation in Switzerland: An Historical and Theological Analysis of the Dialgoues between Anabaptists and Reformers*, ed. C. Arnold Snyder, trans. David Stassen and C. Arnold Snyder (Kitchener, ON: Pandora, 2003) challenges the traditional reading of Mennonites as "passive" and "withdrawn" from public debates. Cf., James M. Stayer, *Anabaptists and the Sword* (Lawrence, KS: Coronado, 1973). I do not wish to enter into the debates of Anabaptist historiography but simply to assert that for pre-Second World War American Mennonites, Hershberger's definition of Mennonite nonresistance is a fair reading.
10. Perry Bush, *Two Kingdoms, Two Loyalties: Mennonite Pacifism in America* (Baltimore: Johns Hopkins Press, 1998), 130ff, has argued that the shift in Mennonite responses to war from the early-twentieth century to the later twentieth century are a result of the movement from

communities" of American Mennonite life gave way to less geographically and socially isolated enclaves, Mennonite thinking concerning involvement in war began to embrace more activist approaches. For example, the traditional "Old Mennonite" congregations (of which Yoder was a member as a boy) began to draw from a more urban and less isolated population, complicating their ability to avoid entanglements with the world.[11] Similarly, the General Conference Mennonite Churches (GCMC) began to divide along generational lines concerning how to articulate their vision for social involvement.

These cultural shifts were accompanied by shifts in the Mennonite relationship to war. During the First World War, Mennonites were largely able to secure conscientious objector status but only after being drafted into the military.[12] Even though a growing number of Mennonites were able to secure conscientious objector status during the Second World War, Mennonites were asked to support war in more indirect ways, such as the acceptance of non-combat service and payment of taxes for war preparations, complicating a divide between church and war that could be more easily predicated by earlier generations.[13]

agrarian life to urban life. Concerning this shift, see J. Howard Kauffman and Leo Driedger, *The Mennonite Mosaic: Identity and Modernization* (Scottdale, PA: Herald, 1991); Albert Keim and Grant Stoltzfus, *The Politics of Conscience: The Historic Peace Churches and America at War, 1917–1955* (Scottdale, PA: Herald, 1988).

11. For Yoder's history among this branch of Mennonites, see Nation, *John Howard Yoder*, 2–9.

12. Bush, *Two Kingdoms,* 52–56. Earlier in the book, Bush details various humanitarian efforts begun between 1920–1927 by the newly founded Mennonite Central Committee, which give voice to Mennonite missions and centralize these efforts in international contexts such as the aftermath of war. Between 1903 and 1916, various versions of the Militia Act made provision for conscientious objection to war, culminating in the 1918 Selective Service Act, which allowed draftees to be exempt from combat if they "belonged to a well-organized religious sect." This exemption, however, did not excuse Mennonites from rendering alternative service in the event that they were drafted; consequently, Mennonites had to choose either non-compliance with the government or submit to the draft and receive a non-combat assignment (ibid., 28–30).

13. Legal provisions did little to shield Mennonites from public insults or attacks. Mennonite churches were burned in place, and by 1918, all German-speaking schools in the jurisdiction of

Complexities indicated by new taxation and new rules concerning conscription began to undermine older modes of simple resistance, and were indicative of other changes taking place in the traditional ways that Mennonites had responded to American wars. Older Mennonites primarily spoke in terms of *nonresistance* (non-cooperation with the government), while the younger generation began using the language of *peace*, a term that called for a more active engagement with the world. For the older generation, the call to peace seemed more reminiscent of early-twentieth century liberal pacifism than of traditional Mennonite teaching.[14] In the interwar period of the 1930s, various Mennonite Brethren handbooks began to speak in terms of "condemning war and advocating peace" instead of, and sometimes alongside, the concept of nonresistance.[15] Within Mennonite ranks, the two distinct positions—the traditional *nonresistance* and the modern activist *peace* nomenclature—retained their own supporters.[16] But as institutional vehicles for a more

the Mennonite General Conference had been closed. See Homan, *American Mennonites,* 64–80. For further documentary evidence concerning Mennonite experience during the First World War, see Peter Brock, *Freedom from Violence: Sectarian Nonresistance from the Middle Ages to the Great War* (Toronto: University of Toronto Press, 1991) and *Pacifism in the United States: From the Colonial Era to the First World War* (Princeton: Princeton University Press, 1969).

14. Reinhold Niebuhr's accusations that the refusal of Christians to engage in war is both sectarian and a Christian heresy lurk in the background of the First World War. See Reinhold Niebhur, "A Critique of Pacifism," *Love and Justice: Selections from the Shorter Writings of Reinhold Niebuhr*, ed. D.B. Robertson (Louisville: Westminster John Knox, 1957), 241–47. Niebuhr's critique is directed primarily at the liberal pacifism of the twentieth century, which derives its animus from a belief in the peaceable progress of history; Niebuhr believes this position lacks a doctrine of human fallenness. However, the charge of "social irresponsibility" would haunt Mennonites throughout the twentieth century, particularly John Howard Yoder, who repeatedly returned to Niebuhr's charge.
15. Leo Driedger and Donald Kraybill, *Mennonite Peacemaking: From Quietism to Activism* (Scottdale, PA: Herald, 1993), 68, describe how a 1939 "Handbook on Peace" speaks of a "program of peace"; formal statements issued by the General Conference of Mennonites speak of the need to "present and interpret our peace principles to others," in contrast to earlier statements that do not treat peace as a "program" or see the need for interpretation of Mennonite teachings. See also Ervin Stutzman, *From Nonresistance to Justice: The Transformation of Mennonite Church Peace Rhetoric 1908–2008* (Scottdale, PA: Herald, 2011).
16. Dreidger and Kraybill, *Mennonite Peacemaking*, 70.

proactive witness to nonviolence emerged, Mennonite thinking began to shift away from passive nonresistance to a more active peace advocacy.[17]

As Mennonite thinking progressed in the 1950s (the time when Yoder began his work in full), *nonresistance*—rooted in a two-kingdom model, had increasingly become a term used by older generations. In its place, talk of the church's "peace" became increasingly common, understanding the totality of the world under the "Lordship of Christ." This phrase, describing a single cosmos under God's providential care in which Mennonites were called to witness to the unbelieving world, went hand in hand with the new emphasis on "peace" over "nonresistance." For Yoder and his generation, the refusal of war was not a distancing of the church from the world but an act that bore witness both to who the church was called to be and to the life the world was meant for.

Ecclesiology and Witness: Uniting and Distinguishing Church and World

In sum, Yoder's earliest work exhibits a concern with moving beyond the dualist worldview of some of his forbearers. Soon after graduation from Goshen College, Yoder began to critique his predecessors' dichotomous solution of "church" versus "world"; in an unpublished essay from his college years, "Cooking the Anabaptist Goose," Yoder

17. These vehicles include the "peace church" moniker—which drew a variety of traditionally pacifist churches together under one umbrella—and the "Peace Problems" Committee, the forerunner to the Mennonite Central Committee, which operated independently until it folded into the Mennonite Central Committee's Peace Section in 1919. Yoder would later be a board member of this committee. In the 1950 Winona Lake Conference (the first inter-Mennonite gathering around peace in North America), the statements issuing from that meeting use *nonresistance* twice, while *Lordship of Christ*, *social order*, and *witness* appear nearly twice as many times, emphasizing a Mennonite calling within the "total social order of which we are a part" (ibid., 85). As early as 1922, the question was being raised at national conventions as to whether *peacemaker* should be read as more than *nonresistance* and involve active forms of advocacy (ibid., 67ff).

explains that the vision of his mentor and Old Mennonite Harold Bender "put us in the comfortable position of being able to talk back to 'compromisers' . . . accusing them of plain and simple disobedience to the pure and clear truth."[18] Similarly, in the 1954 inaugural issue of *Concern* (a journal started by Yoder and his friends), Yoder explains that any withdrawal from society by Christians, though at times necessary, cannot be absolute.[19] As Yoder explains, there is

> real value in God's plan to the "good heathen" . . . on the level of conversation, who through honest application of sub-Christian ethics do carry a real responsibility for justice in the social order . . . The Bible's injunctions to support to the government . . . all indicate that some morality is better than none. But what the Anabaptist-Mennonite dichotomist challenges is the validity of that *kind* of goodness on the redemptive level of Christian ethics.[20]

For Yoder, the ability to speak to the outside world assumes that "God works in the world on two separate levels, one through the conscious obedience of Christians, the other by ruling over and balancing against each other men's disobediences."[21]

18. Yoder, "Cooking the Anabaptist Goose," John Howard Yoder Papers, box 11, Mennonite Church USA Archives, Goshen, IN. Cited in Zimmerman, *Practicing the Politics of Jesus,* 46. This particular document is the first of many tense writings between Yoder and Bender as the pupil began to dissent from the teacher's vision. See Zimmerman 33–37, 42–50, 102–4 for the relationship between Yoder and his mentor Harold Bender. Likewise, this question became the subject of Yoder's first scholarly publication, "Caesar and the Meidung," *Mennonite Quarterly Review* 23 (1949), 76–98, in which Yoder examines the "difficulties of relating the state to minority religious groups," (76). In other unpublished letters, Yoder connects this phenomenon to the growth of Goshen College in relation to Mennonite life; in the absence of active relation to the world, Yoder sees Mennonites as engaging in unnecessary institution-building. In particular, see the Yoder-Bender letters in Yoder Papers, box 7.
19. Yoder, "The Anabaptist Dissent: The Logic of the Place of the Disciple in Society," in *The Roots of Concern: Writings on Anabaptist Renewal 1952–1957*, ed. Virgil Vogt (Eugene, OR: Cascade, 2009): 29–43: "The term as here used should be clearly distinguished from its ecclesiological usage, where it signifies the separation of a church from other churches in order to be pure, as well as from its epistemological sense, where it refers to the claim to be sole possessor of the truth" (30).
20. Ibid., 35.
21. Ibid.

Seen most clearly in his now-famous 1954 "Peace Without Eschatology?," Yoder characterizes these levels as two different "aeons" with two different social manifestations, arguing that human history "outside of Christ" is of "the world" while existence with an eschatological orientation toward "the fullness of the kingdom of God" corresponds to "the church."[22] Jesus founded a "new aeon" characterized not by "government" (a coercive entity of the "old aeon") but by the possibility of "*agape*; self-giving, nonresistant love."[23] Jesus, whose life preeminently exemplifies this ethic, "is not only the Head of the church; He is at the same time Lord of history, reigning at the right hand of God over the principalities and powers."

The difference between the old and new aeon—namely, the difference between the church and the world—plays out in history along multiple lines, but most significantly in the difference between agape and vengeance:

> The essential change which has taken place is not within the realm of the old aeon, vengeance and the state, where there really is no change; it is rather that the new aeon revealed in Christ takes primacy over the old, explains the meaning of the old, and will finally vanquish the old. The state did not change with the coming of Christ; what changed was the coming of the new aeon which proclaimed doom of the old one.[24]

This clash of aeons—between vengeance and agape, between the state and nonresistant love—leads to "the final triumph of God," as nonresistance "anticipate[s] the triumph of the Lamb that was slain";

22. Yoder, "Peace without Eschatology," in *Cartwright, Royal Priesthood*, 146. The essay dates back to a theological study conference in Heerenwegen, Zeist (Netherlands) in May 1954, after which it was reprinted as a part of the *Concern* pamphlet series in 1961, and again in *The Original Revolution: Essays in Christian Pacifism* in 1971.

23. Yoder, "Peace without Eschatology," 147. In letters with J. Lawrence Burkholder, professor of Bible and philosophy at Goshen College, Yoder takes issue with what he calls the "abstractness" of agape language, which he initially concludes lacks "specific clarity." See "Letter to Paul Peachey, June 23, 1956," Yoder Papers, box 7. Yoder will adopt *agape* with modification in his *Christian Witness to the State*.

24. Yoder, "Peace without Eschatology," 149–50 (italics mine).

those belonging to this new sociality participate in nonviolence in anticipation of its eschatological validation. Both aeons stand under the reign of Christ but are divided along the visible line of fidelity to Christ, which is characterized by a refusal of vengeance and violence. Not all bodies calling themselves churches, however, were inclined to accept this distinction. Yoder argues that many bodies confessing Jesus abandoned this nonresistance in favor of a false hope of "effectiveness" or "Constantinianism"; thus, they submitted to the grip of the old aeon (i.e. the realm of the powers) by participating in the legitimization of violence.[25] Those of the new aeon (i.e. those following in the way of Jesus) practice nonviolence, an act often opposed by bodies calling themselves churches.[26]

In his early writings, Yoder continues to describe the distinction between church and world, using the language of "powers and principalities" to this end and distinguishing between the two (in part) by their recourse to violence.[27] In the first paper of *Discipleship* ("The State in the New Testament"), Yoder argues that the "state" (a term which is "the most deeply representative for 'world'")[28] is "an

25. Ibid., 153–57. The most damning point in Yoder's critique involves those Reformers who colluded with the state; they are to blame for a division among the institutional church whereas "some so-called 'sects,' notably the sixteenth-century Anabaptists, the seventeenth-century Quakers, the eighteenth-century Moravians, and the nineteenth-century Open Brethren" are named as faithful witnesses.

26. This logic is central to Yoder's argument with Reinhold Niebuhr's critique of pacifism a year later. See Yoder, "Reinhold Niebuhr and Christian Pacifism," *Mennonite Quarterly Review* 29 (1955), 101–17. Here, Yoder argues for an eschatological approach that, consequently, enables Christians to argue for God's rule over the entire world "within history": "The acceptance of the cross, i.e. the full cost of utter obedience to the loving nature of God, is the path to the accomplishment in history . . . of action which can please God and be useful to men. . . . That this triumph over sin is incomplete changes in no way the fact that it is possible, and that if God calls us to deny ourselves, accept suffering, and love our neighbors, that too is possible" (116).

27. For a full description of Yoder's use of this language and its theological import, see Scott Prather, *Christ, Power, and Mammon: Karl Barth and John Howard Yoder in Dialogue* (Edinburgh: T&T Clark, 2013).

28. The state remains "a deeply representative segment of the 'world'" because of its organization "by the appeal to force as ultimate authority" and is under Christ's triumph, while not the same as the church. See Yoder, *Christian Witness to the State*, 12.

expression of God's grace aimed at redemption, by keeping God's fallen creation in existence . . . with a view toward the God-intended redemption of the fallen creation."[29] But while the state accomplishes great deeds for the common good, it resorts to violence—one of the "powers, rulers, principalities, [and] thrones" identified in the New Testament—to accomplish its ends. Powers such as the state

> responded to Christ with hostility, but Jesus became Lord through his death, resurrection and ascension; his Lordship extends even over these powers, who, as a result will have to bend their knees (Phil. 2:10). Of these Christ made a spectacle, just as a returning victor does in a triumph march (Col. 2:15).[30]

In this sense, Christ's conquering of the powers means that the church can now live in light of Christ's work without resorting to the violence that characterizes the world. The church is known not by simply rejecting the world and its powers but by carrying on Christ's refusal of the world's way of life:

> The cross-carrying following which the church practices, that is the continuing life of Jesus through his Spirit in the members of his body, is not an implication, something tacked on; rather it is part of his saving work. That is what the new Testament means when it speaks of following, of the body of Christ, of the Holy Spirit—that God's continuing work is no less valid, no less divine, no less urgent than it was from the start . . . It is self-evident and never to be forgotten, that the cross of the church has no meaning without Jesus. But we are too reluctant to confess the other side along with the Scriptures, namely, that without the cross of the church, the cross of Christ would be emptied.[31]

29. John Howard Yoder, *Discipleship as Political Responsibility* (Scottdale, PA: Herald, 1964), 18. Yoder distinguishes between the violent practices done by the government and other acts for the common good. See ibid., 40: "Today we make a distinction between a totalitarian and a welfare state. The state is not there only to guard our physical security; the state also builds roads, leads schools, provides medical services, cares for the elderly and delivers everyone's mail . . . Many of the activities of the modern state are only remotely connected, or not connected at all with the exercise of violence to protect what is right. Still even here we are confronted with a difference only in terms of concepts."
30. Ibid., 19.

It is important to note the link that Yoder makes: the church does not exist as an "imitation" of Jesus' ethic, but, continuing in the way of Jesus, the church continues Jesus' own work. However, this is true only insofar as bodies that worship Jesus continue their allegiance to Jesus in a rejection of violence by attesting to and bearing witness to Christ, making known the true nature of the acts of the world as fallen acts, which use violence for erstwhile worthy ends.[32]

As I noted before, though Yoder's formulation here distinguishes between church and world, it is not dualist; because powers are equivalent to modern-day "structures," those of the new aeon are constantly given opportunity to communicate with the old aeon through these ubiquitous powers and structures, with which everyone must deal.[33] The relation between the church and the world—the "coexistence of two ages or aeons"—is not described in terms of essences but "direction":

> The church points forward as the social manifestation of the ultimately triumphant redemptive work of God; the world, however, even though still rebellious, is brought into subjection to the kingship of Christ or the kingdom of the Son. The kingdom of the Son is thus to be distinguished, insofar as we may be permitted to speak systematically, from the kingdom of God.[34]

As his reworked and republished essay, "The Otherness of the Church," makes clear:

31. Ibid., 22.
32. Ibid., 23.
33. Yoder, *Christian Witness to the State*, 8: "In biblical language *powers* would be roughly the equivalent of the modern term *structures*, by which psychological and sociological analysts refer to the dimensions of cohesiveness and purposefulness which hold together human affairs beyond the strictly personal level, especially in such realms as that of the state or certain areas of culture." This work was prepared in 1955 as a work paper, reworked as part of a study assignment by the Institute of Mennonite Studies from 1958–59, and published in 1964.
34. Ibid., 10. Yoder prefers the term "kingdom of Christ" because of the specificity it lends in comparison to the nebulous "Kingdom of God" (ibid., 9–10).

> "World" . . . signifies . . . not creation or nature or the universe but rather the fallen form of the same, no longer conformed to the creative intent. The state, which for present purposes may be considered as typical for the world, belongs with the other *exousiai* in this realm. Over against this "world" the church is visible, identified by baptism, discipline, morality, and martyrdom.[35]

The church (defined by its faithful practices) relates to the world (defined as a set of practices constituting "creaturely order in the state of rebellion") by undertaking common human activities that the church orients toward God rather than away from God.[36]

Thus, Christ's overcoming of the powers makes possible a new aeon characterized by the rejection of violence—a social existence that describes the church as it engages in this work; the church witnesses to the world through this rejection of violence—a world that has already been conquered by Christ but lives in rebellion to the way of Christ. The church witnesses to this victory through the embodiment of an alternative way in witness to Christ's work and in distinction from the world in its most emblematic way: violence.[37] For Yoder, the church cannot be reduced simply to a nonviolent gathering; during this early period of his work, themes of ecumenism, church polity, and pastoral ministry appear as frequently, if not more so, than themes of war and peace.

To grasp more fully how the church engages in this performative witness, we must examine Yoder's ecclesiology more closely, as we are now in a better position to see the careful line that Yoder must tread. On the one hand, a division certainly exists between church and world, as signified by the distance between obedience and

35. Yoder, "The Otherness of the Church," in *Cartwright, Royal Priesthood*, 54–64 (55).
36. Ibid., 56–57.
37. Yoder's own understanding of the "powers" developed most fully during his doctoral studies, especially when he came into contact with Hedrik Berkhof's *Christ and the Powers* through the direction of Karl Barth. See the preface to *Christ and the Powers*, trans. John Howard Yoder (Scottdale, PA: Herald, 1962), 9.

disobedience to Christ's way. On the other hand, this distinction cannot be resolved by way of the dualist tendencies latent in his Mennonite forebearers; the distance between those things under the sway of the powers (the world) and those that have been freed from the powers of death and violence (the church) involves "direction" and not complete division. Positing an absolute distinction between church and world disavows the Lordship of Christ over all creation.

Ecclesiology: The Dialogical Nature of Church Practice and Witness

We will return later to the prophetic border of the church's relation to the world, which Yoder characterizes here as the refusal of the world's violence. First, we must turn more explicitly to the question of witness, specifically, how a social body characterized by release from the powers and peaceability can relate to the wider world. In order to do so, we will turn to Yoder's dialogical ecclesiology. By "dialogical," I mean that Yoder characterizes the church as a form of dialogue that enables it to engage in the practice of dialogue with the world along available common lines. Only after understanding Yoder's terminology can we grasp the significance of his understanding of nonviolence as a dialogical practice that communicates what the church is in comparison to the world.

For Yoder, the church could engage in dialogue because the church *is* a dialogue, a position he asserts dating back to his 1957 dissertation on the Swiss Anabaptists.[38] Whereas the Zwinglian

38. Published initially as *Taufertum und Reformation in der Schweiz I. Die Gesprache zwischen Taufern und Reformatoern 1523–1538* (Karlsruhe, Ger.: Verlag H. Schnedier, 1962). Translated as pt. 1 of *Anabaptism and Reformation in Switzerland: An Historical and Theological Analysis of the Dialogues between Anabaptists and Reformers*, ed. C. Arnold Snyder, trans. David Carl Stassen and C. Arnold Snyder (Kitchener, ON: Pandora, 2004). Part 2, translated as pt. 2 of *Anabaptism and Reformation*, was published initially as *Taufertum und Reformatoern im Gesprach: Dogmengeschichtliche Untersuchung der fruhen Gesprache zwischen Sweizerischen Taufern und Reformatoren* (Zurich: EVZ-Verlag, 1968).

branch of the Reformation utilized a separation of church and world that could not conceive of analogs between unbaptized society and the church, the Swiss Anabaptists did not experience this kind of strict duality.[39] The Anabaptists, rejecting the claim of two orders, understood the arguments of the Zwinglians to be rooted in an "ontological dualism."[40] For the Anabaptists, church and world are related in the same way that perfection is related to the imperfect.[41] However, this external dialogue with the world is predicated on the church's existence *as* a dialogue:

> Was it not necessary to belong to an entity—or better—a series of events that one could call either "community" or "dialogue" for the establishing of [biblical] knowledge? . . . Is it not conceivable that the community's functioning would be constitutive for a theological epistemology as a *fundamental pre-condition for valid knowledge of God*, standing, to be sure, under Scripture, but certainly above the theologians, not as a restriction but rather as an *essential clarification of the scriptural principle*?[42]

Yoder concludes that conversations between other Reformers and the Anabaptists took place not in order "to escape persecution, but out of a fully-developed theological . . . *ecclesiology*."[43] For the Anabaptists, the true church is an entity characterized by a dialogical form that assumes the presence of the Spirit because of the process by which the church operates, as much as because of the center around which it gathers (Scripture).[44] Only by being the church-as-dialogue could

39. Yoder, *Anabaptism and Reformation*, 152. As Yoder explains Zwingli's view: "Existing sinfulness of humanity has, as its consequence, the fact that divine justice cannot be humanity's ultimate standard, for it is ordained for heaven. . . . Sin thus belongs so essentially to humanity that one can never speak of a transfer of divine justice to society."

40. Ibid., 156.

41. Ibid., 190–97. This analogy is also true for the way in which the "true church"—existing in the breaking of bread and baptism—relates to other churches that are created by birth or lineage. In this latter "imperfect" community, Yoder argues that the Anabaptists include Catholicism, which includes children by way of their parent's actions (198–202).

42. Ibid., 219 (italics Yoder's).

43. Ibid., 223 (italics mine).

44. Ibid., 224.

the church model the new aeon to the world.[45] Again, the church's confidence in dialogue (both as the church's performative mode and its mode of witness to the world) is rooted in Christ's victory over the powers, a victory that enables the church to dialogue with the world instead of violently overpowering it:

> The early church knew that the powers of this world (under which must counted the power of the sword) stood under the Lordship of Christ, even though all the statesmen were non-Christian. It knew that the community had to pressure the heathen state to do its duty to be just, in view of the victory Christ had already achieved. The fact that they abandoned the state to the heathens did not mean that the community abandoned it to the Devil, but rather that they had given it over to the Lordship of Christ . . . What truly represents this greater venture of faith, the greater trust in the Lordship of Christ over the powers of this world?[46]

As Yoder argues, "If one asks why the community should be visible and capable of action, then one finds this answer: It has to do with the life of Christ in his members," which enables the community to proceed dialogically rather than violently or coercively.[47]

Yoder continues this argument in a popular three-part series entitled "The Things That Are Caeasar's."[48] The church's advocacy—that the state live up to the practices of the Gospel (specifically in the rejection of war)—was not for the sake of the church's purity but "for our brother's welfare."[49] Yoder argues that

45. According to Yoder, when this model was transposed into the state, the results were disastrous. As the state church of the Netherlands, the Anabaptists "abandoned the dialogical character of the rule of Christ. This puritanical practice of church discipline must understand discipline as punishment that conformed to transgression in a casuistic manner" (227).

46. Ibid., 271.

47. Ibid., 299.

48. Yoder, "The Things That Are Caesar's," *Christian Living,* July 1960, 4, begins with Yoder's familiar bracketing of church and world under the Lordship of Christ, who reigns over "thrones, dominions, principalities and powers." See also "The Things That Are Ceasar's, Part 3," *Christian Living,* September 1960, 18.

49. "The Things That Are Caesar's," 5. Witness is given in all social actions, Yoder argues: "Even if it could not be argued absolutely convincingly that it is the Christian's duty to 'speak truth

because only "one order" exists, Christians can call upon the state for "limitations of the exercise of . . . power within the legal system" in order to operate according to the limits of the constitution and within the state's calling to keep order.[50] As the state, it will act insufficiently with regards to Christian justice, providing all the more reason for Christians to continue challenging state modes of "selfishness" that climax in war.[51] No place outside of a dialogical mode can be found for the church to exist, particularly in regard to war:

> On the one hand, the "whole system" argument, whereby the soldier, the executive, the legislator, the office worker, and the voting citizen are all morally on the same level, is unreasonable when taken seriously. The non-combatant soldier is not the same as the combatant soldier. If the Christian conscientious objector refuses both kinds of military service, it is because both are objectionable, not because one is polluted by the other . . . to follow this view consistently would make of Jesus Himself a sinner, for He, too, was involved in sinful society, its economy, its division of labor, and its politics.[52]

Describing dialogue as intrinsic to church life presents certain difficulties because church language remains in danger of being conscripted by the world. As Yoder remarked in a 1967 address,[53]

to power,' we shall keep on speaking. *Even our silence communicates.* Whether we vote or refuse to vote, we are saying something. Our participation in the economy, in the school system, in the market for newspapers and magazines, already speaks volumes. The difference between a witness to government that is explicit, and one that we give in spite of ourselves by our silence, is not a difference between being involved or not being involved; it is a matter of whether we are conscious and responsibly careful about what we say."

50. Yoder, "The Things That Are Ceasar's, Part 2," *Christian Living*, August 1960, 16.

51. Ibid., 17. Such witness is not equivalent to calling the state to salvation, rather, it is a call for the state to behave in analogous ways to the "perfection" of righteousness mirrored in church life.

52. Yoder, "The Things That Are Caesar's, Part 3," 18. As Yoder argues that if the church does not continue in this witness, it effectively ceases to be "church," in "The Theology of the Church's Mission," *Mennonite Life* (January 1966), 30–33. "This distinction between church and mission . . . is inadmissible. A human community which is not constantly both experiencing and proclaiming the transformation of the human situation by the coming of God among men will immediately degenerate into Judaism or paganism" (31).

53. Yoder, "A People in the World: Theological Interpretation," *Concept of the Believers' Church*, ed. James Leo Garrett (Scottdale, PA: Herald, 1969), 250–83. On 254, Yoder remarks that the

while "men are called together to a new social wholeness [that] is itself the work of God which gives meaning to history," the tendency is to think of the church as a "religious establishment of secular society" rather than a foretaste of human society.[54] Between the extremes of co-option by society and stark institutionalism, Yoder stakes out the church as a model that should be known by its corporate witness, meeting secular questions with responses beyond "reasonable expectations."[55]

Through the era of the Vietnam War, Yoder continued to argue that the dialogical partnership between church and world is facilitated through these dialogical practices.[56] Communal process and renunciation of power manifest themselves externally through the refusal of war and the promotion of reconciliatory initiatives. While the world cannot understand the internal process of Mennonites or the experience of faith present within the body of the church, the world can comprehend the refusal of war.[57]

This communication to the world by the church occurs through the "borrowing" of idioms familiar to the audience, though in a different sense than the borrowing of church practices from pagans, which Yoder rejects in *The Politics of Jesus*.[58] With respect to the

Anabaptist model of separation and freedom of conscience have proliferated to the point that these things can hardly be discussed without being misunderstood.

54. Ibid., 258–59.

55. Ibid., 266–70. Alain Epp Weaver calls this a "diasporic" existence, characterized by instability rather than security, in A. E. Weaver, "On Exile: Yoder, Said, and A Theology of Return," *Cross Currents* 52 (2003), 439–61. The position of tentativeness is, for Yoder, the freedom of the church. Cf., "People in the World," 276: "It would be possible to argue on either side of the thesis that, if Christians are to be in servitude to the powers and principalities, it at least is better that it be the powers of the future than those of the past. But from the context of the covenant community the argument should rather be that such servitude, whether past or future is part of what we have been freed from by the work of Christ and the gift of his Spirit."

56. Yoder, "Anabaptist Vision and Mennonite Reality," *Consultation on Anabaptist-Mennonite Theology* (Fresno: Council of Mennonite Seminaries, 1970), 1–46.

57. Ibid., 4.

58. Yoder, *The Politics of Jesus*, 2nd ed. (Grand Rapids: Eerdmans, 1994), 165ff. This work originally appeared in 1972. While Yoder notes that nothing in the text has changed between editions, I will be referring to the 1994 edition for the most part for its accessibility (vii). Yoder

external replication of Christian faith—as opposed to the adoption of pagan practices for internal church life—borrowing is inevitable and necessary; for Yoder, this practice has been used in missions throughout Christian history.[59] He argues that borrowing for the sake of witness helps the church resist the temptation to be a cultural enclave, enabling it to be more committed to Jesus' way and Jesus' reign in the world, even at the expense of denominational distinctives.[60]

Mission is carried out vis-à-vis these practices of discipleship, performed by a people who are a minority within a larger world.[61] These practices are not incidental to the church—an addition to a substantive definition of church—but rather, intrinsic. From Yoder's earliest work forward, descriptions of the church are centered in a concern for living out the ethics of the New Testament. Moreover, the church is not dependent on an invisible essence; as Yoder states, "Our attitude should be to New Testament *practice*, toward the *example* of the New Testament church."[62] Church, for Yoder, is not the institutions or creedal formulations that give "official voice" to the faith but a people who are brought into being by God's work through these practices of the faith.[63] Though Scripture remains the foundational guide for the church, the practices of the community are

adds epilogues to each chapter as a way of interacting with the twenty-five years between editions, but the developments in Yoder's thought during this period are not our direct concern here.

59. Yoder, "Anabaptist Vision and Mennonite Reality," 10–14. For a full rendering of Yoder on these themes, see *Theology of Mission: A Believers Church Perspective* (Downers Grove, IL: IVP Academic, 2014).

60. Yoder, "Anabaptist Vision and Mennonite Reality," 46.

61. Cf., Yoder, "Anabaptist Dissent," 29–34.

62. David A. Shenk and John Howard Yoder, "Biblicism and the Church," in *The Roots of Concern*, 67–101, (71) (italics in the original). Yoder's concern with the centrality of Scripture is that, apart from Scripture, Christians have no orientation for their witness to Christ. Concerning Yoder on the relation between Scripture and the practices of the church, see "The New Testament View of Ministry," *Gospel Herald*, February 8, 1955: 121–22, 124; "Der Statt im Neuen Testament," *Der Mennonit* (December 1957): 151; "Capital Punishment and the Bible," *Christianity Today*, February 1960, 3–6.

essential to the understanding of and conformation to the commands of Scripture.[64]

In terms of practice, this definition of a social body (whether it be church, world, or government) remains central to Yoder's work. As we have seen, the distinction between world and church does not consist of a timeless essence but of governance practices.[65] Insofar as world and church are composed of practice (which are often analogous), naming the practices of the state as hostile to Christ is a matter of naming their orientation: the state's wars, for example, are illegitimate because they demand an absolute allegiance that a person can give only to God.

What are we to make of these "practice" analogies between church and world and the ways in which they are central to the church's dialogical relation with the world? To be clear, Yoder is not equating the world and church; neither is he boiling down the practice of

63. For Yoder, institutions of the church exist for the sake of facilitating the growth and communal life of the people. See his later essay, "The Hermeneutics of Peoplehood," in *Priestly Kingdom*, 15–45. According to Yoder, those bodies that call themselves "church" are not always true church, i.e. a body that exists as the new community of witness to Christ's way. See *The Ecumenical Movement and the Faithful Church*, and "The Nature of the Unity We Seek," in *Cartwright, Royal Priesthood*, 221–30, in which Yoder states that "it would seem that the only feasible solution to the problem of authority would be to declare inadmissible the attribution of authoritative character to any particular historical development and to recognize, as the only legitimate judge *Christ himself* as he is made known through Scripture to the congregation of those who seek to know him and his will," 225, distinguishing between external structure and the obedient congregation. Yoder makes similar arguments in the later written "The Free Church Ecumenical Style," *Quaker Religious Thought* 10/11 (1968): 29–38.

64. I do not take this to negate Yoder's concern for the church as a place of free confession, but for Yoder, confession is inextricable from a life of discipleship that conforms to the confession of Christ as Lord. For this reason, the pastors of the church—who guide the practices of the church—have priority over teachers. Yoder delineates between the offices of "pastor" and "teacher," arguing that the pastor guides the church in its practical reasoning and congregational issues, while the teacher who speaks to the body on doctrinal issues should have no authority in terms of congregational life. The teacher directs the congregation to what Scripture says, but the act of helping a congregation conform to this model falls to the pastor and elders, in Shank and Yoder, "Biblicism and the Church," 85–88.

65. Yoder, *Christian Witness to the State*, 19–20. Yoder distinguishes between benign practices such as building roads and administering public works and more subversive practices, such as violence.

discernment within the church to a round-table, town hall discussion.[66] Insofar as one practice issues forth from obedience to Jesus and the other from the desire to come to a civic decision, the difference could be construed in terms of a substantialist ontology—namely, that a thing is what its essence is, independent of practice. Defining the church in these terms was particularly dissatisfying for Yoder because to speak of the church as having an essence independent of its practice is to speak of Jesus as a symbol and not a person who calls disciples to a narrow and difficult way.[67] Yoder does not eschew ontology altogether; rather, he rejects a particular ontology that secures the essence of a thing *behind* the enactment of a thing—whether it be a church as "faithful" independent of its obedience or a state as "good" independent of its violent practices. As such, Yoder articulates an ontology-of-practice: a thing *is* insofar as it *practices* in a certain way.

Having come to this understanding, we can see how the practices of the church, when performed as acts of obedience to Christ, are superior to analogous activities of the unbelieving state,

> if we believe along with the New Testament that through their Gospel proclamation, their prayers of supplication, their discipleship in the context of suffering, and their service of loving the neighbor, Christians contribute not less, but far more to human solidarity and therefore to the state than the political officials themselves.[68]

The state remains outside the perfection to which the church is privy—not simply because of deficient practice but because the church practices bear witness to a different kind of understanding of human sociality. The state-as-deficient-practice produces a society

66. On this promise and limits of the analogy, see Yoder, "The Christian Case for Democracy," in *Priestly Kingdom*, 151–71.

67. "The Constantinian Sources of Western Social Ethics," in *Priestly Kingdom*, 135–50.

68. Yoder, *Discipleship as Political Responsibility*, 32.

that withdraws from God in violence, as opposed to the church-as-true-practice, which bears witness to Christ through its practices of peaceableness.[69] Other aspects of the Scriptures—such as the commands—enable the church to know the force of the practices and direct the hearer of the commands to the practices of obedience; independent of engaging in the practices, coming to understand the commands of Scripture is impossible.

This description of the church-as-practice not only enables mission to the world but is also critical for reading Yoder's ecclesiological concerns, whether in ecumenism, polity, or discipleship. In "The Nature of the Unity We Seek" (1957), for example, Yoder writes that true ecumenism is taken up not on the basis of common structural alignment or doctrinal uniformity but on common discipleship, arguing that "unity in ethical commitment was for the apostolic church no less central than unity in faith and worship."[70] At least as far back as his 1957 essay "What Are Our Concerns?," we find Yoder arguing that the church's practices of discipleship form the church:

> On this basis (and not on any other) discipline is possible within the fellowship: i.e., on the basis of the common conviction that the unity of the church is unity *in discipleship*. This discipline is . . . on an individual, local, Spirit-led process of growth together. If someone is finally excluded from the fellowship, it is not because he broke such and

69. For Yoder, this does not mean distinguishing between commands and practices, as if one were more normative than the other, but rather that the commands find their normativity within the context of the practices. Shank and Yoder, "Biblicism and the Church," 72–73: "We must further recognize the obvious fact, so self-evident we fail to take sufficient account of it, that if the New Testament example is not normative, some other example is. If we do not pattern our life after the early church, we pattern it after some other church. That other church . . . comes thus to have greater normative authority than the apostolic church. This is difficult to justify Biblically to say the least."

70. Yoder, "The Nature of the Unity We Seek," 228. Via the subheadings of the this article, Yoder argues that the unity we seek is not a "common denominator" but "a discipline." Similarly, in *The Ecumenical Movement and the Faithful Church* (Scottdale, PA: Mennonite Publishing House, 1958), 34, Yoder defines Anabaptist ecumenicity as "[practicing] Biblical baptism, communion and discipline in your local congregation, and [accepting] Scripture as the criterion for future discussion."

such a rule, but because he shows himself no longer desirous of living in the unity of the group's commitment to discipleship.[71]

Though dialogue with the world occurs through these practices, it should be noted that, for Yoder, the practices internal to the church are not identical to the practices externalto the church with simply a different name. For example, take the process of fraternal admonition known as "binding and loosing,"[72] which refers to the interlocking process of communal discernment and forgiveness found in Matthew 18. A practice similar to democratic process, it enables "the group's standards [to] be challenged, tested and confirmed, or changed as it is found necessary, in the course of their being applied."[73] In this creation of a people, the binding/loosing practice promises the presence of Christ, efficacious prayer, and the direction of the Holy Spirit; in and through this new community's ethical existence, the work of God is visible.[74] Through this practice, the people of the church learn to be reconciled to one another, enacting an alternate form of communal formation that does not require violence. In the context of the gathered church, the people learn to discern a correct direction, to correct and challenge one another; in turn, they model this toward the world, which can recognize how this practice relates to its own democratic practices.

71. Yoder, "What Are Our Concerns?," in *The Roots of Concern*, 164–76 (167), italics mine.

72. Yoder, "Binding and Loosing," in *Cartwright, Royal Priesthood*, 323–58. Yoder considered "rule-based" ethics antithetical to binding and loosing since the church as a "peoplehood" exists through the process: "God speaks where his people gather and are free to be led. The marks of the validity of the conclusions are to be sought not alone in the principles applied but in the procedure of the meeting," in Yoder, "Hermeneutics of Peoplehood," 23.

73. Yoder, "Binding and Loosing," 328. Forgiveness, which is indicative of the "interpersonal nature" of this binding/loosing process, produces a people out of fragmented individuals. See ibid., 329: "Differences of conviction and behavior are unacceptable *when they offend* . . . If the difference destroys fellowship, it is for that reason a topic for reconciling concern. Any variance not dealt with, on the grounds that it is unimportant, becomes increasingly important with the passage of time. Unattended, it magnifies the next conflict as well." Italics original.

74. Ibid., 331.

While the differentiation between practices despite their analogous form may seem like special pleading, Yoder believes that Scripture—rather than another procedural norm—forms and informs the practices of the church. If the church fails to maintain its own distinct internal practices, it ceases to be "a missionary church"; because the world/state and church share occasional analogous practices, which the church performs in light of the Lordship of Christ, the church can act as a minority model for the larger society, as long as it continues these practices.[75] So long as the church *remains* the dialogue that it is called to be, it can continue *in* dialogue with the world.

Yoder concedes that this mode of witness risks confusing church practices with those outside the church.[76] However, in both international missions and witness to the state, disobedience must be dealt with "on whatever level" it can hear the singular call of Christ:

> We would wrongly understand the witness to a person in authority as a sort of second best, as if we had first called him to believe in Jesus Christ, and then, when he had said he would not, we would go on to plead, "Well all right then, but will you please at least be decent and honest?" What we ask of him does not cease to be gospel by virtue of the fact that we relate it to his present available options. It is rather the gospel itself in relationship to his present situation, that situation being determined largely by his earlier disobedience.[77]

75. Yoder, *As You Go: The Old Mission in a New Day,* Focal Pamphlet 5 (Scottdale, PA: Herald, 1961),22: "Likewise an investigation of the possibilities of migration as a possibly more effective way of spreading the Gospel calls for some consideration of the cultural significance of such an undertaking. Would such an approach mean that Christians taking it would thereby lose their chance to make an effective social contribution because they would find themselves a small minority and representative of an unpopular race in other parts of the world? Insofar as we can learn from history in realms such as this, it is clear the most significant social and cultural contributions have usually been made by minority groups."
76. Ibid., 18–21. See also Yoder, "Discipleship as Missionary Strategy," *Christian Ministry* (January–March) 1955, 26–31. This is not to say that the state cannot misunderstand the nature of its good deeds, taking its acts of goodness as divine authorization. See Yoder, "When the State is God," *Gospel Herald*, February 16, 1954, 153.
77. Yoder, "Discipleship as Missionary Strategy," 25.

This witness to the world proceeds on a "level of involvement in which the message finds the man to whom it speaks," whether speaking to the world involves war or proper farm practices.[78] The world-as-disobedient is unable to hear the commands of Christ in their explicit nature but is able to "hear" the church's practices because of their analogous form to the practices of the world.

A reading of the three penultimate chapters of *The Politics of Jesus* (chapters 9–11) will help illustrate this process. In these chapters, Yoder discusses a variety of church practices, showing how each of them bears witness through the common practices of their secular analogue. Yoder's discussion of the *haustafeln* in chapter 9 describes Paul's household codes as teachings that call Stoic morality to a higher standard.[79] Rather than simply borrowing from Stoicism, Paul puts forth "the relationship itself that we are called upon to live up to." Codes that reflect the church's internal life, the *haustafeln* serves as "testimony" to other configurations of social ordering, thereby subverting the powers of the world.[80] Far from reifying the practices of the world, the *haustafeln* "relativizes and undercuts this order."[81]

Chapters 10 and 11 are marked by the same pattern: though they resemble pagan practices, Christian practices bear witness to a different social order, challenging not only the pagan practice but also the underlying sociality that the pagan practice attests to. Regarding Christian life as it relates to the government (chapter 10), Yoder discards the secular options of a "just rebellion" and "government as divine revelation" in favor of "nonresistant attitude

78. Ibid., 22, 25.

79. Yoder, *Politics of Jesus*, 169.

80. Ibid., 173: "For the apostles to encourage slaves and women to be subordinate, there must have been some specific reason for them to have been tempted to behave otherwise . . . Only if something in the life or the preaching of the church had given them the idea that their subordinate status had been challenged or changed would there be any temptation to the kind of unruliness to which these texts are addressed."

81. Ibid., 181.

toward a tyrannical government."[82] Because present governments are "subject to the ordering of God, and Christians are to be subject to them all," Yoder argues that "we can judge and measure the extent to which a government is accomplishing its ministry by asking namely whether it persistently . . . attends to the rewarding of good and evil according to their merits," affirming the government when it lives up to its vocation as created by God and resisting the government when it fails to live up to that measure.[83] Likewise, the justification of both Jews and Gentiles (chapter 11)—cast in terms of a Christian practice of communal reconciliation—serves to critique "social activism" and "pietist" versions of human perfection; only through the communal transformation-as-salvation do other social problems cease, most pre-eminently, the division of the world into friend/enemy.[84]

We will return to this issue of dialogical witness in due course, but first let us unpack how nonviolence functions as a form of witness embodied by the church, as seen in Yoder's work. The world—characterized by violence—lives as it does because it misunderstood the purpose of its own best practices. Creation —which consists of the church and that which is not yet the church—constitutes a dialogical relation between the body, which is freed from the violence of the powers, and the rest of the world, which is still intoxicated by the promise of violence. However, all is not lost for the world: insofar as the church is a performative body constituted and known by its practice, the church in its performance—its very social life—exists as a witness to the deficient practices of the world, and most centrally, its violence.

82. Ibid., 205–8.
83. Ibid., 205
84. Ibid., 229–31.

Nonviolence: The Knowledge of God and the Church's Performative Witness

As I have suggested earlier, the engagement between the church (the witness to the "new aeon") and the world takes place along any number of lines, practices that can be oriented toward Christ or away from Christ. Chief among those acts that signify the world's misdirection is violence. Because violence and war name the deepest points of rebellion against God, the church must engage the world most vigorously in these areas. An act of national idolatry, war is met by the call to accept "providential workings, to renounce other means of defense . . . to accept even captivity . . . and to learn through these events that stillness in which there is strength."[85] As the church engages in nonviolence—acts made possible by virtue of Christ's conquering of the powers—the "new humanity" of the church is made visible. Insofar as this represents the character of Christ's church (the refusal of violence), this "new humanity" colors multiple aspects of the church's self-identification and theology. When Vietnam moved more fully into the national conscience, the church's vocation to embody this confession in its practice and in its confession became more pressing.[86]

85. Yoder, *Christian Witness to the State*, 16.

86. During the period of 1964–1970, Yoder begins to engage more stringently with just war arguments in a number of formats, exploring what it means to say that Vietnam cannot rightly be called rightly a just war. See "Developing a Christian Attitude Toward War," *Journal of the Methodists for Church Renewal* (April 1966): 8–12; "Vietnam: A Just War?," *His*, April 1968, 1–3; "Vietnam: Another Option," *His*, May 1968, 8–11; "Another Option to a Just War," *This Day*, July 1968, 4–7, 30; "The Way of the Peacemaker," in *Peacemakers in a Broken World*, ed. John A. Lapp (Scottdale, PA: Herald, 1969), 111–25. Yoder's *Karl Barth and the Problem of War* (Nashville: Abingdon, 1970) is Yoder's most in-depth example from this period. Through the late 1970s and 1980s, engagement with just war thinking is one of the predominant themes of Yoder's writings.

While engagements with just war thought would seem to be a departure from his advocacy for nonviolence as I have been describing it, I would argue that engaging with the just war tradition is a natural outgrowth. If, as Yoder argues, wars are made on the basis of calculations and end results, then Christian advocacy against war in a world under Christ's reign cannot be accomplished by advocating that the state—committed to a logic of violence—follow Christians

Take, for example, Yoder's description of the church in *The Original Revolution.* Here, Yoder argues that Jesus established a "new peoplehood, the being-together with one another and the being different in style of life" in a way that contrasts with other violent and coercive methods of revolution.[87] A new society, "with its own deviant values," is the "judgment of God" upon injustice and violence; in other words, the alternative society characterized by different practices *is* the witness that performs *acts* of witness. This community, which is the "judgment and promise" of God, is "God's people gathered as a unit . . . to find what it means here and now to put into practice this different quality of life which is God's promise to them and to the world and their promise to God and service to the world."[88]

Nonviolence and reconciliation with one's neighbors are central, insofar as these practices are intrinsic to Jesus' own life.[89] By these practices (more than others), this community witnesses to the world:

> What do I communicate to a man about the love of God by being willing to consider him an enemy? What do I say about personal responsibility by agreeing to consider him my enemy when it is only the hazard of birth that causes us to live under different flags? What do I say about forgiveness if I punish him for the sins of his rulers? . . . The idea that human life is intrinsically sacred is not a specifically Christian thought. But the gospel itself, the message that Christ died

in nonviolence on principle, but that the state come to this presumption against violence by means of the practice of calculated risks and benefits. I will explore Yoder's just war arguments briefly in a later section, but for now, I will simply assert that the movement toward practical engagement with peacemaking as seen in his early writings on just war are intelligible in light of the framework I am tracing here: if church and state exist under a single reign of Christ, with the church witnessing to the state's practices in hope that the violent practices constituting "state" will adhere to the "absolute norm which is valid for both," Yoder must proceed by appealing to a common language of practices.

87. Yoder, *The Original Revolution* (Scottdale, PA: Herald, 1971), 30. For other options of revolution, see ibid.,18–27.

88. Ibid., 31.

89. Ibid., 34.

> for His enemies is our reason or being ultimately responsible for the neighbor's . . . life.[90]

By exhibiting this refusal of violence in its public acts, the community does not point to itself but to the way of Jesus who is, significantly, what God is like: "We do not, ultimately, love our neighbor because Jesus told us to. We love our neighbor because God is like that. It is not because Jesus told us to that we love even beyond the limits of reason, even to the point of refusing to kill and being willing to suffer—but because *God is like that too.*"[91]

In other words, the church's performative nonviolence coheres to the being of God, such that a true witness to Christ depends upon faithfully depicting what God is like in the church's practice—an argument Yoder deepens in *The Politics of Jesus.*[92] Before Yoder describes Jesus' engagements with the powers of his day, he enters into an exploration of the Old Testament war narratives in what appears, at first, to be an unrelated chapter. Chronicling the manner in which Moses' disobedient call for war and "Elisha's nonviolent misdirection" point toward Israel's continual call to trust God, Yoder argues that a rejection of violence is intrinsic to the Old Testament.[93]

90. Ibid., 41–42. Concerning nonviolence as the culmination of the Old Testament laws on vengeance, see ibid., 42–45.

91. Ibid., 52 (italics mine). Here, we see the interrelation of the love of God and the act of God focused in the refusal of violence. As such, the statement focuses on the ethical act and not the attribute of love; it is the act of neighbor love in nonviolence that expresses the character of God. See Yoder's discussion of Jesus and revelation in terms of Jesus as prophet, which refers to Jesus' "communicative character, not only through his words as prophet but in his person," in Yoder, *Preface to Theology*, 332–33. The ascription of Jesus' "person" as revelation does not mean ontological substance but rather Jesus' character. See *Preface to Theology*, 306, for Yoder's aversion to "substance" language with regards to Christology. He states that "history is the only reality we know; we do not think about essences anymore, about substances or *hypostases,* about realities "out there" having being in themselves. We think of reality as happening in personal relationships, in institutional relationships, and in the passage of time."

92. Yoder, *The Politics of Jesus*,2. In this work, Yoder intends to investigate the relevance of Jesus to contemporary political acts, in keeping with his concern for witness. As Yoder puts it, if "Jesus was not like everyone else a political being, or if he demonstrated no originality or no interest in responding to the questions which his sociopolitical environment put to him, it would be pointless to ask about the meaning of his stance for today" (11).

Teasing out a lineage of Old Testament discipleship, he asserts that the pattern of rejection of violence (as seen with Elisha) would have been expected by Jesus' audience as "a paradigm of the way God would save his people now."[94] By doing this, Yoder makes a controversial point: Jesus' audience—far from expecting a warrior Messiah—would have actually been looking for a nonviolent deliverance of God commensurate with how they would have understood God acting in the Old Testament:

> When, therefore, Jesus used the language of liberation and revolution, announcing a restoration of "kingdom" community and a new pattern of life, without predicting or authorizing particular violent techniques for achieving his good ends, he need not have seemed to his listeners to be a dreamer; *he could very easily have been understood as updating the faith of Jehoshaphat and Hezekiah*, a faith whereby a believing people would be saved despite their weakness, on condition that they "be still and wait to see the salvation of the Lord."[95]

Thus, when we read Yoder's characterization of nonviolence as a description of the way God acts in the world, nonviolence is not simply the church's act of obedience (meaning discipleship) but the very *modus operandi* of the divine life; the practice of nonviolence by Jesus reveals God's way in the world.

As a result of God being known in the refusal of violence and the practice of reconciliation—which Jesus displays in his own life and commends to the church—Yoder argues that Jesus' death is not only

93. Ibid., 76–82. Throughout his work, Yoder is careful to distinguish between authorized violence by the community and what John C. Nugent calls the "phenomenon of Yahweh war," in Nugent, *The Politics of Yahweh: John Howard Yoder, the Old Testament, and the People of God* (Eugene, OR: Cascade Books, 2011), 218. In *Politics*, violence by the community is depicted as unfaithful, while the delivering act of God is not. Interestingly, Yoder is ambivalent toward these texts, noting that "now whatever be the 'actual historical shape' of the events lying behind the story, we can be assured that . . . it was a least *possible* if not *normal* for those 'waiting for the consolation of Israel' to see in these miraculous deliverances of the Old Testament story a paradigm of the way God would save his people now" (84).

94. Yoder, *Politics of Jesus*, 84.

95. Ibid. (emphasis mine).

an act that "disarms" the powers of violence and governance but that his "act of obedience" in submission to the powers also constitutes"the firstfruits of an authentic restored humanity"—the exemplification of a new community that is anticipated in the Old Testament but fulfilled in the New Testament.[96] Thus, the refusal of violence represents the "restored humanity," present as the church:

> What can be called the "otherness of the church" is an attitude rooted in strength and not in weakness. It consists in being a herald of liberation and not a community of slaves. It is not a detour or a waiting period, looking forward to better days which one hopes might come a few centuries later . . . The church accepted as a gift being the "new humanity" created by the cross and not by the sword.[97]

In this passage, we hear echoes of Yoder's early work, amplified in a significant way. As we have seen, the church's identification as the "new humanity" depends on its continuation of Jesus' work; by following Jesus' way, the church witnesses to the world. In addition to this, Yoder contends that not only is the refusal of war and violence intrinsic to the church's witness but it also allows the church to identify Jesus as the one who images God's nonviolent ways to the world.

In its existence as the community carrying forth the life of Jesus, this new humanity exists as the alternative to the "violence which governs society,"[98] However, it does not describe all the bodies that

96. Ibid., 148.

97. Ibid., 148–49.

98. Ibid., 157. The emergence of this community as "new" or eschatologically-oriented (which is distinct from the social possibilities prior to Christ) has been named "apocalyptic." For this interpretation, see David Toole, *Waiting for Godot in Sarajevo: Theological Reflections on Nihilism, Tragedy, and Apocalypse* (Boulder, CO: Westview, 1998), 210; Douglas Harink, *Paul among the Postliberals: Pauline Theology beyond Christendom and Modernity* (Grand Rapids: Brazos, 2003); Daniel Colucciello Barber, "The Particularity of Jesus and the Time of the Kingdom: Philosophy and Theology in Yoder," *Modern Theology* 23 (2007), 63–90; Nathan R. Kerr: *Christ, History, and Apocalyptic: The Politics of Christian Mission* (Eugene, OR: Cascade Books, 2009). For the most part, the followers of Toole's approach have identified the singularity of Jesusas apocalyptic rather than—as Yoder argues—the presence of the churchas the apocalyptic

worship Jesus but only those churches that know Jesus as the nonviolent one who overcomes the powers, enacting a standard of nonviolence for both church and world.[99] With the naming of God by the nonviolence of Jesus, we move into the heart of the relationship between the refusal of war and ecclesiology. For Yoder, the Christian refusal of war bears witness to the peaceable grain of the universe—to the heart of the church's life and to who God is.

Nonviolence can, and has, been construed as an entirely negative proposition—the simple refusal of one act (going to war) without a corresponding positive act—but as we have seen in Yoder, the call for nonviolence involves the embodiment of another way of life that is characterized by dialogue and reconciliation on the basis of who God is in Christ. For Yoder, bearing witness to this means showing how other approaches to war find their fullness in the practice by which the church is known to be the church and Jesus is known to be God: nonviolence.

In *The Politics of Jesus* (1972), it becomes more clear how Yoder was able to draw his conclusions in *Nevertheless: A Meditation on the Varieties and Shortcomings of Christian Pacifism*; in *Politics*, those who participate in the nonviolence that is seen in Jesus' life also bear witness to the eschatological truth of all created order. The final chapter of *Politics* describes the eschatological vision of a nonviolent Christ, drawing the "argument of the entire book" together—which could be read simply to mean that eschatology is the ultimate justification of the church's witness. However, the logic is far more

inbreaking of God. While Jesus remains at the center of the church for Yoder, the community "*is* the alternative" and thus, the true center of Yoder's apocalyptic approach.

99. Though Yoder was involved in a variety of ecumenical discussions throughout his life, he does not believe that all institutions that call themselves "church" live up to his definition of "church" as the "new humanity," which is characterized by nonviolence. See Yoder, *The Ecumenical Movement and the Faithful Church* (Scottdale, PA: Mennonite Publishing House, 1958), 38–42, in which Yoder views ecumenical divisions over war and nonviolence as indicative of the manner in which certain churches have refused an ethic of obedience to Jesus.

powerful: if the nonviolence seen in the life of Jesus of Nazareth is not a practice that coheres to the eschatological vision of Christ, the entire dialogical project of *Politics* must be held in question, insofar as the Christ who will come in the eschaton is utterly unrelated to temporal discipleship.[100] But if Christ—incarnate and eschatological—speaks to a refusal of violence, not only is nonviolence more than wishful thinking, but the other practices of *Politics* are possible as well. Christ's own refusal of violence makes possible a community of "revolutionary subordination," of giving, and of reconciliation inside the church. Beyond the church, the refusal of violence—embodied in the church—also proves to be a more compelling practice.

The culminating chapter of *Politics*, in which Yoder contrasts a variety of approaches to changing society in contrast to what is presented in the life of Jesus, makes this logic clear. Yoder argues that Moral Rearmament, Marxist revolutions, and conservative evangelicalism similarly desire a "handle" by which to violently leverage one aspect of society against others in an attempt to save society.[101] Convinced that one can manage the outcomes of one's actions—having been adequately informed in order to make effective choices—these movements ignore their limitations and fail to see that their violent and forceful measures are ultimately self-defeating.[102]

In offering nonviolence as an alternative, Yoder connects the refusal of violence to a good historical existence; if God has acted in history, sent Jesus as the validation of God's work, and established a church that embodies the message of Jesus, then nonviolence must historically be a tenable way to live.[103] For Yoder, the eschatological vision of Revelation, which identifies the Lord of History with the

100. Yoder, *Politics of Jesus* (1972), 228.
101. Ibid., 229–30.
102. Ibid., 230ff.
103. Ibid., 230–31. See 232: "If God is the kind of God-active-in-history of whom the Bible speaks, then concern for the course of history is itself not an illegitimate or an irrelevant concern."

nonviolent Jesus of Nazareth, reveals this truth; if the nonviolent God of Revelation is concerned with our present history, nonviolence is both normative and desirable, and the practices described in chapters 9–11 of *Politics* become possible.[104] Thus, nonviolent resistance to war is not the last ethical option but an opening into the meaning of history. Those who would follow Jesus (who is the preeminent exemplar of human existence) must take up an ethic of nonviolence that finds its meaning as the ultimate truth of history.[105]

Though predicated on an explicitly Christian confession and ecclesial life, this logic makes sense to non-Christians; as we discovered in *Nevertheless*, the truth of the "messianic community" can be articulated in partial form through a variety of idioms.[106] In the context of Vietnam, the affirmation of nonviolence we find in *Politics* (which presents the way forward in the world) seems decidedly against the moral grain in the face of the escalating draft. Given the plurality of nonviolent movements that emerged during this time, the arguments for an ecclesial-specific nonviolence (much less an argument that proposed to make sense of *other* forms of

104. Ibid., "The triumph of the right is assured not by the might that comes to the aid of the right, which is of course the justification of the use of violence and other kinds of powers in every human conflict. The triumph of the right, although it is assured, is sure because of the power of the resurrection and not because of any calculation of causes and effects, nor because of the inherently greater strength of the good guys. The relationship between the obedience of God's people and the triumph of God's cause is not a relationship of cause and effect but one of cross and resurrection."

105. Ibid., 234–35. This is not to say that Yoder has a vision of Christ as either divine or human. In his exploration of the manner in which Jesus is "Lord" and "equal with God" (ibid., 234–36), Yoder shies away from the language of "essences" and "substances." I take the Christology of Yoder vis-à-vis the Chalcedonian orthodoxy to be an open question and do not directly explore the topic here. However, in the earlier chapters of the book, it is in keeping with his vision of Jesus to refer to the effects of Jesus' human nature and not to explore Jesus in terms of subsistence or persons.

106. Ibid., 237: "Almost every other kind of ethical approach espoused by Christians, pacifist or otherwise, will continue to make sense to the non-Christian as well. Whether Jesus be the Christ or not, whether Jesus the Christ be Lord or not, whether this kind of religious language be meaningful or not, most types of ethical approach will keep on functioning just the same. For their true foundation is in some reading of the human situation or some ethical insight which is claimed to be generally accessible to all people of goodwill."

nonviolence) must have appeared, at the very least, presumptuous. As Yoder argued in *Nevertheless*, not all varieties of nonviolence operate as witness to Christ or speak *in and of themselves* of God's presence. The dialogical nature of Yoder's work, which draws together the church and the world for the sake of witness, seeks to identify the light of the eschaton in the fragmentary places where it appears. It is to these dialogical engagements that we now turn.

Nonviolence in Dialogue

Yoder's writing on nonviolence has been the subject of no little discussion in recent years. Much of the work surrounding Yoder's thought, however, investigates his nonviolence as a kind of epistemology or a general stance, though rarely with regards to specific practices.[107] Having already described the manner in which a rejection of social violence is central to both an identifying practice of Jesus and the true church, I will now return to how the practice of the church operates dialogically for Yoder, bearing witness to the partial and deficient practices of the world. As I have suggested with regards to the practices of *Politics of Jesus*—that various church practices engage with their secular counterparts for the sake of calling the world to the church—nonviolence is the capstone of the church's

107. Chris K. Huebner, *A Precarious Peace: Yoderian Explorations on Theology, Knowledge, and Identity* (Scottdale: Herald, 2006) contains two chapters on Yoder's nonviolence—one that focuses on the epistemic conditions of Yoder's nonviolence (97–114) and the other that makes mention of the dialogue between just war and pacifism in Yoder's work (129)—but goes into no real detail on the particular practices of nonviolence. The same is true with Cynthia Hess, *Sites of Violence, Sites of Grace: Christian Nonviolence and the Traumatized Self* (Lanham, MD: Lexington Books, 2009), which describes Yoder's nonviolence within his discussion of the powers but does not discuss the practices of nonviolence (11–32). Similarly, the volume *A Mind Patient and Untamed: Assessing John Howard Yoder's Contribution to Theology, Ethics, and Peacemaking*, ed. Ben C. Ollenburger and Gayle Gerber Koontz (Telford, PA: Cascadia, 2003) contains no examinations of Yoder's actual descriptions of nonviolence. The *festschrift* for Yoder, *The Wisdom of the Cross: Essays in Honor of John Howard Yoder*, ed. Stanley Hauerwas et al. (Grand Rapids: Eerdmans, 1999) contains discussion on policing and selective conscientious objection but focuses on Yoder's post-Vietnam work.

practices, bearing witness both to the way in which Christ lived and in which the church is called to live. Unsurprisingly, we find Yoder engaging in these conversations more than others.

Yoder's writings on war dates back at least to 1948 as part of his assignment through the Mennonite Central Committee (MCC) to help recover the Anabaptist peace tradition in France, which had recently survived the ravages of the Second World War; for Yoder, this undertaking presented an eye-opening experience.[108] Yoder's mentor Harold Bender had argued for the centrality of nonviolence to the Anabaptist tradition in *The Anabaptist Vision*, but the Anabaptist churches Yoder worked with did not immediately understand that a commitment to nonviolence represented an intrinsic ecclesiological commitment.[109]

However, all evidence from these meetings indicates that, for Yoder, the relationship between ecclesiology and nonviolence was eminently obvious. The initial 1948 meeting with French Mennonites evolved into an ongoing dialogue, during which Yoder inquired what reason there was for not making the rejection of war an ecclesial norm for all Christians. Reformed ethicist Hendrik van Oyen responded that "[the proposal of Yoder's] goes much too far further [in the direction] of legalism and perfection, of thinking that in a church of true believers you are completely out of the old world."[110] As we have seen, Yoder did not consider nonviolence to be an idealist fantasy because Christ had created a new community

108. Zimmerman, *Practicing the Politics of Jesus,* 73–74. Zimmerman emphasizes the background of emerging Russian nuclear power as a "new specter of war" that confronted the French congregations.

109. Ibid., 77. As Zimmerman has shown, Yoder contends that the "peace ethic," as a gift to all the churches, must be fleshed out in the varieties of contexts and cannot be enforced on a church prior to it coming to the conclusion of nonviolence for itself. For Yoder's letters to Bender detailing the difference between American Mennonites and European Mennonites, see ibid., 73–74.

110. Donald F. Durnbaugh, "John Howard Yoder's Role in the 'Lordship of Christ over Church and State' Conferences," *Mennonite Quarterly Review* 77 (2003): 371–86 (378).

in the world for which the refusal of war is christologically indispensible:

> The "pacifism" of the Anabaptists . . . are explained from this starting point, and not from the Sermon on the Mount. The Anabaptists speak remarkably seldom about the Sermon on the Mount . . . Their position does not stand or fall with considerations regarding the likelihood of a peaceful and brotherly world order, but rather, with the conviction that Jesus Christ was fully God and fully human, not only in his preaching and in his actions, but also and most particularly in his obedience unto death, precisely in order to reveal there the ultimate basic orientation of God-willed human obedience: an offence for some, and folly for others, but the power and wisdom of God for those who believe.[111]

The church as "the bearer of the meaning of history" is the body that bears forth Jesus' work, making the logic of nonviolence intelligible as the "power and wisdom of God." The growing cloud of the Vietnam War provided a context that put these convictions to the test in a variety of ways, which I will now briefly describe.

In Yoder's career, one of the most significant opportunities to attest to nonviolence as Christ's way came with the issue of conscientious objection (CO).[112] For years, Yoder had argued that "our peace testimony, and our conscientious objection to war, is abundantly grounded in the very heart of the Gospel"; consistent with his vision of the connection between church and world, Christian conscientious objection involves solidarity with other conscientious objectors, in keeping with Jesus' "solidarity of men in their sinfulness."[113] For traditional Mennonites, engaging the conscientious

111. Yoder, *Anabaptism and Reformation*, 288–89.

112. Yoder's work on this question dates back to "The Peace Testimony and Conscientious Objection," *Gospel Herald*, January 21, 1958, 57–58. Yoder agues that, scripturally, the act of conscientious objection with respect to the draft is consistent with Paul's admonition to be "crucified with Christ" and to wrestle "against principalities and powers" (ibid., 58).

113. Ibid., 58: "This 'peace testimony' is no 'pacifism,' as the term is used in political discussion today. It does not stand or fall with the possibility or the predictability of political peace. It only has value because no political peace is possible or predictable. In a world where there are wars and

objector question was natural, but for a society becoming more and more uneasy with the draft and the escalations in Vietnam, conscientious objection provided a way into a dialogue about the nature of war and its consequences.

As a part of the Peace Section of the Mennonite Central Committee (MCC) throughout the 1960s, Yoder was deeply involved with how this "solidarity" happens. Particularly, the way in which the MCC should address the question of draftees with an I-W status (those registered as conscientious objectors during Vietnam) was considered.[114] Having registered as objectors, these draftees were still obliged to provide alternative service to the government; as part of a group of church bodies seeking to aid these objectors, the MCC sought to provide opportunities for Mennonites to faithfully bear witness to the government. Specifically, religious projects such as "church schools" and "church-related agencies" were not considered options for I-W workers because these projects did not fulfill the government requirements.[115] However, the lack of specifically religious projects for Mennonite conscientious objectors was not a problem; as the committee argued, "our understanding of Christian vocation is moving more toward the essential wholeness and indivisibility of 'service' and 'witness.'"[116] This linking of "service" to

rumors of wars, the church whose citizenship is not of this world calls the believing Christian because of his faith to love for his neighbor which is worthy of a disciple; she also calls the unbelieving state, its unbelief not withstanding, to righteousness and the preservation of peace." Yoder continues this argument in two 1961 articles: "The Place of Peace Witness in Missions," *Gospel Herald*, January 3, 1961, 14–15, 19–20, and "The Way of Peace in a World of War," *Gospel Herald*, July 18, 1961, 25.

114. "MCC Peace Section Minutes 1963–1968," Yoder Papers, box 25 1/b. Among these minutes, one can find a consistent discussion of the I-W status given to conscientious objectors (CO) during the Second World War. The 1948 Selective Service law was amended in 1951 to read that COs had to contribute "civilian work contributing to the maintenance of the national health, safety, or interest" in lieu of military service, for approximately twenty-four months.

115. Ibid., "I-W Project Approval Criteria," appended to "Report to Peace Section Executive Committee on the Washington Witness to Government by John D. Unruh, Jr.," September 6, 1963.

116. Ibid., 4. This criteria is repeated in the minutes on January 16, 1964.

"witness" is consistent with Yoder's thought, particularly his emphasis that witness to the world occurs through common practices that the world can "hear."

During this time, Yoder continued to dialogically argue for nonviolence as the perfection or conclusion of other approaches to war, most famously with Barth's understanding of war—*Karl Barth and the Problem of War*.[117] According to Yoder, Barth saw the church and state as related, insofar as the church provides the model of a true society for the state.[118] In light of this church/state relation and because a population must be alive in order to receive the Word of the church, Barth maintains that wars could conceivably be commanded by God in the defense of secular polities; to exclude war would be to exclude God's absolute freedom and to endanger the world in which discipleship occurs.[119]

Yoder argues, however, that Barth's emphasis upon the human Jesus as the center of God's revelation to humanity excludes even the remote possibility of war, to the extent that Barth's "near pacifism" becomes, for all practical purposes, pacifism.[120] Built upon a freedom of God that is visible in Jesus, Barth's view of war is logically pacifist, though Barth would never declare this. In later developments of this

117. Yoder, "The Pacifism of Karl Barth," initially published in French (1963) and later translated for Herald Press (1968). Also, *Karl Barth and the Problem of War* (Nashville: Abingdon, 1970). Both studies are reprinted in Mark Thiessen Nation, ed., *Karl Barth and the Problem of War and Other Essays on Barth* (Eugene, OR: Cascade, 2003). For a different take on Barth and war, see Rowan Williams, "Barth, War, and the State," in Nigel Biggar, ed., *Reckoning with Barth: Essays in Commemoration of the Centenary of Barth's Birth* (Oxford and London: Mowbray, 1988), 170–90.

118. Ibid., 116–17. For Barth, this approach means that while "there will therefore be a Christian message addressed to the State; there will not be a Christian ethic for the State."

119. Ibid., 122–23.

120. Ibid., 125–26. Yoder's reading of Barth on the humanity of Christ reflects a questionable reading of Barth on this point. See Paul Daffyd Jones, *The Humanity of Christ* (Edinburgh: T&T Clark, 2008), in which Jones contends that Barth's concern with Christ's humanity is, in part, to maintain Jesus as the free locus through which the eternal Word is revealed (26–59). Because Barth is concerned more centrally with Jesus as the revelation of God the Son (a topic Yoder rarely addresses), Yoder's concern with the normativity of Jesus' nonviolence seems to be missing the point of Barth's Christology.

original work—particularly the one published as *Karl Barth and the Problem of War*—Yoder's argument rests on the incompatibility of ecclesiology and war.[121]

In his conversation with just war argument, Yoder employs a similar dialogical approach in a series of 1968 articles. He begins the conversation by assuming three possible stances for Christians regarding government undertaking of war: crusade, just war, or "blank check."[122] Rejecting the first and third options out of hand as unbiblical, Yoder shows that the just war—the median approach between these extremes—does not justify the Vietnam War on either Protestant or Catholic grounds.[123] Yoder's follow-up article, "Vietnam: Another Option," then argues that Christian nonviolence accomplishes the ends of the just war (social involvement) without sacrificing obedience to the commands of Christ.[124] As Yoder phrases it:

> I believe Jesus doesn't tell his disciples to abstain from the realm of social conflict. Nor does he tell them to worship Him in a corner of their lives and let the government dictate their action in the realm of social conflict. He leads them right into the eye of the storm of social conflict, but tells them to take a different position: to be a reflection of what He was, the incarnation of the cross-bearing love of God who gives His life for His enemies.[125]

121. In the original pamphlet presented to Barth in 1963, Yoder begins with the difference between church and state in Barth's early dogmatics, describing how the difference between church and world creates an ethical difference on the question of war. The christological argument, as discussed above, appears at the end of the pamphlet. In the later work (1970), the Christological criticism of 1963 is placed at the beginning with the ecclesiological comparison of church and world the predominant focus of Yoder's analysis; he concludes the later work with an analysis of whether war is a legitimate option for the church and whether the teachings of Christ can be embodied faithfully by the church. See Yoder, *Karl Barth and the Problem of War*, 99ff.

122. Yoder, "Vietnam: A Just War?,"1–3. "Blank check" is Yoder's term, which refers to an open-ended approval of war.

123. Ibid., 3.

124. Yoder, "Vietnam: Another Option," 8–11.

125. Ibid., 11.

In a modification of his earlier writing in which nonviolence depends upon a particularly dialogical context, Yoder describes how this kind of discipleship can be funded by a number of ecclesial contexts, noting that nonviolence in imitation of Christ is found among Catholic monks, Quakers, and Mennonites. Jesus is no "tribal deity"—by which he means the Western "military and political establishment"—but rather the Lord of all who suffers in Jesus' name on behalf of the Vietnamese.[126]

Beyond engaging with alternate approaches to war, Yoder's dialogical approach involves bearing witness to other (albeit imperfect) forms of war resistance, the most paradigmatic being *Nevertheless: A Meditation on the Varieties and Shortcomings of Religious Pacifism*, in which Yoder explores over twenty different constructions of pacifism.[127] In *Nevertheless*, Yoder outlines a variety of nonviolence positions adopted by religious adherents, ranging from pragmatic approaches to the pacifism of the messianic community (assumed to be Yoder's own position).[128] Laying out over twenty varieties of religious nonviolence, the work finishes with a discussion of the "messianic community," a variety of nonviolence that does not depend on pre-ordained rules as much as "the full humanity of a

126. Ibid., 10.

127. John Howard Yoder, *Nevertheless: A Meditation on the Varieties and Shortcomings of Religious Pacifism* (Scottdale, PA: Herald, 1971).

128. In consensus with the majority of scholarship, I take Yoder's position to be best described by the "messianic community" option, but Yoder does not designate this as his own position in the chapter. Significantly, he notes that delineating between various options "does not necessarily mean that the borders between them are airtight" (ibid., 13). Yoder is often slippery in these dialogical circumstances, writing that "one could argue x" or some variant, giving cause for caution in asserting this form straightforwardly as Yoder's own. For the assertion of the "Messianic Community" as Yoder's own brand of nonviolence, see Paul Ramsey and Stanley Hauerwas, *Speak Up for Just War or Pacifism: A Critique of the United Methodist Bishops' Pastoral Letter "In Defense of Creation"* (State College, PA: Penn State Press, 1988), 116ff; Craig Carter, *The Pacifism of the Messianic Community: The Social Ethics of John Howard Yoder* (PhD diss., St. Michael's College, 1999); Nation, *Yoder*, 127. Though Yoder never makes this claim in the work, this reading seems to have originated in Paul Toews, review of *Nevertheless* by John Howard Yoder, *Direction* 1 (1972): 134–35.

unique and yet complete human being" who opens up a "human community experiencing in its shared life a foretaste of God's kingdom."[129] This "messianic community" is "a necessary reflection of the true meaning of Jesus," and only those initiated into "that authentic human existence" are able to grasp the logic of this way.[130]

As we have seen in his engagements with various kinds of just war reasoning, the "messianic" variety of nonviolence—lived as a part of being in the community that reflects the "true meaning of Jesus"—completes the concerns of other types of nonviolence, answering their concerns from within the messianic form of nonviolence.[131] Significantly, the "messianic community" is not only able to fulfill their intentions but to extend their limited insights alongside other forms of nonviolence that are contradictory to one another. For example, the messianic community approach includes the intention of the command-based nonviolence of the Old and New Testaments (types 3 and 8), which is rule-based, and the "believer's church" (type 9), which suffer (in the case of type 9) from "a withdrawal from history."[132] This is in addition to a non-ecclesial "programmatic" view of nonviolence (type 2), which is the nonviolence of political pragmatism (type 4), since messianic pacifism "includes the practical concern of the programmatic views . . . without placing its hope there."[133] By itself, the claim that "messianic

129. Toews, Review of *Nevertheless*, 134–35.

130. Ibid., 136. Yoder says that one must undergo "that reorientation of the personality and its expression which Jesus and his first followers called repentance and new birth." As we have seen, these terms involve a reorientation of one's life toward incorporation in the "new humanity," with "repentance" and the accompanying signs of "new birth," (i.e. the gifts of the spirit) furthering this primary anthropology of being part of a humanity.

131. Ibid., 137. The kinds of pacifism that "pacifism of the messianic community" encompasses include pacifisms of absolute principle (type 3), utopian purism (type 8), the pacifism of the virtuous minority (type 9), the pacifism of cultic law (type 13), pacifism based in case studies (type 2), the pacifism of political alternatives (type 4), and the pacifism of nonviolent social change (type 5).

132. Ibid.

133. Ibid.

community" nonviolence is the fulfillment of other varieties of nonviolence is astounding; however, Yoder additionally claimed that the messianic variety draws together varieties that otherwise would be incompatible.[134] In other words, a nonviolence that bears witness to a new social order (the messianic community) is able to incorporate the hopes and aspirations of contradictory forms of nonviolence that emphasize pragmatism on the one hand and rule-based approaches on the other by orienting their common hope through the corporate witness of a people.[135]

Through Yoder's various engagements, it becomes increasingly clear that the embodied life of the church who rightly follows its Lord is not merely the possession of the church. If Jesus is known to us as the one who refused violence—calling forth a church who will do the same—and if this Jesus is the Lord of all creation, then it should not surprise us that nonviolence appears in a variety of places outside the church.[136] Yoder's dialogical approach—in which other forms of war require fulfillment by the church's own practice—enters into the public arena, calling Christians to embody nonviolence as the heart of the church's practice and public witness in a time of war.

Conclusion

Yoder's conviction that the church *is* the witness against war is a powerful formulation. Insofar as the world is characterized at its most

134. Ibid., 143: "These various pacifisms are sometimes compatible with one another, sometimes even mutually reinforcing (13–16; or 1–2, 4), and sometimes directly contradictory in their assumptions (4 versus 8–9, 16)."
135. Ibid., 138: "One cannot avoid either messianism or the claim to chosen peoplehood by setting Jesus or his methods aside."
136. What happens beyond the mid-1970s with regards to Yoder's own development of thought is not in the purview of this book. However, I am largely sympathetic to Paul Martens's view that the acknowledgment of analogous social forms to the church leads Yoder to narrate theology more and more in terms of ethics, to the extent that the question should be posed: "If an ethic is available ubiquitously beyond the church, why must one belong to the church to adhere to this ethic?"

virulent as an ongoing practice of violence, the church stands—in its confession, embodied practice, and argument—as a body of witness to Christ's peace. For Yoder, the connection between the church's internal life and the habits and practices of the world is, quite simply, that analogies exist between the practices of the church and elsewhere; many people seek to answer the question of war, and Christians answer it not by resorting to violence but by embodying a peaceable and dialogical posture toward the world. In this way, the character of the church—as a body characterized by nonviolence—is intrinsic to its missional character: if the church *is* the witness, the practices of the church are placed alongside analogous practices, showing the world (in the words of St. Paul) "a more excellent way."

From Yoder's perspective, the centrality of practice for defining ecclesiology is in keeping with the biblical narrative. In addition to sustaining church life, this emphasis on practices such as nonviolence sustains engagements with the world, enabling the church to move out of a sectarian space and into conversation with the wider world. But, as others have noted, faithful practice can begin to lead the way for what constitutes doctrine; note the way, for example, that nonviolence indicates whether a confessional body has taken up an appropriate doctrine. In Yoder's work, as I have laid it out here, nonviolence appears as the measure of appropriate Christology, ecclesiology, and eschatology. In light of the way in which certain modes of practice become central to faithful ecclesiology, the preface to his 1971 *Original Revolution* becomes more clear:

> There is a growing awareness in churches and seminaries that the problem of war is at the heart of much of the sickness of modern society, and a growing recognition that the traditional Christian approaches to this problem . . . are becoming increasingly inadequate as sources of moral guidance and are beginning to look as if they never were adequate . . . I have accepted the invitation to gather a body of essays which seek to restate in various moods and modes the conviction that

> *the renunciation of violence is the key to the rest of the problems of Christian faithfulness and to the recovery of the evangelical and ecumenical integrity of the church in the age of the atom.*[137]

As I have argued in this chapter, the relationship between ecclesiology and nonviolence for Yoder can be summed up as follows:

1. To be of the church is to be committed to the way of Jesus.
2. To be of the way of Jesus is to commit to, among other things, the refusal of war, insofar as understanding the commands and person of Jesus requires that one is committed to certain practices.
3. To engage in christologically-authorized nonviolence is to embody a way of life that speaks of the true grain of the universe.
4. This way of the church is seen in refracted ways in a variety of places, some of which do not confess Jesus.[138]

Before moving on, we must assess what affects the strong identification of the church *as* a body of nonviolence has on other aspects of theology, especially if the refusal of violence becomes a central way of identifying not only what God is like but who the

137. Yoder, *Original Revolution*, 7–8 (italics mine).

138. Though I will not pursue this statement here, it is arguable that Yoder's work on nonviolent resistance to war does not end with the formation of a faithful church, as important a connection as this is. For Yoder, the difference between church and world is one of "direction." Given Yoder's affirmation of other non-ecclesial forms of resistance to war, in combination with statements such as "those who bear crosses are working with the grain of the universe," we must consider whether practice does not only overdetermineother considerations of ecclesiology but also overrunsecclesiology. If, in fact, the practice of refusing violence and war speaks of the eschatological truth of creation, Yoder leaves open the possibility that, ultimately, the practice is sufficient independentofits context, i.e. the church. Since Yoder's death, much has been made of how to read Yoder's legacy, and claims to his mantle have been made by those committed to nonviolence as the central defining characteristic of the church as well as by those who argue that nonviolence remains secondary to a christologically-ordered polity. See J. Denny Weaver, "The John Howard Yoder Legacy: Wither the Second Generation?," *Mennonite Quarterly Review* 77 (2003), 451–71 for one rendering of this question.

church is to be. For example, "binding/loosing" cannot be simply a juridical process of the church but rather a process of social reconciliation in which the non-coercive way of Jesus is borne out; the Eucharist cannot be seen as only the sacramental presence of Christ but as the communication of a nonviolent presence of God within history; baptism must be rethought as a renunciation of a life of violence and an embrace of a new life of dispossession.

The impacts of such a view of nonviolence upon ecclesiology extend to issues of church unity as well. Ecumenism—defined as the unity of the church—occurs on the basis of their common (if unacknowledged by non-pacifist traditions) root: nonviolence is not only the heart of the church's performance but also the sign of the eschaton. However, Yoder's account of nonviolence begs the question as to whether practice ultimately overreads other aspects of doctrine and church life. While Yoder is careful not to narrate nonviolence as the central doctrine of the church's existence, it is unclear whether or not nonviolence's role in establishing the church's vocation, confessions, and hope does not overdetermine other aspects of ecclesiology, placing the weight of a church's identity as a community of the "new humanity" on this ethic.

In terms of opening up an ecumenical discussion in which resistance to war is not the property of any one communion, Yoder's formulation presents some immediate difficulties. What happens, for example, when a confessing body decides differently on the absolute nature of resistance to war? As we shall see with the remaining figures of this study, the refusal of war is not always a moral absolute and does not rise to the level of doctrine. In evaluating doctrine by practice, however, Yoder cannot avoid the conclusion, I think, that the refusal of war is the measure of the faithful church. Turning to Dorothy Day, we find a person for whom nonviolence is one practice among others that bears witness to the social existence given in the church. Like Yoder, Day's life is characterized by dialogue with those outside the church; but while nonviolence is ultimately consistent with Catholic ecclesiology, it is not, for Day, the determinate factor for what the church is.

3

The Church *Forming* Nonviolence: Dorothy Day, The Mystical Body, and the Logic of Tradition

In the work of Dorothy Day, we find a second voice offering an account of the interrelation between ecclesiology and nonviolence, albeit in a distinctly different manner. For Day, Christ's Mystical Body assumes all human existence and directs all humanity toward its full communion: the visible body of Christ, the Catholic Church.[1] In certain ways, Day's thesis agrees with Yoder, insofar as Yoder also measures the church's nature and witness according to Christ's humanity. For Yoder, the church (Christ's body) is inextricably related to nonviolence, to the extent that the faithful church could not be narrated as other than nonviolent. For Day, nonviolence is descriptive of Christ's "Mystical Body," but the Church forms and frames this nonviolent witness, as opposed to naming nonviolent

1. In this chapter, I will be capitalizing Church in keeping with Day's usage.

resistance to war as an intrinsic and necessary characteristic of proper ecclesiology. While Day emphasizes many of the same themes as Yoder, she worked within an American Catholic tradition largely ill-equipped to speak to the practice of Christian nonviolence in her time. For many years, the issue of Catholic non-participation in war in the twentieth century received decidedly little attention.[2] It is widely acknowledged that, in American Catholic life, the work and life of Dorothy Day acted as a catalyst in the recognition of a nonviolent option for Catholics.[3]

Following the pattern of the previous chapter, I will begin with an account of the governing concept in Day's work that illuminates both her ecclesiology and her reasons for nonviolent resistance to war: the Mystical Body of Christ.[4] For Day, the Mystical Body of Christ—the way in which Christ's person is the measure and meaning of all humanity—points to a refusal of war; if all human nature finds

2. Historians such as Ronald Musto and Catholic peace movements such as the Catholic Peace Fellowship have attempted to ascertain an unbroken tradition of Catholic nonviolence. While Catholic witnesses have appeared in every generation arguing for Christian non-involvement in war, prior to the Second Vatican Council (1962–1965), the question of non-participation received almost no attention.
3. United State Conference of Catholic Bishops, *The Challenge of Peace: God's Promise and Our Response, A Pastoral Letter on War and Peace,* United States Conference of Catholic Bishops Website, May 3, 1983, http://www.usccb.org/upload/challenge-peace-gods-promise-our-response-1983.pdf: "In the twentieth century, prescinding from the non-Christian witness of a Mahatma Gandhi and its worldwide impact, the nonviolent witness of such figures as Dorothy Day and Martin Luther King has had profound impact upon the life of the Church in the United States. The witness of numerous Christians who had preceded them over the centuries was affirmed in a remarkable way at the Second Vatican Council," (117). It appears that Day's witness to the Christian practice of nonviolence, stretching back to the 1930s, was validated at Vatican II, thirty years later, http://www.usccb.org/upload/challenge-peace-gods-promise-our-response-1983.pdf.
4. Other studies have evaluated the impact of Day's nonviolence. See Charles Chatfield, "The Catholic Worker in the United States Peace Tradition," in *American Catholic Pacifism: The Influence of Dorothy Day and the Catholic Worker Movement*, ed. Anne Klejment and Nancy L. Roberts (Westport, CT: Praeger, 1996), 1–13. For thorough expositions of radical Catholic social witness in the wake of Dorothy Day *and The Catholic Worker*, see Mel Piehl, *Breaking Bread: The Catholic Worker and the Origin of Catholic Radicalism in America* (Philadelphia: Temple University Press, 1982); Patricia McNeal, *Harder than War: Catholic Peacemaking in Twentieth-Century America* (New Brunswick, NJ: Rutgers University Press, 1992).

its center in Christ's humanity, then war is a theological offense, a rending of Christ's own body. In turn, Day's arguments against war are inseparable from her commitment to human life as ordered by Christ's person toward its true end: the communion of the Church's worship. While worked out within the bounds of Catholic teaching, Day's arguments for nonviolent resistance to war press the Church to reconsider the radicality of its own tradition.[5]

For Day, the Church and its wisdom *forms* nonviolence, by which I mean that the ecclesial telos of human life gives form and shape to a charity that (for Day) is the graced orientation of all persons. However, though nonviolence attests profoundly to the nature of the human communion in Christ, nonviolence it is not the only practice that speaks of this communion or the only way in which a person might be directed toward their true end. According to Day, nonviolence speaks of the peaceable logic of the Church, but it is one act among others that bears witness to Christ's work and humanity's true end in christological communion.

The Mystical Body of Christ: Present, Potential, and Peaceable

Day's theology rests upon the intimacy of God to natural life, such that the communion of the Church is the fullness of the loves, affections, and desires of natural life given by God. For Day, this truth is expressed in no place more clearly than the doctrine of the "Mystical Body of Christ," in which all humanity—either in actuality or potentially—are taken up by Christ's person; all human desires

5. This is not to say that Day learned of nonviolence through only Catholic sources. As Anne Klejment points out, Day's roots in the radical left during the First World War contributed to her initial critique of involvement in war, in "The Radical Origins of Catholic Pacifism: Dorothy Day and the Lyrical Left During World War I," in *American Catholic Pacifism*, 15–32. Additionally, her own appreciation for nonviolence stretched beyond Catholic sources to Marxist, Gandhian, and anarchist forms. I will show, however, that Day's appreciation of the limits of these critiques occurs with the limits of Catholic teaching, creating an ecclesial bracket for her thought on the ends and means of nonviolence.

and loves thus yearn for God. Humanity's creation in Christ calls, in turn, for humanity to receive the visible form of that unity: the Church. After briefly describing the meaning of the Mystical Body of Christ in the encyclical tradition of the early-twentieth century, I will describe how Day's use of the term expands beyond the traditional use of the doctrine.

The doctrine of the Mystical Body of Christ (*corpus mysticum*) has a long and involved history of interpretation; in short, it refers to how Christ is present in the world in a way inseparable from the celebration and liturgy of the Church.[6] In pre-twentieth-century formulations, the Mystical Body of Christ refers to three interlocking "bodies": the physical body of Christ, the gathered body of the people of the Church, and the Eucharist. In this way, the resurrected body of Christ is present through its corresponding and interlocking present-day "bodies"—the gathered people of the Church and the Eucharist.[7]

Pius XII's 1943 encyclical *Mystici Corporis Christi* steps into this tradition to articulate how the Mystical Body of Christ "is the Church," a "society . . . [which] resembles its divine Founder."[8] For

6. For overviews of this ecclesiological history, see Bernard P. Prusak, *The Church Unfinished: Ecclesiology through the Centuries* (Mahaw, NJ: Paulist, 2004), 148–69, 230–42, 279–86. See also J.-M.-R. Tillard, *Flesh of the Church, Flesh of Christ: At the Source of the Ecclesiology of Communion*, trans. Madeliene Beaumont (Collegeville, MN: Liturgical, 2001); Robert S. Pelton, ed., *The Church as the Body of Christ* (Notre Dame: University of Notre Dame Press, 1963). For major medieval shifts in this doctrine, see Henri Cardinal de Lubac, SJ, *Corpus Mysticum: The Eucharist and the Church in the Middle Ages*, trans. Gemma Simmonds, CJ, with Richard Prace and Christopher Stephens (Notre Dame: University of Notre Dame Press, 2006); Ernest Kantorowicz, *The King's Two Bodies: A Study in Medieval Political Theology* (Princeton: Princeton University Press, 1957).

7. De Lubac, *Corpus Mysticum*, 4–7 demonstrates the manner in which these "bodies" are connected, determined in large part by what is understood to be the role of the gathered people. The full theological and political history is complex and beyond the scope of this discussion. See also ibid., 34–39, 269–75; William Cavanaugh, *Torture and Eucharist: Theology, Politics, and the Body of Christ* (Malden, MA:Wiley-Blackwell, 1998), 210–21.

8. Pius XII, *Mystici Corporis Christi* [Encyclical on the Mystical Body of Christ], Vatican Website, June 29, 1943, para. 1, 3, http://www.vatican.va/holy_father/pius_xii/encyclicals/documents/hf_p-xii_enc_29061943_mystici-corporis-christi_en.html. All citations from *Mystici Corporis Christi* will be from the Vatican translation. In the wake of the ecclesiology put forth in the

Pius XII, the union between the gathered body of Christ and the risen Christ was inconceivable apart from the juridical structures of the Church facilitating that union.[9] The "ineffable flow of graces" was willed by Christ to come the Church "only through a visible Church made up of men";[10] the logic of *body* in Pius's writing implies an institutional visibility of the body that visibly orders its parts, with laity and hierarchy functioning together in defined orders.[11] Belonging to the visible body of Christ facilitates the "mystical" bond between believers, namely, the Church as seen in its juridical and institutional aspects. Addressing the historical context of *Mystici Corporis*, it should be noted that the Second World War had thrown the visible unity of the Church into question, and Catholics found themselves divided by national lines. Therefore, Pius sought to emphasize the manner in which the singular work of Christ is secured in mystical, juridical, and liturgical ways—particularly in an age when political divisions among nations in which the Church had a presence threatened to compromise this visible unity.[12]

First Vatican Council, some were concerned that ecclesiology had been too strictly defined in terms of its hierarchical institutions, neglecting the laity. See Richard McBrien, *The Church: The Evolution of Catholicism* (New York: HarperOne, 2008), 122–23.

9. Pius XII, *Mystici Corporis Christi*, para. 9: "For while there still survives a false rationalism, which ridicules anything that transcends and defies the power of human genius, and which is accompanied by a cognate error, the so-called popular naturalism, which sees and wills to see in the Church nothing but a juridical and social union, there is on the other hand a false mysticism creeping in, which, in its attempt to eliminate the immovable frontier that separates creatures from their Creator, falsifies the Sacred Scriptures." Mystical Body ecclesiology, revived in part through the writings of theologian Emile Mersch, stresses the spiritual aspects of this union between Christ and the members of the Church, though not the juridical features. See Emile Mersch, *The Whole Christ*, trans. John R. Kelly (Milwaukee: Bruce, 1938). The great irony of Mersch's role in the revival of Mystical Body ecclesiology is that *Mystici Corporis Christi* (published three years after Mersch's death) emphasizes the institutional dimensions of ecclesiology that Mersch himself downplays. See Ralph Del Colle, *Christ and the Spirit: Spirit-Christology in Trinitarian Perspective* (Oxford: Oxford University Press, 1994), 51–54.
10. Pius XII, *Mystici Corporis Christi*, para. 12.
11. Ibid., para. 17. The Eucharist, according to the encyclical, is not the "Mystical Body" proper but that by which "the faithful are nourished and strengthened . . . and by a divine, ineffable bond are united with each other and with the Divine Head of the whole Body" (para. 19).

William Cavanaugh argues that by emphasizing the juridical nature of the Church, Pius's work trades in a visible, transpolitical unity for an invisible, supratemporal unity that could be achieved in a world divided by war.[13] However, this seems to be in context the best one could hope for without negating the validity of a nation's sovereignty. The encyclical goes to great lengths to argue that through the juridical nature of the Church, the Church is able to be a visible and unified political body, provided that national sovereignty is not abolished.[14] The unity of the "social body" of Christ is visible "through their profession of the same faith and their sharing the same sacred rites, through participation in the same Sacrifice, and practical observance of the same laws," accompanied by the faith, hope, and love of its members. According to *Mystici*, the visible unity of the Church is located in shared liturgies that do not negate national claims, in contrast to Cavanaugh's proposal.[15]

In *Mystici*, the work of Christ—available through the visible Church—establishes the Mystical Body of Christ in an institutional body made visible through the Sacraments and the juridical structures of the Church.[16] As a result, the Mystical Body is described in juridical

12. Ibid., para. 31: "For both the juridical mission of the Church, and the power to govern and administer the Sacraments derive their supernatural efficacy and force for the building up of the Body of Christ from the fact that Jesus Christ . . . opened up to His Church the fountain of those divine gifts, which prevent her from ever teaching false doctrine and enable her to rule them for the salvation of their souls through divinely enlightened pastors and to bestow on them an abundance of heavenly graces."
13. Cavanaugh, *Torture and Eucharist*, 211. Placing Pius XII in line with Jacques Maritain and others of the "New Christendom" school who perceived the spiritual and temporal worlds to be on "two planes," Cavanaugh charges Pius XII with abandoning a visible stance within the world on political issues by retreating into a supratemporal plane. See ibid., 191–94.
14. Pius XII, *Mystici Corporis Christi*, para. 65: The work of the Church, to "perpetuate on earth the saving work of Redemption," is "far superior to all other human societies . . . surpass[ing] them as grace surpasses nature, as things immortal are above all those that perish. Such human societieis, and in the first place civil society, are by no means to be despised or belittled."
15. Ibid., para. 69–70.
16. Ibid., para. 12–14, 17–19. See also para. 31: "For both the juridical mission of the Church, and the power to teach, govern and administer the Sacraments, derive their supernatural efficacy and force for the building up of the Body of Christ from the fact that Jesus Christ, hanging

terms, denoting contours of the gathered and visible community united in the Vicar of Christ as the circumscribed limits of the Mystical Body.[17] To establish how the Mystical Body of Christ was unified and visible in an age of war, the encyclical plays up the juridical features of the Church, having the dual effect of re-emphasizing the juridical aspects of the Church as central to the Church's identity and unity and reinforcing the Mystical Body of Christ as an exclusively Roman Catholic liturgical body.

Day's usage of the doctrine of the Mystical Body also emphasizes the visible nature of Christ's body; to be a member of Christ's body is to visibly receive one's own true form. However, Day's usage emphasizes that, before it is a statement about liturgical belonging or juridical actuality, the Mystical Body of Christ is an anthropological reality that cuts across national, ecclesiastical, and political divisions. As such, to speak of Christ's Mystical Body is not first and foremost to speak of the Church's liturgy (though this is indispensible) but to speak of the way in which the humanity of Christ is the normative and ontological account of all human life, behavior, and virtues. I will now turn to Day's use of this doctrine.

The Mystical Body and the Unity of Humanity: Day's Usage of "Mystical Body"

Day's introduction to the doctrine of the Mystical Body of Christ occurred shortly after her 1927 conversion to Catholicism and, as Roger Statnick rightly observes, became foundational to her theology.[18] Her earliest writings in *The Catholic Worker* contain no

on the Cross, opened up to His Church the fountain of those divine gifts." In para. 65, *Mystici* "deplores and condemns the pernicious error of those who dream of an imaginary Church . . . to which somewhat contemptuously, they oppose another, which they call juridical."

17. Ibid., para. 34, 40.

18. Roger A. Statnick, "Dorothy Day's Religious Conversion: A Study in Biographical Theology," (PhD diss., University of Notre Dame, 1983), 310–14. The sources for Day's understanding of the doctrine of the Mystical Body are in all likelihood beyond reconstruction; the doctrine

overt reference to the Mystical Body of Christ as such, emphasizing Jesus' historical identification with human suffering instead.[19] By 1935, she began explicitly making the connection between the suffering state of humanity and the Mystical Body of Christ:

> It is because we forget the Humanity of Christ (present with us today in the Blessed Sacrament just as truly as when He walked with His apostles through the cornfields that Sunday long ago, breakfasting on the ears of corn)—that we have ignored the material claims of our fellow man during this capitalistic, industrialist era. We have allowed our brothers and sisters, our fellow members in the Mystical Body to be degraded, to endure slavery to a machine, to live in rat-infested holes. This ignoring of the material body of our humanity, which Christ ennobled when He took flesh, gives rise to the aversion for religion evidenced by many workers.[20]

In this early quote, we can discern three points that become foundational for Day's understanding of the Mystical Body. First, as seen in the Eucharist, the "humanity of Christ" is the basis of thinking about material life—in that bodily life is to be understood and justified Christologically, prior to any other political claims on human life. Second, Christ's humanity vicariously "ennobles" all

appears in the Baltimore Catechism, which was a part of Day's formation, and Day recounts being given literature by a number of Catholic mentors during the time leading up to her conversion but prior to her meeting Peter Maurin. We can say with certainty, however, that Day did not know of the doctrine prior to her own conversion. See Dorothy Day, *From Union Square to Rome* (Silver Spring, MD: Preservation of the Faith, 1938; reprint, Maryknoll, NY: Orbis Books),142: "Teresa was baptized, she had become a member of the Mystical Body of Christ. I didn't know anything of the Mystical Body or I might have felt disturbed at being separated from her."

19. Dorothy Day, "Co-operative Apartment for Unemployed Women Has Its Start in Parish," *Catholic Worker* (*CW*), December 1933, 5: "However, we hug to ourselves the assurance that 'all these things' such as blankets 'will be added unto us,' so we are not dismayed. Come to think of it, there are two rugs on *The Catholic Worker* floor, which, if energetically beaten out, will serve as covers. Christ's first bed was of straw." See also, Day, "Catholic Worker Program,," *CW*, December 1933: "There was social justice in the demands made by the Communists—they were the poor, the unemployed, the homeless. They were among the ones Christ was thinking of when he said, 'Feed my Sheep.' And the Church had food for them, that I knew."
20. Dorothy Day, "Wealth, The Humanity of Christ, Class War," *CW*, June 1935, 4.

persons—Christian or not—meaning that all human life is to be read through the lens of Christ's humanity.[21] Third, those who Christ has "ennobled" are seen as either actual or potential members in the Mystical Body, which exists prior to its fracturing into categories of "worker" or "citizen."

Day's use of the term *Mystical Body* is often ambiguous in its designations. At times, she uses the term to include all people, regardless of church affiliation, as members in the Mystical Body: "All the nation, I mean, that is made up of the poor, the worker, the trade unionist—those who felt most keenly the sense of solidarity—that very sense of solidarity which made me gradually understand the doctrine of the Mystical Body of Christ whereby we are the members of one another."[22] At other times, she describes the Mystical Body as belonging to only the baptized.[23] In other words, two senses of the

21. Day will often speak of "potential members" of the body of Christ, indicating that while Christ's humanity holds purchase for all people, their visible belonging to this body in time and space is a belonging that is seen in hope. See Day, "On Pilgrimage," *CW*, December 1963, 2, 6: "The entire world has acclaimed Pope John, and he increased the sum total of love in the world and renewed the health of the Mystical Body of which we are all members, or potential members." This terminology is used throughout Day's writings. See Day, "Catholic Worker Celebrates Third Birthday; A Restatement of C.W. Aims and Ideals," *CW*, May 1936; Day, "Fall Appeal—November 1957," *CW*, November 1957; Day, "Fall Appeal—October 1963," *CW*, October 1963; Day, "On Pilgrimage,," *CW*, January 1970 for a few representative instances.
22. Dorothy Day, *The Long Loneliness: An Autobiography* (New York: Harper and Row, 1952), 147. Unless Day is writing her memoir for an explicitly Catholic audience, her use of "we" leaves open how she means this term. In her description of labor strikes, Day made a similar claim: "Take a factory where fifty per cent of the workers themselves content, do not care about their fellows. It is hard to inspire them with the idea of solidarity. . . . That is why there is coercion, the beating of scabs and strikebreakers, the threats and the hatreds that grow up. That is why in labor struggles, unless there is a wise and patient leader, there is disunity, a rending of the Mystical Body,," in Day, *From Union Square to Rome*, 14.
23. Day, *The Long Loneliness*, 144: In *The Long Loneliness*, she writes that, after having her daughter baptized, "Teresa had become a member of the Mystical Body of Christ. I didn't know anything of the Mystical Body or I might have felt disturbed at being separated from her." In the same sense, Day describes her own conversion as "[becoming] a member of the Mystical Body of Christ" (ibid., 10). A more divisive nature of the Mystical Body is emphasized by Day's frequent use of "members and potential members" when describing social movements involving Catholics and non-Catholics. See, in particular, Day, "Catholic Worker Celebrates Third Birthday"; Day, "On Pilgrimage," *CW,* October–November 1972.

Mystical Body seem to be in play for Day: sometimes, she refers to all persons as the Mystical Body, while at other times, she seems to draw distinctions between Catholics and non-Catholics—with only the former as the Mystical Body. What are we to make of Day's seemingly contradictory uses of the term?

A 1948 article provides some guidance. Here, she argues that what is visible in the Church as the Body of Christ is the culmination of a larger process that people began as a consequence of the incarnation:

> But our unity, if it is not unity of thought, in regard to temporal matters, is a unity at the altar rail. We are all members of the Mystical Body of Christ, and so we are closer, to each other, by the tie of grace, than any blood brothers are. . . . We are our brothers' keeper, and all men are our brothers whether they are Catholic or not. But of course the tie that binds Catholics is closer, the tie of grace. We partake of the same food, Christ. We put off the old man and put on Christ. The same blood flows through our veins, Christ's. We are the same flesh, Christ's. But all men are members or potential members, as St. Augustine says, and there is no time with God, so who are we to know the degree of separation between us and the Communist, the unbaptized, the God-hater, who may tomorrow, like St. Paul, love Christ.[24]

In other words, while all persons have been "ennobled" by Christ, Day understands this ennobling to be the first step in a process pointing toward the culminating work of participation in the Eucharist. The joining of Christ's humanity to ours is not simply a matter of God accompanying humanity in misery but directing humanity toward its true end: the renewed sociality of the Mystical Body, found in the worship of Christ in the Church.

In many ways, this description of the way in which Christ calls us through our natural loves and desires summarizes Day's own conversion. While Day was provided no religious training by her parents, she was introduced to Scripture, Sunday school, hymns, and

24. Day, "On Pilgrimage," *CW*, May 1948.

the liturgy through the influence of a Methodist neighbor, becoming "a regular churchgoer" following the family's move to Oakland, California.[25] Nevertheless, she describes this early exposure to Christianity in ambiguous terms, saying that "in all the first years I remember nothing about God except that routine chapter and prayer in school which I did not feel.[26] Day longed for was for "every home to be open to the lame, the halt and the blind," for the institutional Church to cohere to her vision for the good society.[27] Though by the time Day entered the university at 16, she "no longer [felt it] necessary to go to church," having "distrusted all churches after reading the books of London and Sinclair," she remained drawn to Christian authors such as Dostoevsky and Tolstoy, though her "faith had nothing in common with that of Christians around me."[28] Despite Day's aversion to "religion, as it was practiced by those I encountered," the language of the Church she learned as a child continues to haunt her descriptions of the world:

25. Day, *Long Loneliness*, 9–23. Day writes of her exposure to Catholics and Episcopalians (with whom she was confirmed) throughout her itinerant childhood (28–29). Neither William Miller, *Dorothy Day: A Biography* (San Francisco: Harper and Row, 1982) nor Robert Coles, *Dorothy Day: A Radical Devotion* (Reading, MA: Addison-Wesley, 1989) make much of these experiences. Miller's 525 page biography devotes a single page to Day's early religious influences, and Coles's biography devotes none. The fullest treatment of the literary and intellectual sources Day refers to as formative for herself and for her vision of the Catholic Worker movement is Mark and Louise Zwick, *The Catholic Worker Movement: Intellectual and Spiritual Origins* (Mahwah, NJ: Paulist, 2005).

26. Day, *From Union Square to Rome*, 21. Day makes this statement despite acknowledging that, in reading Scripture as a child, "a new personality impressed itself on me . . . I knew almost immediately that I was discovering God" (20).

27. Day, *Long Loneliness*, 39.

28. Day, *From Union Square to Rome*, 41–43. June O'Connor, "Dorothy Day's Christian Conversion," *Journal of Religious Ethics* 18 (1990): 159–80 argues that Day's conversion to Catholicism was primarily affective—consisting of primal affections to which cognitive content are added later. If O'Connor's account of Day's conversion is correct, however, we would not find Day referring to Christian categories prior to her adult conversion. In fact, Day's early contact with Christians, as detailed by Day herself, indicates that her conversion was not one of affection followed by cognitive content but one in which she reconciled the cognitive content with her affections.

> Christ no longer walked the streets of this world. He was two thousand years dead and new prophets had risen up in His place. I was in love with the masses. I do not remember that I was articulate or reasoned about this love, but it warmed my heart and filled it. It was those among the poor and the oppressed who were going to rise up, they were collectively the new Messiah, and they would release the captives.[29]

During her post-university years, the division between her early religious influences and her activism became the most pronounced; as Day would later reflect, religion exhibited a "pie in the sky" as opposed to the Socialists' work against poverty and war.[30] As she explains in *The Long Loneliness,* however, the Church was inseparable from "the masses":

> Without even looking into the claims of the Catholic Church, I was willing to admit that for me she was the one true Church. She had come down through the centuries since the time of Peter, and far from being dead, she claimed and held the allegiance of the masses of people in all cities where I had lived. They poured in and out of her doors on Sundays and holy days, for novenas and missions.[31]

Prior to her conversion, Day had begun going to mass and praying on a regular basis.[32] In time, Day would see that her engagement with the liturgy did not compete with her social commitments but was the

29. Day, *From Union Square to Rome*, 51.
30. Day spent 1914–1922 among Marxist and Socialist groups, first as a student member of a university Socialist club, then as a staff writer for *The Call*, a Socialist newspaper based in the lower East Side of New York City, and later for *The Masses*, a similar publication. See Miller, *Dorothy Day,* 31–86. Day was never a "card-carrying member" of these groups but engaged in numerous strikes and protests on behalf of socialist causes out of a belief that the varied groups, despite their conflicting social visions, were working on behalf of the masses in some respect. As Day would describe her commitments, "I wavered between my allegiance to socialism, syndicalism (the I.W.W.s) and anarchism" (*Long Loneliness,* 62). For Day's involvement with these various groups, see Miller, *Dorothy Day,* 62–75.
31. Day, *Long Loneliness*, 139.
32. Day, *From Union Square to Rome*, 125–27. One could argue that *apologias* such as *Union Square* or *Loneliness* are merely post-event nostalgia overlaying the circumstances surrounding her conversion, except that in noting these events, Day is drawing on her diaries from the period and not retrospectively retelling the story.

logical culmination of her natural loves. During her pre-conversion period of social activism, Day felt that "religion would only impede my work . . . I felt I must turn from it as from a drug."[33] In her two subsequent autobiographies, Day remarks that her conversion was the culmination of her other desires.[34]

The love that drew Day to the poor and to lay Catholic voices found its culmination when she joined the institutional Church where these insights find their visible, historical form. As Day puts it in her description of the coherence between the love of God and her love of the masses:

> The problem is, how to love God? We are only too conscious of the hardness of our hearts, and in spite of all that religious writers tell us about *feeling* not being necessary, we do want to feel and so know that we love God . . . The final object of this love and gratitude was God. No human creature could receive or contain so vast a flood of love and joy as I often felt after the birth of my child. With this came the need to worship, to adore. I had heard many say that they wanted to worship God in their own way and did not need a Church in which to praise Him, nor a body of people with whom to associate themselves. But I did not agree to this. *My very experience as a radical, my whole make-up led me to want to associate myself with others, with the masses, in loving and praising God.*[35]

As her earliest statements on the Mystical Body show, the unity of Christ's humanity with human nature implicates all humanity; for Day, however, this implies a fulfillment of this work in the life of the Church.[36] In numerous places, she expresses her belief in the visibility and truth of the Church's claim to be "Christ made visible,"[37] with

33. Day, *Long Loneliness,* 43. During these early years, Day wrote her first memoir, a controversial and thinly-veiled autobiographical volume named *The Eleventh Virgin* (New York: Boni, 1928).In the work, Day describes her early life in lurid detail, including her youthful affairs and an abortion.

34. Day, *From Union Square to Rome*, 132–33. Following the birth of her daughter Therese in 1927, Day chose to have Therese baptized, much to the chagrin of Day's husband Forester.

35. Day, *Long Loneliness*, 139, emphasis mine.

the work of Christ's humanity present in all humanity, drawing them toward their true end. However, Day's description of human nature as "ennobled" by Christ does not diminish the need for this nature to be perfected. Rather, "ennobling" emphasizes the manner in which humanity—as that which has been already taken up by Christ in crucifixion and resurrection—exhibits a graced orientation toward its true end, though the natural loves that a person exhibits (such as Day's love for the masses) still must be clarified and reoriented in light of Christ.[38]

As a result of viewing Christ's humanity as the telos of human life, drawing all people to their fullness, Day is able to affirm the adductive work of Christ in a variety of places, and particularly with those who differed from her on the question of war. For example, after her grandson's return from Vietnam in 1970, Day reflected upon what it would mean to participate in the Vietnam War from the other side, in service to Ho Chi Minh. Stating that "we believe that we are all members or potential members of the Mystical Body of Christ, members of one another as St. Paul said," Day affirmed Ho's "vision" and defense of his people against danger.[39]

36. In many ways, this is in line with Henri de Lubac's claim in *Catholicism: Christ and the Common Destiny of Man* (San Francisco: Ignatius, 1988) that "salvation for this body, for humanity, consists in its receiving the form of Christ, and that is possible only through the Catholic Church. For is she not the only complete authoritative interpreter of Christian revelation? . . . And, lastly, is she not responsible for realizing the spiritual unity of men insofar as they will lend themselves to it?" (223).

37. Day, *Long Loneliness*, 149.

38. Day was committed to the need for human nature to be "mortified," as seen in her relationship to the Lacouture retreat movement, a controversial movement held by some to be Janesinst for its emphasis on the mortification of the flesh. On the Lacouture Movement and its controversies, see Brigid O'Shea Merriman, *Searching for Christ: The Spirituality of Dorothy Day* (Notre Dame: University of Notre Dame, 1994), 137–69. See also, Zwick and Zwick, *The Catholic Worker Movement*, 235–49; Jean Dolet, "Un Mouvement de Spiritualitie Sacerdotale au Quebec au 20e Siecle (1931-1950): le Lacouturisme," *Societie Canadienne d'Histoire de L'Eglise Catholique* 40 (1974): 55–91.

39. Dorothy Day, "On Pilgrimage—January 1970," *CW*, January 1970, 1, 2, 8.

Day employed a similar approach in discussing "movements to deepen the spiritual life of men of good will," as encouraged by Pope John XXIII.[40] In these cases, Day found non-Catholic movements that were aiding in the fields of education and agriculture in Central America and among North American migrant populations. She reaffirmed that the material aspects of these works was never the primary work but that "the basic need is for a change of hearts and souls, and when we write of destitution and voluntary poverty as one of the means to combat it, it is to emphasize the primacy of the spiritual."[41] In both this case and the case of Ho Chih Minh, we find an affirmation of those instances in the non-Catholic world that were, for Day, indicative of the Christ who has redeemed all humanity and calls to humanity through human desires and virtues.

In these writings, we find Day's understanding of the Mystical Body as consistent with *Mystici Corporis* but also an expansion of it. *Mystici* states that the doctrine of the Mystical Body is "acceptable and useful to those who are without the fold of the Church," but the unity of the Mystical Body is not given to humanity at large; rather, *Mystici* states that the Mystical Body is only given "if [the world] turn their gaze to the church, if they contemplate *her* divinely-given unity."[42] For *Mystici*, the unity of the Mystical Body refers one to the institutional Church. But for Day, one cannot speak of Christ's Mystical Body without speaking of the ways in which this body appears in shadowy form within all persons, including non-Christian exemplars of social action, because Christ's Mystical Body refers first to the incarnate Christ who assumes human flesh.

40. Dorothy Day, "On Pilgrimage—December 1963," *CW*, December 1963, 2, 6.

41. Ibid, 6.

42. Pius XII, *Mystici Corporis Christi*, 5 (emphasis mine). *Mystici* does allow that some "by an unconscious desire and longing . . . have a certain relationship with the Mystical Body of the Redeemer." However, this relation is conceived only as longing and not participation in the gifts of full Catholic communion, which the encyclical sees as controvertible with belonging to the visible body (para.103).

This solidarity between persons is spoken of most fully in the Eucharist, by which our vision of Christ is clarified and the particular character of Jesus is made known:

> Why did Christ institute this Sacrament of His Body and Blood?. . . . It was because He loved us and wished to be with us. "My delights are to be with the children of men." He made us and He loves us. His presence in the Blessed Sacrament is the great proof of that love . . . It took me a long time as a convert to realize the presence of Christ as Man in the Sacrament. He is the same Jesus Who walked on earth, Who slept in the boat as the tempest arose, Who hungered in the desert, Who prayed in the garden . . . Jesus is there as Man. He is there, Flesh and Blood, Soul and Divinity. He is our leader Who is always with us.[43]

In its more controversial moments, this vision of the Mystical Body allows for an inclusion of Mohandas K. Gandhi and Communist rebels in Cuba as "filling up the sufferings of Christ."[44] However, Christ's humanity is not simply an example for socio-political changes. As Day wrote concerning her tentative approval of the Cuban revolution, "putting on Christ" is more than imitation of the works of Christ:

> Man is a creature of body and soul, and he must work to live, he must work to be co-creator with God, taking raw materials and producing for man's needs. He becomes God-like, he is divinized not only by the sacrament but by his work, in which he intimates his Creator, in which he is truly "putting on Christ" and putting off the old man, who is fearful and alienated from his material surrounding.[45]

43. Day, *From Union Square to Rome*, 166–67. Day continues:"And if you and I love our faulty fellow-human beings, how much more must God love us all? . . . You may say perhaps: 'how do we know he does, if there is a He!' And I can only answer that we know it because He is here present with us today in the Blessed Sacrament on the altar, that He never has left us, and that by daily going to Him for the gift of Himself as daily bread, I am convinced of that love."
44. Dorothy Day, "We Mourn Death of Gandhi Non Violent Revolutionary," *CW*, February 1948, 1; Day, "On Pilgrimage in Cuba: Part III," *CW*, November 1962, 1–8.
45. Day, "On Pilgrimage in Cuba,"

By limiting the Mystical Body to its juridical form and not its anthropological form, Day saw that the Church's own celebrations of the Mystical Body often moved in a different direction from the doctrine's intent. Particularly, the Church affirmed aspects of human life that enabled structural survival of the Church, such as war. In a speech to the Eucharistic Congress in 1976, Day explains that "penance comes before the Eucharist" and that we oppose the "life" of the Eucharist by "world instruments of death," that the universal salvation proclaimed by Christ is opposed by massacres, wars, and holocausts.[46] As such, any Mass for the military should be a mass dedicated to penance in recognition that the telos of "natural life" has been turned into a celebration of death.[47] If the Eucharist is the presentation of Christ's life, insofar as the Church turns the Mass into a celebration of the military, the Church not only misunderstood the life of Christ but also its own constitution as the Church. Thus, not only does the Church receive the "living presence of Jesus" in the Eucharist, but the Church is reminded of the Jesus whose humanity is at work in the whole of humanity as well. During the Vietnam War era, Day lamented the lost connection between the humanity of Christ as displayed in the Eucharist and secular protests on behalf of humanity, blaming the Church for the fact that the protesters could not see that "God was Father of all, that all men are brothers." As a result, Church teaching was pitted against those who sought common ground to preserve society.[48]

At this point, we can see how Day's understanding of the Mystical Body of Christ frames the Church's relationship to the world: all humanity is made one in Christ—a unity that is meant to be borne out through the visible body of Christ, the Church. As we move

46. Dorothy Day, "Bread for the Hungry," *CW*, September 1976, 1, 5.
47. Ibid.
48. Dorothy Day, "On Pilgrimage," *CW*, February 1967, 2, 6, 7.

forward, we will see how the visible body of Christ continues to be the end toward which advocacy for the world in the form of nonviolence is ordered, as well as the frame within which Day's witness against war found an uneasy home.

Ecclesiology: The Culmination of Natural Life and the Orientation of Witness

Day's ecclesiology remains an understudied aspect of her thought, as most studies focus on her "permanent dissatisfaction" with the Catholic Church.[49] This rendering of Day's view of the church is one-sided, neglecting Day's repeated affirmations of obedience as well as the central role the institutional Church played in the Catholic Worker movement she co-founded with Peter Maurin.[50] Thomas Frary helpfully describes her ecclesiology as an "intuitive understanding of the relationship of the Church to the world," thereby underscoring how, for Day, the institutions of the Church cannot be understood apart from the "natural life" about which the Church claims to speak authoritatively. To approach Day's ecclesiology, thus, is to not only attend to the difficulties Day had with her Church, but to her belief that the Church authoritative claims on the orientation of human life.[51] Therefore, the manner in which the Church—as the telos of the Mystical Body meant for

49. See Coles, *Dorothy Day*, 52ff. Day does call her stance one of "permanent dissatisfaction," in *The Long Loneliness*, (150), but she brackets this protest against various failures of the Church by emphasizing her love of the Church and Roman Guardini's statement that "the Church is the cross upon which Christ is crucified." In other words, for all the Church's failures, it is still the body of Christ in the world and cannot be abandoned.

50. Debra Campbell's "The Catholic Earth Mother: Dorothy Day and Women's Power in the Church," *Cross Currents* 34 (1984): 270–82 captures some of Day's dynamic as "deeply traditionalist" and radical but examines Day's ecclesiology only as it relates to her dealings with Church authorities.

51. Thomas Frary, "The Ecclesiology of Dorothy Day"(PhD diss., Marquette University, 1972), 8. For Frary, Day's ecclesiology is characterized by a tension between the spiritual and social dimensions of faith; the institutional Church, according to Frary, is concerned primarily with the immaterial (spiritual), while Day longed for social involvement.

all humanity—frames Day's discussions of war and peace will be of central interest.

The Catholic Worker as Apostolate

After her introduction to Peter Maurin in 1932, Day established the first Catholic Worker house, a setting that drew together the liturgy and institutions of the Church with "the masses." Through Maurin, Day was introduced to Catholic social teachings, including the works of mercy—acts of charity meant to orient the person's loves and actions toward God.[52] This practice of joining the teachings of the Church with "natural life" is best summed up in Peter Maurin's "Houses of Hospitality":

> We need Houses of Hospitality / to give to the rich / the opportunity to serve the poor.
>
> We need Houses of Hospitality / to bring the Bishops to the people / and the people to the Bishops.
>
> We need Houses of Hospitality / to bring back to institutions / the technique of institutions.
>
> We need Houses of Hospitality / to show what idealism looks like when it is practiced.
>
> We need Houses of Hospitality / to bring Social Justice / through Catholic Action / exercised in Catholic Institutions.[53]

As Maurin and Day envisioned them, the Worker homes were places where the institutions of the Church and the masses could come together.[54] Instead of simply propagating "good works," the Worker homes were designed to be a meeting ground between institutional

52. See Day, "The Scandal of the Works of Mercy," in *Selected Writings*, ed. Robert Ellsberg (Maryknoll, NY: Orbis Books, 2001), 98–99.
53. Day, *House of Hospitality* (London: Sheed & Ward, 1939), xxiii.
54. Ibid., xxxiv–xxxvi.

Catholicism and the world: "This work of ours toward a new heaven and a new earth shows a correlation between the material and the spiritual, and, of course, recognizes the primacy of the spiritual. Food for the body is not enough. There must be food for the soul."[55] Although the Catholic Worker houses emphasized Catholic social teaching and the works of mercy, Day saw these houses as part of the apostolate—not under the direct supervision of the Church, but an extension of it.[56]

Within the houses, instruction and formation took place as more of a round-table "clarification of thought" than strict catechesis, to use Peter Maurin's terminology; open discussions were hosted on various topics such as poverty, war, and Catholic social teaching, with members of the houses engaging in lively discussion on the meaning of the central commitments of the Catholic Worker movement.[57] Even concerning nonviolence, the pages of *The Catholic Worker* newsletter were rife with diverse approaches. The arguments for pacifism wrought by the anarchist Ammon Hennacy and Day's confessor John Hugo exemplify this "round-table" format, offering divergent theological articulations of nonviolence, even though both were committed pacifists.[58]

55. Ibid.

56. See ibid., 225; Day, "Letter to Our Readers at the Beginning of Our Fifteenth Year," *CW*, May 1947; Day, "On Pilgrimage," *CW*, May 1948. This is in keeping with Maurin's original vision which included, in addition to the works of mercy and the establishment of the houses of hospitality, "building up a lay apostolate through round table discussions for the clarification of thought" ("Letter to Our Readers," 1).

57. The only exception to this open process was Day's commitment to nonviolence, which she saw as normative for all of the houses. From the start, Day saw the social teachings providing a range of acceptable practice, but nonviolence—the "revolution . . . without the use of force"—was a non-negotiable. Day's stance on nonviolence was normative for all houses, leading to a schism during the Second World War among the Catholic Worker houses. See Francis J. Sicius, "Prophecy Faces Tradition: The Pacifist Debate During World War II," in *American Catholic Pacifism*, 66–76; Angie O'Gorman and Patrick G. Coy, "Houses of Hospitality: A Pilgrimage into Nonviolence," in *A Revolution of the Heart: Essays on the Catholic Worker*, ed. Patrick G. Coy (Philadelphia: Temple University Press, 1988), 239–71.

For some such as Hennacy, a frequent columnist for *The Catholic Worker*, this "clarification of thought" led to a departure from the Catholic Church; but for many others, conversion to Catholicism followed in the wake of these discussions.[59] Hennacy left the Church for reasons of conscience. Rather than condemn him, Day applauded his courage, in much the same way that she found reason to praise Ho Chi Minh's leadership. Though Hennacy departed from the physical sign of his love's perfection, Day curiously describes him as a "non-Church Christian." Day herself struggled in joining to the visible, institutional Church,[60] but in contrast to Hennacy, her adherence to the authority and juridical structures of the Church allowed her to bear witness to a different way of thinking about Catholic involvement in war.

Day's occasional writings, particularly on social issues of the day, are peppered with accounts of going to Mass, her prayers, and her relationship with her confessors.[61] Once more, this was not out love

58. Ben Peters, "Nature and Grace in the Theology of John Hugo," in *God, Grace, and Creation*, ed. Philip J. Rossi, Annual Publication of the College Theology Society 55 (Maryknoll, NY: Orbis Books, 2010), 59–79 describes Hugo's work as an American example of the *nouvelle-theologie* approach, comparable to Henri de Lubac. The comparison of Hugo to Hennacy—who advocated rebellion against the institutional Church—highlights the "round-table" format that characterized not only Catholic Worker houses but also *The Catholic Worker* paper.
59. For Ammon Hennacy's departure, see Day, "Ammon Hennacy: 'Non-Church' Christian," *CW*, February 1970, 2, 8.
60. Day, *From Union Square to Rome,* 159–69.
61. Day, "The Scandal of the Works of Mercy," 99–102. On her confessors, see Miller, *Dorothy Day*, 367ff. John Hugo became the most influential of these confessors, leading several retreats that helped form Day's vision of the supernatural culmination of the natural. Day would call this encounter with Hugo's retreats "a second conversion," in William Miller, *All Is Grace: The Spirituality of Dorothy Day* (Garden City, NY: Doubleday, 1987), 58ff. Ultimately, this would lead Day to become a Benedictine oblate in the early 1940s, a commitment that arguably shaped her understanding of the Catholic Worker houses. As Brigid O'Shea Merriman has shown, Day's movement toward becoming a Benedictine oblate provides a hermeneutical lens by which to understand Day's commitments, in O'Shea, *Searching for Christ*, 73–74, 100ff. Between Maurin's teaching and Day's exposure to Benedictine publications and priests, the influence on Day's earliest articulations of the Catholic Worker houses as "houses of hospitality" is evident.

for the institution as such but the culmination of the love Day had for God and the "masses":

> It was all very well to love God in His works, in the beauty of His creation which was crowned for me by the birth of my child . . . The final object of this love was God . . . With this came the need to worship, to adore. I had heard many say that they wanted to worship God in their own way and did not need a Church in which to praise Him, nor a body of people with whom to associate themselves. But I did not agree to this. My very experience as a radical, my whole make-up, led me to want to associate myself with others, with the masses, in loving and praising God.[62]

For Day, moving in the direction of social radicalism means accepting the guidance of Christ's visible body—the Church.[63] Because of her love of the Christ present in the Church, Day learned to love Christ's Church through the discipline of obedience.

Through obedience to Christ's Church, one's conscience is rightly formed away from transient desires and toward God, making oneself available to God as a part of the visible body of Christ.[64] Such obedience, Day reasons, has a leavening effect on the Church at large; as the laity models obedience to God, the hierarchy can better understand the Church's true mission.[65] Because obedience belongs ultimately to God in Christ—and subsequently to the Church—we can see the tension in Day's position: though obedience is due to Christ (whose life speaks against war), the institutional Church (which often affirms and celebrates just wars) is the place where

62. Day, *Long Loneliness,* 139.

63. Ibid., "What if they were compelled to come in by the law of the Church, which said they were guilty of mortal sin if they did not go to Mass every Sunday? They obeyed that law. . . . They accepted the Church. It may have been an unthinking, unquestioning faith, and yet the chance certainly came, again and again, 'Do I prefer the Church to my own will' . . . And the choice was the Church."

64. Day, "Holy Obedience," in *Selected Writings*, ed. Robert Ellsberg (Maryknoll, NY: Orbis Books, 2001), 168.

65. Ibid., 169. Day recounts how the bishop of Kansas City told Peter Maurin: "You lead the way, and we [the bishops] will follow."

Christ is spoken and the Eucharist—Christ made visible—is celebrated.[66]

By rendering obedience to the Mystical Body of Christ made visible in the Church, Day found herself able to inhabit the authority of Tradition in such a way that allowed her to read the Tradition dialogically, mining the internal logic for a new witness against war. One of the best examples of this dialogical dynamic is seen in Day's interpretation of the Catholic teachings on war. Day regularly sided with what she perceived to be the true meaning of the papal teachings, over against the bishops, which can be seen in her conflicts with Cardinal Spellman, Archbishop over New York.[67] As the chaplain to the Armed Forces, Spellman visited the military overseas during conflicts in Korea and Vietnam and did not approve of the Catholic Worker's adamant pacifism.[68] While Day notes on several occasions that she would cease her writings on war if asked to by the Cardinal, she never expected him to do so. That said, she felt no fear in criticizing Spellman for his involvement with the military.[69]

66. On the coinherence of individual conscience and the teachings of the Catholic Church, see Vatican Council II, *Gaudium et Spes* [Dogmatic Constitution on the Church in the Modern World], July 12, 1965, 14: "However in forming their consciences the faithful must pay careful attention to the holy and certain teaching of the church. For the Catholic Church is by the will of Christ the teacher of truth." Accessed at www.vatican.va/archive/hist_councils/ii_vatican_council/documents/vat-ii_cons_19651207_gaudium-et-spes.html.

67. Francis Joseph Cardinal Spellman was the Archbishop of New York from 1939–1967, as well as the chaplain of the military during that time. On Spellman, see John Cooney, *The American Pope: The Life and Times of Francis Cardinal Spellman* (New York: New York Times Books, 1984).

68. Spellman, who attended Vatican II, opposed the inclusion of pacifism in the wording of *Gaudium et Spes*. See Eileen Egan,"The Struggle of the Small Vehicle, Pax," in *American Catholic Pacifism*, 136.

69. "I have often thought it a brave thing to do, these Christmas visits of Cardinal Spellman to the American troops all over the world, Europe, Korea, Vietnam. But oh, God, what are all these Americans, so-called Christians, doing all over the world so far from our own shores? But what words are those he spoke—going against even the Pope, calling for victory, total victory? Words are as strong and powerful as bombs, as napalm," in Day, "In Peace Is My Bitterness Most Bitter," in *Selected Writings*, 338.

In examining Day's understanding of the encyclical tradition on war, we can see this slantways approach to Church teaching more clearly.[70] Beginning in 1934, Day took the encyclicals as one of her key sources for articulating a Catholic response to war; and for the next forty years, she continuously turned to the encyclical tradition for guidance on war and peace.[71] However, her interpretation of these encyclicals certainly does not always agree with the application of the bishops. During the Second World War, Day cites Pius XI's

70. Likewise, Day's reading of the lives of the saints carried out this strategy. Day's use of Thérèse of Liseux will serve as but among many poignant examples here, a saint whom Day turned to throughout her life, most fully in Day's biography of Thérèse, *Therese: A Life of Therese of Lisieux* (1960; reprint Springfield, IL: Templeton, 1990). On the importance of Thérèse for Day's own narrative, see Leon J. Hooper, "Dorothy Day's Transposition of Therese's 'Little Way,'" *Theological Studies* 63, no. 1 (2002): 68–86; Frederick Christian Bauerschmidt, "The Politics of the Little Way: Dorothy Day Reads Therese of Lisieux," in *American Catholic Traditions: Resources for Renewal*, ed. Sandra Yocum Mize and William Portier (Maryknoll, NY: Orbis Books, 1996), 77–95.

Instead of emphasizing Thérèse's obedience to her order or theology, Day emphasizes Thérèse's disciplined life, desire to aid the poor, and clashes with Catholic authorities. Recounting Thérèse's visit to Pope Leo XIII to plead for her admittance to her order, Day notes that "she had gone against Church and State, one might say, in disregarding the orders of the Vicar General. One might almost say that she had made a scene, that she had clung to the Holy Father, trying to force him to say yes to her request, so that it had taken two guards and Father Reverony himself to disengage her hands and lift her to her feet," 119. Similar use is made of Francis, who for Day became a model of devotion and social action, in "Francis and Ignatius," *CW,* September 1956. See also "Poverty Is to Care and Not to Care," *CW*,April 1953, 1, 5,; "Poverty and Precarity," *CW*, May 1952, 2, 6. Likewise, Day praises Benedict of Nursia—not for founding an order but for his communal life. See Day, "Peter's Program," *CW*, May 1955, 2; "Catholic Worker Ideas on Hospitality," *CW*, May 1940, 10; "On Pilgrimage," *CW*, September 1970, 2, 5. In the same way, Catherine of Sienna is acclaimed for her social activities rather than her well-documented mystical experiences. See Day, *Loaves and Fishes* (New York: Harper and Row, 1963), 12ff; "On Pilgrimage," *CW*,December 1971, 2.

71. Day's use of the encyclical tradition in thinking about war and nonviolence will be addressed in a subsequent section. For examples of Day's use of the encyclical tradition in reasoning about war and peace, see "Wars Are Caused by Man's Loss of Faith in Man," *CW*, September 1940, 1-2; "Day after Day," *CW*, December 1942, 1, 6; "Letter to Our Readers at the Beginning of Our Fifteenth Year," *CW*, May 1947, 1, 3; "The Pope and Peace," *CW*, February 1954, 1, 7; "The Pope Is Dead. Long Live the Pope/Viva John XXIII," *CW*, November 1958, 1-2; "On Pilgrimage," *CW,* June 1963, 1, 2, 6, 8; "On Pilgrimage," *CW*, June 1966, 2, 6, 8. During the 1960s, Day's use of the encyclical tradition to address war increases dramatically; prior to this time, her use of the encyclicals focuses primarily on their teachings on poverty and property (which was the primary focus of the papal encyclicals during this time), with a few notable exceptions such as Pius XI's *Ubi Arcano Dei Consilio* and Pius XII's *Optatissima Pax*, *Mirabile Illud*, and *Laetamur Admodum*.

1931 encyclical, *Nova Impendet,* in her article defending nonviolence during a time of conscription: "In various issues of the *Catholic Worker*, we have reaffirmed this stand. We have quoted the Pope on the 'fallacy of an armed peace.' We have quoted Pope Pius XI, who urged the press and the pulpit to oppose increased armaments (adding sadly, 'and up to this time our voice has not been heard')."[72]

Quoting Pius XI alongside other sources, Day applies his words to justify *The Catholic Worker's* continued defense of pacifism. However, the encyclical that Day cites does not explicitly refer to nonviolence but rather to the "fallacy of an armed peace" that diverts money from other more immediate public needs.[73] Day routinely cites encyclicals such as *Divini Redemptoris* and *Nova Impendet*, which couch their approach to armed conflict within the concern for right social order; whereas the American bishops applied these works in their economic teachings, the papal encyclicals' words on the horrors of war were tantamount to a rejection of war for Day.[74]

72. Day, "Our Stand,," *CW*, June 1940, 1, 4. See also Day, *House of Hospitality*, 257.

73. Pope Pius XI, *Nova Impendent* [Encyclical on the Economic Crisis], Vatican Website, February 10, 1931, para.8, http://www.vatican.va/holy_father/pius_xi/encyclicals/documents/hf_p-xi_enc_02101931_nova-impendet_en.html. Pope Pius XI: "As an effect of rivalry between peoples there is an insensate competition in armaments which, in its turn, becomes the cause of enormous expenditure, diverting large sums of money from the public welfare; and this makes the present crisis more acute. Therefore, we cannot refrain from renewing and from making Our own the solemn warnings of Our predecessor . . . which have, alas! not been heeded." During World War II, a number of American Catholic conscientious objectors opposed involvement in wars of any kind, but this position had not yet become officially recognized by Catholics. For the Catholic conscientious objection during World War II, see Gordon Zahn, *War, Conscience and Dissent* (New York: Hawthorn Books, 1967) as well as his *Another Part of the War: The Camp Simon Story* (Amherst: University of Massachusetts, 1979). During the Second World War, neutrality was the preferred position in papal writings, but as Peter C. Kent argues, the Vatican was not without its preference for the democratic Allies, whose politics presented themselves as most conducive to the promotion of religion within public life, in Peter C. Kent, "The War Aims of the Papacy," in *FDR, The Vatican, and The Roman Catholic Church in America, 1933-1945*, ed. David B. Woolner and Richard G. Kurial (New York: Palgrave MacMillan, 2003), 163–65. On the conflicts Catholics felt between their American and Catholic commitments, see George Q. Flynn, *Roosevelt and Romanism: Catholics and American Diplomacy* 1937–1945 (Westport, CT: Greenwood, 1976), 189–97; John McGreevy, *Catholicism and American Freedom* (New York: W.W. Norton, 2003).

Are we to take Day's argument for nonviolence from the encyclicals as selective readings of the encyclicals' meaning and authority? Rather, I would suggest that Day viewed the papal witness as one voice among others within the Church, with obedience to Christ in the Church as the governing rationale for her obedience. Alongside her citations of Leo XI and Leo XII, Day regularly cites the witness of the saints, Scripture, and other Catholic writers; in keeping with her commitment to moral formation in the Catholic Worker houses as a "clarification of thought" rather than a catechesis, it is not surprising that she viewed papal writings as part of a "larger cloud of witnesses."[75] In sum, the encyclicals function as theological markers within which Day's reasoning about war operates. Her use of these teachings never openly contradicts the encyclicals even while her exegesis draws out an implicit affirmation of nonviolence in places where an explicit condemnationof nonviolence cannot be found.

Nonviolence: Witness of the Mystical Body, Witness to the World

In this section, we will explore both how nonviolence is described as an act envisioned by Day as a necessary extension of the logic of the Mystical Body and by which a person is conformed to Christ's image as they undertake it, drawing them to the Church, Christ made visible. Early in Day's life, opposition to war and nonviolent behavior were not necessary counterparts.[76] Because the pre-Catholic Day

74. On this concern in the American context, see Michael Warner, *Changing Witness: Catholic Bishops and Public Policy, 1917-1994* (Grand Rapids: Eerdmans, 1995), 37–46, 52–54. For Day's use of these encyclicals, see "The Church and Work," *CW*, September 1946, 1, 3, 7, 8; "Days with an End," *CW*, April 1934, 3–4; "On Distributism: Answer to John Cort," *CW*, December 1948, 1, 3. Kent notes that in 1939, *Summi Pontificatus* rearticulated Pius XII's concern for justice; though justice comes through "the demons of violence," it should ultimately be pursued assuming that Divine Law is guiding civil authorities. Kent, "The War Aims of the Papacy," takes this to assume tactit papal support for the Allied forces during the Second World War (166).

75. Hebrews 12:1

saw war as an extension of an unjust economic system, nonviolent resistance to war was one possible tactic used in protest, but she did not exclude the use of violence.[77] Following her conversion, Day recognized that while Socialism and Catholicism both claim the allegiance of the masses, they greatly diverge in terms of what nonviolence is. Whereas Socialism speaks of temporal human order with nonviolence as a possible tactical means toward that end, Catholicism provides a way to see nonviolence as an act by which a person is sacramentally formed in love and faith.[78]

Post-conversion, Day continued to make use of a variety of forms of nonviolence, albeit with different ends in mind. Insofar as war represents a comprehensive social division, participating in marches or active forms of resistance are significant acts but do not represent a sufficient witness to match the comprehensive reach of war's influence. While Day participated in marches and other demonstrations against war—encouraging others to do so if her own conscience did not permit her[79]— her nonviolence encompassed a variety of tactics such as non-payment of taxes and non-compliance

76. As Day recounts her arrest during a suffrage strike in 1917, "a guard tried to grab me when I was going from one side of the room to another and I resisted. He grabbed me by the arm and started to drag me. I fought back—I wasn't being non-violent—I fought back," in Miller, *Dorothy Day*, 96. See also *Long Loneliness*, 58–59.

77. Miller, *Dorothy Day*, 22: "As a revolutionary socialist, Day opposed an imperial war without rejecting violence as an instrument of workers in a class war." Those pacifists who went to jail for Socialist causes were seen by Day as extending their protest actively in prison as living embodiments of their cause (21); however, this reading of pacifism simply emphasizes the utility of nonviolence in certain instances, though not all. See Day's comments on Trotsky's view of war as necessary to "win the state," in *Long Loneliness*, 65. In retrospect, Day was keenly aware that her utilitarian view of nonviolence was indicative of her inconsistency during these early years; in the same way, she "lined [herself] up on the side of the 'capitalist-imperalist' press" in her vocation as a journalist "rather than on the side of my poor friend" (*Long Loneliness*, 59).

78. Though Day agrees that, fundamentally, God's love of the person takes logical primacy over sociopolitical order, she struggles with how to think about Communists who were enacting the "actual works of mercy that the comrades had always made part of their technique in reaching the workers," (*The Long Loneliness*, 165). Again, notice the manner in which nonviolence and other "works of mercy" are for the Communists "technique" rather than activities that form a person's loves.

with civilian air-raid drills.[80] As the Vietnam War continued to unfold, Day's tactics grew to encompass the question of draft resistance and conscription; while she refused to absolutely counsel others to defy the draft as she herself would, she encouraged them to seek peace according to the dictates of their consciences.[81] The comprehensive nature of war creates a manifold conscription of humanity away from its true end, resulting in both physical and spiritual divisions within humanity. By contrast, through various forms of nonviolence, witness is borne to a comprehensively different vision of human sociality, namely the Mystical Body of Christ.

From her earliest writings, Day names all acts of social division that result in violence as visibly antithetical to the Mystical Body.[82] Insofar as the act of war is named as the "opposite of the works of mercy," the social conflict that war creates and perpetuates stands in direct

79. On occasion, tactics taken by protesters were beyond Day's conscience. Such was the case with regards to the burning of draft cards. See Day, "On Pilgrimage," *CW*, March/April 1967, 2, 7, 8.

80. Day, "Where Are the Poor? They Are in Prisons, Too" *CW*, July-August 1955, 1, 8; Day, "On Pilgrimage," *CW*, September 1973, 1, 2, 6. For resistance to air-raid drills, Day, "On Pilgrimage—June 1960," *CW*, June 1960, 2, 7. In a 1960 protest of air raid drills, Day and twenty-nine others were arrested for non-compliance, for refusing to seek shelter during the drills. Subsequent actions by Day and others were so well-attended that no arrests were made because of the infeasibility of arresting 1,000 participants. For Day's involvement in marches against war, see "On Pilgrimage," *CW*, July-August 1957, 1, 3. Day's final march and arrest took place in 1973, marching with Cesar Chavez in California, in Day, "On Pilgrimage," *CW*, September 1973, 1, 2, 6.On taxes, see in particular Day, "The Pope and Peace," 1,7; "On Pilgrimage," *CW*, June 1972, 2, 7; "Poverty is to Care and Not to Care," *CW*, April 1953, 1: "If one raises food or irrigates to raise food, one may be feeding troops or liberating others to serve as trops. If you ride a bus, you are paying taxes. Whatever you buy is taxed so you are supporting the state in the war which is 'the health of the state.'" On refusing to pay taxes, see "On Pilgrimage," *CW*, June 1972, 2, 7; "We Go On Record: CW Refuses Tax Exemption," *CW*, May 1972, 1, 3, 5. In 1972, the Catholic Worker received a letter indicating they owed the federal government nearly $300,000 in back taxes. This could have been easily avoided had the Worker house filed as a non-profit entity. However, Day was adamant that she would neither pay the taxes nor register as a non-profit, as both of these stances would indicate compliance with a war-making government.

81. Day, "On Pilgrimage," *CW*, May 1951, 3, 6; "If Conscription Came for Women," *CW*, January 1943, 1, 4.

82. Day, *Houses of Hospitality*, 148–49.

opposition to the unity present through Christ's Mystical Body.[83] As a perversion of human sociality, war parodies the unity of the Church, uniting humanity only after first deeply dividing humanity:

> War is deviltry. It calls for sacrifices indeed, but not at the altar of love. "Greater love hath no man than this." A great blasphemy this, to use Christ's words in connection with me going to war. They go because they are drafted, because they are afraid of what their neighbors will say, because the benefits accruing afterward . . . are great. And they are told by press and pulpit that they are going because they love their fellows, and they are filled with a warm glow of self-love.[84]

Instead of producing human communion in the pursuit of God, war yields new divisions among humanity; the virtues that affirm a divided humanity are then replicated through the structures and desires created by war.[85] Day consistently describes war as symptomatic of larger problems within society, namely, a wrong

83. Day argues that fractures in Christ's Mystical Body are present in other social permutations, such as nationalism and class wars, which impose artificial barriers and create false understandings of human unity and unnecessary (possibly sinful) social divisions, with war as the final result. See Day, "The Mystical Body and Spain," *CW*, August 1936, 4. A similar crisis emerged for the paper during the Second World War. See "Why Do the Members of Christ Tear One Another?," *CW*, February 1942, 1, 4, 7. By arguing on this basis, Day is not rejecting the material causes of these conflicts (e.g., nationalism, labor disputes) but rather deepening these critiques; the love of nation or right use of labor is more basically an issue of how humans have rightly or wrongly been united. As Michael Baxter has suggests, Day's understanding of the unity between the "public" world and "private" religious activity runs counter to the theologies of the predominant Catholic voices of her day, namely John Ryan and John Courtenay Murray, who provide justification for Catholic involvement in the Second World War, in Michael Baxter, "'Blowing the Dynamite of the Church': Catholic Radicalism from a Catholic Radicalist Perspective," in *Dorothy Day and the Catholic Worker Movement: Centenary Essays*, ed. William J. Thorn, Phillip M. Runkel, and Susan Mountin (Marquette: Marquette University Press, 2001), 82–83.
84. Day, "Things Worth Fighting For?," *Commonweal*, May 21, 1948, 136–37.
85. To this end, war is described as creating its own economy, which in turn creates an inextricable bond between economic injustice and war. Day recalls speaking to a woman who said, "At least war will teach me new trades, which the public school system has failed to do," in *On Pilgrimage* (Grand Rapids: Eerdmans, 1999), 171. Day continued these arguments throughout the contentious years of the Second World War, during which time subscriptions to *The Catholic Worker* dropped by half due to Day's continued pacifism. See Day, "Our Country Passes from Undeclared War to Declared War; We Continue Our Christian Pacifist Stand," *CW*, January 1942, 1, 4; Day, "Why Do the Members of Christ Tear One Another."

social anthropology. Rooted in a corrupted social anthropology, war proves to be a graphic example of that which is more commonly seen in class warfare:

> We oppose class war and class hatred, even while we stand opposed to injustice and greed. Our fight is not "with flesh and blood but principalities and powers." We oppose also imperialist war. We oppose, moreover preparedness for war, a preparedness which is going on now on an unprecedented scale and which will undoubtedly lead to war.[86]

For Day, nationalism (as well as social analysis that relies upon class divisions) is of the same species as war; both encourage a false division of human society contrary to Christ's own body, which unites opposites and reconciles enemies domestic and abroad.[87]

George Weigel's assessment of Day—that she mistakenly assesses political deformations by the same measure as she measures personal relationships, conflating personal and political charity—poses an important criticism to Day's work at this point. Insofar as nonviolence (as a work of love) is not only a personal act but an act that bears witness to an alternate social arrangement without class wars or international wars, one cannot separate the required interpersonal unity from the political charity that should characterize human politics.[88] As Weigel poses the question, should we see political divisions among nation-states as inherently opposed to the unity of the Mystical Body of Christ?[89] *Mystici Corporis* assumes that

86. Day, "Pacifism," *CW*, May 1936, 8.
87. Ibid. In this article, Day advocates "preparing for peace" by renouncing maritime borders and banking practices that support war. While her proposals bear resemblance to certain Marxist proposals, they are derivative of the premise that war follows from the division of humanity—that which Christ has called into the Mystical Body—into artificial groups such as "class" or "nation."
88. George Weigel, Tranquillitas Ordinis: *The Present Failure and Future Promise of American Catholic Thought on War and Peace* (Oxford: Oxford University Press, 1987), 150ff.
89. For example, the just war tradition sees political arrangements that do not necessarily lead to conflict as part of a prudentially organized world. Paul Ramsey, one of the better-known thinkers within the twentieth century just war tradition, criticizes John XXIII's *Pacem in*

the Mystical Body and nationalism are not inherently contradictory: the unity between juridically-united churches is not threatened by the presence of multiple nation states, as the Catholic Church's visibility is articulated as appropriate within various social arrangements.

Day would agree with Weigel that the particularities of various nations make possible the conditions under which the visibility of the Mystical Body may be known. However, Day disagrees with Weigel (and in this way, with the assumptions of *Mystici Corporis Christi*) in her claim that the Mystical Body relativizes considerations of nationality, to the extent that one cannot have personal charity apart from political charity, insofar as all people potentially belong to the same body of Christ.[90] Indeed, Day did voice hope for a unified national response to the Vietnam War in her writings, in order that public policy might shift to a more just arrangement.[91] But for Day, a Catholic opposition to war did not need to wait for national actions, insofar as the unity of Christ supersedes that of nations both ontologically and ethically. Looking to Catholics already in Vietnam, Day applauded the Christian witness of the Brothers and Sisters of Brother Charles de Foucauld, who were present in the midst of great suffering.[92] A similar commendation is offered to Americans opposing the production of napalm. There are those who

Terris for improperly conflating divine realities with temporal life. In this way, the Pope excludes force from proper governance. See John XXIII, *Pacem in Terris* [Encyclical Letter on Establishing Universal Peace in Truth, Justice, Charity, and Liberty], April 11, 1963 (New York: Abingdon, 1963).

90. In her famous "In Peace Is My Bitterness Most Bitter," Day argues that national interests oppose the practices of the Church in precisely this manner: "We are the most powerful nation, the most armed, and we are supplying arms and money to the rest of the world where we are not ourselves fighting. We are eating while there is famine in the world. . . . we are not performing the works of mercy but the works of war. We cannot repeat this enough" (337).
91. Day, "Spring Mobilization," *CW*, May 1967, 1,4.
92. Day, "On Pilgrimage," *CW*, February 1967, 2, 6, 7: "If peace were declared in Vietnam tomorrow, there would still be world suffering, famine, injustice on a giant scale and the war between the rich and the destitute would go on."

> share the life of prisoners, to lighten in some small way the heavy burden of misery . . . these Catholic Worker prisoners who see in their brothers and sisters the suffering Christ, are helping to lighten the sum-total of anguish in the world. They are reminders; they are news, good news, of another world. They are the gospel in other words, and carrying to its ultimate meaning, they are the Word, they are other Christs.[93]

In other words, witness to the peace found in the Mystical Body is achieved from within the misery of war as a new sociality "within the shell of the old," unified in Christ visibly and politically, with or without the aid of national policy.[94]

This conclusion of nonviolent resistance to war as a logical consequence of the Mystical Body leaves Day in a relatively weak position, in that the relationship between nonviolence and the Mystical Body of the Church is not a necessary connection, or for most of Day's life, one affirmed by the Church. While Day reasons about nonviolence from within the resources of the Church toward a conclusion of nonviolence, there seems to be an implied conclusion between nonviolence and the Mystical Body, and not a necessary one for communion. As we move forward, Day's work, then, is under the burden of arguing for the relation between nonviolence and Catholic ecclesiology, a position which in her own age had neither the support of the state or the Church.

Nonviolence and Ecclesiastical Reasoning

Before I can further illustrate how Day saw Catholic ecclesiology as the framework for her nonviolence arguments, I must briefly describe her arguments within the twentieth-century encyclical tradition on war. What follows is not intended as a comprehensive reading of these documents but rather a sketch within which to contextualize

93. Day, "On Pilgrimage," *CW*, June 1966, 2, 6, 8.
94. Day understood that what she was proposing would not be without a measure of suffering. See Day, "Theophane Venard and Ho Chi Minh," *CW*, May 1954.

Day's writings. The papal tradition on war in the twentieth century dates back to Pius X's *Une Fois Encore*, in which he writes:

> Founded by Him who came to bring peace to the world and to reconcile man with God, a Messenger of peace upon earth, the Church could only seek religious war by repudiating her high mission and belying it before the eyes of all . . . the whole world now knows that if peace of conscience is broken in France that is not the work of the Church but of her enemies. Fair-minded men, even though not of our faith, recognize that if there is a struggle on the question of religion in your beloved country, it is not because the Church was the first to unfurl the flag, but because war was declared against her.[95]

Pius X's approach is paradigmatic of writings during this era in that he emphasizes a presumption against violence while recognizing that times of violence demand prudential participation in war.[96] Though the Church proclaims the peace of Christ, situations may arise that demand a response by Catholics in form of force.

Through the twentieth Century, the encyclical tradition continued to emphasize these two points: 1) Christ calls Christians to peace and charity, but 2) involvement in wars on behalf of the common good is a viable option for Catholics. This approach is repeated throughout papal writings during both the First and Second World Wars; in *Ad Beatissimi Apostolorum*, for example, Benedict XV argues that the twin evils plaguing humanity are war and the "absence of respect for the authority of those who exercise ruling powers", with the absence of right authority inevitably leading to divisions within

95. Pius X, *Une Fois Encore* [Encyclical on the Separation of Church and State], Vatican Website, June 1, 1907, para. 8, http://www.vatican.va/holy_father/pius_x/encyclicals/documents/hf_p-x_enc_06011907_une-fois-encore_en.html.

96. The question as to whether Catholic tradition on war should be characterized as a presumption against violence or as a presumption for justice is still being debated. See J. Daryl Charles, "Presumption against War or Presumption against Injustice? The Just War Tradition Reconsidered," *Journal of Church and State* 47 (Spring 2005): 335–69; Tobias L. Winright, "Two Rival Versions of Just War Theory and the Presumption Against Harm in Policing," *Annual of the Society of Christian Ethics* 18 (1998): 221–39.

society characterized by war and class division.[97] The similarity to Day's arguments is striking, except that Benedict calls for relative deference to the state in the judgments of war: "Whenever legitimate authority has once given a clear command, let no one transgress that command, because it does not happen to commend itself to him; but let each one subject his own opinion to the authority of him who is his superior, and obey him as a matter of conscience."[98] For Benedict XV, as for Pius X before him, the conscience must be subject to the "common good" found in the legitimate authority of the state.[99] Accordingly, limited space existed for Catholics to protest involvement in war until after the Second World War.

During the Second World War, however, the tone of papal encyclicals began to change, emphasizing care for those affected by wars.[100] Pius XII encouraged Catholics to continue their involvement in public life, because without an education "to virtue and right social living," dissension among humanity would persist, causing further wars.[101] Accompanied by the rise of American Catholic conscientious objection during the Second World War, the question of Catholic involvement in war became a more pressing issue, though often these issues were more vigorously addressed in papal writings than by American bishops.[102] For example, Pius XII's condemnation of

97. Benedict XV, *Ad Beatissimi Apostolorum* [Encyclical Appealing for Peace], Vatican Website, January 11, 1914, para. 5, 9, http://www.vatican.va/holy_father/benedict_xv/encyclicals/documents/hf_ben-xv_enc_01111914_ad-beatissimi-apostolorum_en.html.

98. Ibid., para. 22.

99. Ibid., para. 10. For charity to be promoted by Catholics within society, deference must be given by the Catholic conscience to the national authority as ordained of God.

100. In both *Optatissima Pax* and *Auspicia Quaedam*, themes of conscience or involvement by Catholics in war are muted. Rather, he emphasizes "the first and most urgent need . . . to reconcile the hearts of men, to bring them to fraternal agreement and cooperation," in Pius XII, *Optatissima Pax* [Encyclical on Prescribing Public Prayers for Social and World Peace], Vatican Website, para. 3, December 18, 1947, http://www.vatican.va/holy_father/pius_xii/encyclicals/documents/hf_p-xii_enc_18121947_optatissima-pax_en.html.

101. See Pius XII, *Summi Maeroris* [Encyclical on Public Prayers for Peace], Vatican Website, para. 12, July 19, 1950, http://www.vatican.va/holy_father/pius_xii/encyclicals/documents/hf_p-xii_enc_19071950_summi-maeroris_en.html.

the Nagasaki and Dresden bombings, toward the end of the Second World War was not echoed by the American bishops, who remained mostly silent on the war atrocities.[103] In contrast to the Pope's measured tones, the National Catholic Welfare Conference (NCWC) issued a statement expressing their intention to "transmute the impressive material and spiritual resources of our country *into effective strength*, not for vengeance but for the common good."[104] A year later, citing the "virtues of patriotism, justice and charity," the NCWC lauded Catholic soldiers who deserved "unstinted gratitude for their heroic services to our country and high commendation for the faithful practice of their religion."[105]

Even without explicit papal support for nonviolence, Day made use of these papal writings in support of various Catholic Worker positions, often in stark contrast to the NCWC's statements. Despite her disagreements with Pius XII's conclusions, Day sees in his basic commitments a presupposition that coheres to her vision of nonviolence: the fundamental unity of humanity under God—a humanity needing to be directed toward its spiritual telos. Upon this common ground, Day built her writings during this time.[106]

102. Zahn, *War, Conscience and Dissent*, 149, notes that while only 135 Catholics in Civilian Public Service programs were enacted during the Second World War, only one was enacted during the First World War. As Zahn notes, the actual figure during the Second War was probably much higher, as the135 listed programs came from one particular designation (IV-E), which accounted for approximately one-quarter of the 50,000 total objectors. McNeal, *Harder than War*, 55–56, documents the presence of nearly two hundred others imprisoned in the same period for conscientious objection. Unlike the "peace churches," no church-sponsored program existed for objectors, leaving the burden of support and objection upon the objectors and their families (McNeal, 57–59). Whatever the true numbers, Catholic objectors were outnumbered by Catholic military chaplains alone, who numbered over 3,000, in Hugh Joseph Nolan, ed., *Pastoral Letters of the United States Bishops, Vol. 3: 1962–1974* (Washington, DC: National Catholic Council of Bishops, 1998), 13.

103. "Atomic Bomb," l'Observatore Romano, August 10, 1945, cited in McNeal, *Harder than War,* 50–51. As Michael Warner has observed, the American bishops during this time were more concerned with the threat of emerging totalitarian regimes, which affected their view on the necessity of war (*Changing Witness*,52–55).

104. "Catholic Support in World War II," in Nolan, *Pastoral Letters*,36 (italics mine).

105. "Victory and Peace," in Nolan, *Pastoral Letters*, 39.

In Day's opinion, John XXIII's *Pacem in Terris* represented a sea change in this tradition; as she stated, "there was no end to what one could say about the encyclical."[107] According to Day, the encyclical was "a . . . radical condemnation of the instruments of modern warfare."[108] *Pacem*'s affirmation that "representatives of the State have no power to bind men in conscience, unless their own authority is tied to God's authority, and is a participation in it," was a position Day had held for years, but it had never been articulated that explicitly in papal writings.[109] While *Pacem* still acknowledges the role of government authority as a "postulate of moral order," Day welcomed the conclusion that the state and the good did not necessarily coincide.[110] With the emergence of Vatican II's statement, *Gaudium et Spes,* Day received the explicit justification for conscientious objection and nonviolence that she had sought for nearly thirty years. In sections 77–80, not only is nonviolence commended by the council, but countries are encouraged to make provision for conscientious objectors to war.

106. In a 1954 statement of confidence concerning the ability of nation states to foster right exercise of Catholic conscience, Pius XII writes that "the Christian statesman does not serve the cause of national or international peace when he abandons the solid basis of objective experience and clear cut principles . . . It is perhaps necessary to demonstrate that weakness in authority more than any other weakness undermines the strength of a nation . . . [imperiling] the general peace." To this, Day responds: "How obey the laws of a state when they run counter to man's conscience? . . . St. Peter disobeyed the law of men and state that he had to obey God rather than man. Wars today involve total destruction, obliteration bombing, killing of the innocent . . . We are all involved in war these days." Cited in Day, "The Pope and Peace."

107. Day, "War without Weapons," *Selected Writings*, 328.

108. Day, "On Pilgrimage—June 1963," *CW*, June 1963, 6.

109. John XXIII, *Pacem in Terris*, para. 49, http://www.vatican.va/holy_father/john_xxiii/encyclicals/documents/hf_j-xxiii_enc_11041963_pacem_en.html.

110. Ibid., para. 51. *Pacem et Terris* has been roundly criticized by Christians, both Catholic and non-Catholic, for its disarmament advocacy, See Paul Ramsey, *The Just War*, 70–90; George Weigel, *Tranquilitus Ordinis: The Present Failure and Future Promise of American Catholic Thought on War and Peace* (Oxford: Oxford University Press, 1987), 78–92. Ramsey, in particular, argues that such a blanket deterrence undermines politics, taking deterrence to be an essentially defensive political tactic. For Day, however, this objection is entirely beside the point: humanity is fundamentally a single entity that "politics" is an addendum—and in the instance of its militarist and nationalist manifestations, a barrier—to natural unity.

While *Gaudium* still operates within a broadly just-war framework, the inclusion of conscientious objection and pacifism as institutionally commended represented a large victory for Day, who had made pilgrimage to Italy with the "Mothers of Peace" during the council to pray for the peace movement's validation by the council's proceedings.[111] Interestingly, Day was untroubled that the council had not completely rebuked all involvement in war: "If a man truly thinks he is combating evil and striving for the good, if he truly thinks he is striving for the common good, he must follow his conscience regardless of others. But he always has the duty of forming his conscience by studying, listening, being ready to hear his opponents' point of view."[112] As we have seen, mandating nonviolence apart from a free and conscientious recognition of nonviolence's validity undercuts the formation of the conscience through a reliance on mere institutional conformity.[113]

Day's engagements with the encyclical tradition ultimately identified a logic of nonviolence underlying papal writings that would not be fully recognized until Vatican II. As she argued during a retreat with the Pax Peace Fellowship in 1963, freedom *within* the Church allowed her to make the arguments for nonviolence that she found intrinsic to ecclesiastical writings.[114] By treating the hierarchy as simply a number of Catholic voices among others on the issue of war, Day was able to articulate the underlying logic of the encyclicals toward what she saw as their supernatural culmination: the calling

111. Day, "On Pilgrimage," *CW*, October 1965, 1, 8.

112. Day, "On Pilgrimage," *CW*, December 1965, 1, 2, 7.

113. Ibid., 7: "The primacy of conscience in the life of a Catholic is more and more brought out by the deliberations in the Council and by the very conflicts that take place there . . . Of course we consider enlightening the ignorant and counseling the doubtful works of mercy, as indeed they are. As for 'rebuking the sinner' we are told not to judge, by our dear Lord, and we are only too conscious of our own all too imperfect state. However, our positions seem to imply a judgment, a condemnation, and we get the 'holier than thou' accusation often enough."

114. "Fear in Our Time," in *Peace through Reconciliation: Proceedings of the Pax Conference at Spoke House* (Eugene, OR: October 1963), 14–15.

of the Church to beat swords into plowshares.[115] However, to fully understand Catholic social teaching on nonviolent resistance to war, we must explore how nonviolent resistance is not only a viable ethical act but a full renovation of the person's loves and conscience directing them toward the fullness of these virtues, the Church.

Nonviolent Resistance, Conscience, and the Works of Mercy

Because full participation in Christ's humanity is the telos of all persons, resistance to war is not an end unto itself but an act by which persons bear witness to the unity of human life in Christ; in doing so, they are morally formed toward their true end. Insofar as nonviolent resistance to war is an act of an ecclesially-framed conscience, resistance proves to be not only an act that is framed and formed by the Church (which witnesses to the world by doing so) but one that challenges the Church tradition to live into the fullness of its own witness.

Those committed to Christian nonviolent resistance must be exemplars of a different understanding of the way human life is organized and, therefore, bearers of a different set of virtues appropriate to that vision:

> If we are calling upon nations to disarm, we must be brave enough and courageous enough to set the example . . . Do we believe we help any country by participating in an evil in which they are engaged? We rather help them by maintaining our own peace. It takes a man of heroic stature to be a pacifist and we urge our readers to consider and study pacifism and disarmament in this light. A pacifist who is willing to endure the scorn of the unthinking mob, the ignominy of jail, the pain of stripes and the threat of death, cannot be lightly dismissed as a coward afraid of physical pain. A pacifist even now must be prepared for the opposition of the next mob who thinks violence is bravery. The pacifist in the next war must be ready for martyrdom.[116]

115. Vatican Council II, *Gaudium et Spes,* para. 78.

Thus, opposition to war for Day means developing not only ideological positions but actively loving one's neighbor in ways that do not secure the "common good" by excluding part of humanity, to the extent of showing that love to the point of death.[117]

Ordered toward participation in Christ's visible body (the Church), nonviolent opposition to war therefore involves reforming the person toward the love of God in Christ.[118] The formation of conscience is central to this vision of charitable nonviolence in its cultivation of a humanity ordered toward God that can love comprehensively; for example, a rightly formed conscience is intrinsic to keeping the Scriptural command against killing one's neighbor, insofar as one cannot will not to kill unless one first desires not to do so.[119] If the conscience of the individual—the ability to desire and act in a manner consistent with the perceived good—is neglected, conscription toward ends alien to the person's christological orientation is inevitable.[120] As Day writes:

> One must follow one's own conscience first before all authority, and of course one must inform one's conscience. But one must follow one's conscience still, even if it is an ill-informed one. All those young ones and older ones, who are committing themselves to violent revolution as the only way to overcome evil government, imperialism, industrial

116. Ibid.
117. Day, "The Use of Force," *CW*, November 1936, 4: "They knew then that not by force of arms, by the bullet or the ballot, they would conquer. They knew and were ready to suffer defeat—to show that great love which enabled them to lay down their lives for their friends . . . And now the whole world is turning to 'force' to conquer. Fascist and Communist alike believe that only by the shedding of blood can they achieve victory. Catholics, too, believe that suffering and the shedding of blood 'must needs be' as Our Lord said to the disciples at Emmaus."
118. Day, "Fight Conscription," *CW*, September 1939.
119. With this freedom comes "the duty of forming his conscience, by studying, listening, being ready to hear his opponents' point of view." See "On Pilgrimage," *CW*, December 1965, 1, 2, 7.
120. Day, "Are The Leaders Insane?," *CW*, April 1954, 1, 6: "St. Peter was ordered by lawful authority not to preaching the name of Jesus, and he said he had to obey God rather than man . . . Over and over again, man had to disobey lawful authority to follow the voice of their conscience. This obedience to God and disobedience to the State has over and over again happened through history."

> capitalism, exploitation—in other words evil—are not only following their conscience but also following tradition.[121]

However, Day recognized that even *mutatis mutandis*, the conscience would not inevitably lead to the nonviolence exemplified in *The Catholic Worker*.[122] Participation in the resistance to war was certainly not an entirely open question for Day: if one's conscience, rightly formed, exists for the formation of a person toward God in Christ, then the fullness of conscience would, according to Day, lead in the direction of keeping Christ's commands to love one's enemy. But as much as Day remained persuaded by nonviolence and maintained it as the official stance of *The Catholic Worker*, compelling someone toward this act apart from their conscientious participation would be a mirror form of the draft, a forcing of the will to actions alien to it.[123] All the more, then, the formation of conscience is an ecclesiological concern for Day; the Church—as that body in which Christ is made visible—should most of all be held accountable and called to a right formation of the conscience of its members.[124] Day did not see this as a choice between the institutional Church and a conscientious nonviolence, but rather a coherence of Church and conscience. As she wrote in a 1951 article on the issue, long before Vietnam:

121. Day, "On Pilgrimage—Our Spring Appeal," *CW*, May 1970, 1, 2, 11.

122. Day, "Are the Leaders Insane," 6: "Each one of us must make our decisions as to what he should do; each one must examine his conscience and beg God for strength. Should one register for the draft? Should one accept conscientious objector status in the army or out of it, taking advantage of the exceptions allowed, but accepting the fact of the draft? Should one pay tax which supports this gigantic program? I realize how difficult this is to decide . . . It is not for any one to judge his fellow man on how far he can go in resisting participation in preparation for war."

123. To this end, Day frequently disagreed with the silencing of priests who disagreed with the Church at large. See "The Case of Father Duffy," *CW*, December 1949; "The Case of Cardinal MacIntyre," *CW*, July–August 1964. Both men were censured for their support of Catholic Worker activities, in the areas of poverty and race relations respectively.

124. Day, "The Case of Father Duffy."

> When we are being called appeasers, defeatists, we are being deprived of our dearest goods, our reputation, honor, the esteem of men and we are truly on the way to become the despised of the earth. We are beginning perhaps to be truly poor. We are trying to spread the gospel of peace, persuade others, to extend the peace movement, to build up a mighty army of conscientious objectors, such as Archbishop McNicholas called for in the last war, though I do not think he meant it in the same way we do. And in doing this we are accounted fools and it is the folly of the cross in the eyes of an unbelieving world which was scandalized in Him.[125]

As an act that bears witness to the unity of Christ—an act by which a person is formed in the love of God—nonviolence is an act of conscience that bears witness to both Church and state.[126] The Church is shown the radical implications of its teaching on conscience and the full implications of the doctrine of the Mystical Body: to be a member of the Mystical Body could mean embracing nonviolence in christological worship. Likewise, the state finds itself populated by people whose consciences do not immediately coincide with the demands of the state.

As a matter of conscience, Day's concept of nonviolence is also a matter of virtue, connected to the reformation of one's loves. Specifically, Day understood her various nonviolent activities related to war as an outworking of the works of mercy[127]—which are

125. Day, "Inventory," *CW*, January 1951.

126. Day, cited in William D. Miller, "Dorothy Day," in *Saints Are Now: Eight Portraits of Modern Sanctity, ed.* John J. Delaney(Garden City, NY: Doubleday, 1981), 37: "We are an example of the tremendous liberty that there is in the Church . . . We must have the courage to form our conscience and follow it regardless of the point of view of cardinal or bishop." In the 1973 "Declaration on Conscientious Objection and Selective Conscientious Objection," the United States Catholic Conference affirmed conscientious objection (Nolan, *Pastoral Letters*, 283–86).

127. Day, *Loaves and Fishes: The Story of the Catholic Worker Movement* (San Francisco: Harper and Row, 1963), 87: "Do we get much help from Catholic Charities? We are often asked this question. I can say only that it is not the Church or the state to which we turn when we ask for help in these appeals. Cardinal Spellman did not ask us to undertake this work, nor did the Mayor or New York. It just happened. It is the living from day to day, taking no thought for the morrow."

described in various ways by Day through her writings but typically follow the traditional formulation found in the Catechism of both spiritual and corporeal works.[128] The works of mercy, as acts that minister to tangible needs while reforming the affections of the one practicing them, constitute a participation in the work of Christ for the sake of the world.[129] As Day puts it, insofar as the works of mercy are both those acts that reform the soul and minister to the world, they "are the opposite of the works of war."[130] Through one's participation in the Mystical Body and enactment of the works of mercy, the desire emerges to see the truth of the Mystical Body permeate the world in myriad ways, including the cessation of war. As Day argues in *Loaves and Fishes*: "We . . . spoke of the works of mercy and called attention to the fact that war is inevitably the opposite of them. Laying waste the fields, it brings famine; destroying homes instead of sheltering the harborless, it drives people even out of their own country."[131] Done in a spirit of charity, nonviolence is a means by which the love of God is shown to one's enemy, though these actions cause one to "be in sympathy with the great mass of the poor, the men in revolt, those in jail, the men of color throughout the world," rather "than . . . with imperialists, the colonials, the industrial capitalist, the monopolists."[132]

128. Baltimore Catechism, Q. 223: "What are the chief corporal works of mercy?" (*Saint Joseph Baltimore Catechism*. Catholic Book Publishing Corp., Baltimore, 1995). The formulation of Catholic works of mercy originate from Jesus' words in Matthew 25. According to Aquinas, mercy is the spontaneous product of charity, though distinguishable from charity (Thomas Aquinas, *Summa Theologica* [Translated by Fathers of the English Dominican Province. New York: Benzinger Brothers, 1981], II-II.30). It is not likely that Day has Aquinas's formulation in mind, but it is significant that, for Day, love precedes her articulation of the necessity of the works of mercy.
129. Day, "On Pilgrimage," *CW*, March–April 1967, 2, 7, 8.
130. Day, "Penance," in *Selected Writings*, 180. See also Rosalie G. Riegle, *Dorothy Day: Portraits by Those Who Knew Her* (Maryknoll, NY: Orbis Books, 2003), 44. This connection dates back as early as the 1930s, as articulated in Day's *Houses of Hospitality*, 138ff.
131. Day, *Loaves and Fishes*, 210.
132. Day, "On Pilgrimage," *Catholic Worker*, March 1957, 3, 6.

Viewing nonviolence in this way involves expanding upon the traditional works of mercy, the roots of which can be found in Matthew 25 and later amplified and expanded by Augustine and Aquinas.[133] Not limited to resistance to war, Day and Maurin understood their work on *The Catholic Worker* paper as the task of "correcting the sinner."[134] Early on, Day found it necessary to emphasize the corporeal works of mercy over the spiritual ones in order "to arouse . . . those indifferent Catholics to the crying need of a return to the spirit of Franciscan poverty and charity;" however, the ultimate goal remains the incorporation of both kinds of works into a person's life, as participation in the Mystical Body is a matter of both body and soul.[135]

This description of nonviolence as one of the works of mercy is significant for two reasons. First, the works of mercy fulfill immediate practical needs, such as feeding the hungry and sheltering the homeless. Beyond this, the works reaffirm the spiritual communion that exists even between enemies through the affirmation of their common love, which lies at the root of their competing conceptions of the good.[136] The works of mercy are not only a radical spiritual act, in that they conform the one performing them more fully to the love of God), but also a radical political act, in that they speak of a polity of human unity that transcends national differences. The placement of nonviolence among the works of mercy reinforces the insight that,

133. Gilmore Guyot, *Scriptural References for the Baltimore Catechism: The Biblical Basis for Catholic Belief* (New York: Joseph F. Wagner, 1946), 56–58. The list is amplified in Augustine's *Enchiridion* and then later in Aquinas's *Summa Theologicae.* See James Keenan, SJ, *The Works of Mercy: The Heart of Catholicism*, (Lanham, MD: Sheed & Ward, 2008) for a history of specific works and the interpretative history of those works.

134. Day, "Letter to Our Readers at the Beginning of our Fifteenth Year." The works of mercy were integral to Peter Maurin's initial formulation of the Catholic Worker movement; through these works, people are directed toward their true spiritual end. See ibid., 1, 3.

135. Day, "Why Write About Strife and Violence," in *Selected Writings*, 63.

136. Day, "Letter to Our Readers at the Beginning of our Fifteenth Year," 3: "If your enemy hunger, give him to eat. There is always a solution in the practice of the works of mercy, at a personal sacrifice."

for Day, nonviolence is not first and foremost about social change. As Harry Murray argues, the works of mercy (including nonviolence) first move a person toward spiritual communion with God and with one another.[137]

Secondly—and significantly—viewing nonviolence among the works of mercy means that nonviolence alone can never be the sole measure of a person's growth into the fullness of the Mystical Body or of what it means to belong to the Mystical Body; as we have seen, Day's communion with and obedience to the Church was not contingent upon its agreement with her vision of war. For Day, nonviolence manifests itself alongside other equally important practices, such as "correcting the sinner," hospitality, prayer, and sheltering the homeless. Thus, her nonviolence is one of a nexus of practices that addresses a person's need for personal transformation in a comprehensive fashion and acknowledges that, ultimately, societal transformation occurs only hand in hand with personal transformation.[138]

Viewing nonviolent resistance as a kind of spiritual pedagogy, Day does not separate nonviolence from the sociality (the Mystical Body

137. Harry Murray, *Neglect Not Hospitality: The Catholic Worker and the Homeless* (Philadelphia: Temple University Press, 1990), 74–77.

138. As the Vietnam War wore on into the late 1960s and early 1970s, other Catholics developed more radical tactics for opposing war. Roger Laporte, a Catholic Worker, immolated himself in protest. See McNeal, *Harder than War,* 122, 146–48. In 1968, Daniel and Philip Berrigan, Catholic priests and friends of Day, participated in the destruction of draft records using homemade napalm. Mel Piehl has identified these examples as part of the emergence of a "Catholic Left," breaking with Day's form of witness in favor of more aggressive forms of protest (*Breaking Bread,* 235–37). The divergence between Day and the Berrigans would be played out on a meta-level in the split between the Catholic Peace Fellowship, which focuses on Day's combination of spiritual practices and protest, and Pax Christi, which focuses primarily on institutional advocacy. See McNeal, *Harder than War,* 230–35. However, Day and the Berrigans were not strictly divided. Day spoke at a 1963 rally that involved, among other things, some of the first instances of draft card burnings. During this time, Day reiterated her own vision of nonviolence, stating "[Jesus] spoke of the instruments of peace, to be practiced by all nations; feeding the hungry, clothing the naked, not destroying crops," in William Miller, *A Harsh and Dreadful Love: Dorothy Day and the Catholic Worker Movement* (New York: Liveright, 1973), 320.

of Christ) toward which nonviolence directs the practitioner. For this reason, Day's nonviolence is concerned first with the reformation of its participants toward a new kind of spiritual communion. As participants engage in actions that witness to an alternate social arrangement that transcends state apparatuses, a kind of "anarchy" (as Day describes it) emerges, calling the Church to a deeper understanding of itself as the Mystical Body of Christ and the world to the recognition that true unity can be found only in this body of Christ.

The question that remains in this formulation is this: If nonviolence is an act of conscience, but one's own conscience does not necessarily cohere with the explicit teaching of the Church on war, what role does ecclesiology play in articulating a Christian nonviolence? Day responds in two ways. First, because Day understands nonviolence as the culmination of the encyclical tradition on war, a conscientious adherence to nonviolence is not excluded but rather encouraged, even if it is not explicitly addressed within the encyclical tradition.[139] Insofar as the Church is the Mystical Body of Christ, the judgments of the Church are authoritative but not exhaustive. Nonviolence is never specifically ruled out but neither is it specifically commended, turning Day's witness into a kind of leaven within the Church to a fuller way of understanding the Body of Christ. Second, insofar as Christ is witnessed to within the Church, belonging to the Church is indispensible to the articulation and enactment of this nonviolence; the peace and unity of Christ in the Church is the basis for any act of Christian nonviolence.

139. See *Gaudium et Spes*, para. 16: "Through loyalty to conscience, Christians are joined to others in the search for truth and for the right solution to so many moral problems which arise both in the life of individuals and from social relationships." However, this assumes that the individual conscience and the revealed teachings of the Church are not competitive choices if (as I have argued) the Mystical Body speaks to the person of Christ, who for Day is the basis of nonviolence.

However, since the majority of the Church did not understand nonviolence in this way, the question remains unresolved. While the Church possessed the resources for Christian nonviolence, it did not recognize them. Therefore, the position of nonviolence as an act of conscience often did not receive support from an explicitly authoritative voice within the Church that Day could appeal to as justification for her position. Consequently, nonviolence persists not as a strict identification of Day's ecclesiology (as it does with Yoder) but as a persistent witness to what the Church's communion should be teleologically.

Conclusion

The interrelationship between Day's nonviolence and ecclesiology relies upon her understanding of the Mystical Body, which speaks to humanity's telos. Present as the visible Church, the Mystical Body is connected to the whole of natural life, in that Christ's humanity (which ennobles human life) orients humanity toward its fulfillment in the Church. That being said, the Church's teachings does not always draw the connection between the unity of the Mystical Body and the divisions caused by war. While ecclesiological doctrine does not automatically cohere to a commitment to nonviolent resistance, ecclesiological concerns are, for Day, the indispensible framework for a proper approach to resisting war, accounting not only for how nonviolence should be carried out but what kind of person the practitioner of this resistance is called to be.

In regard to Day, I have posed two questions in particular. First, Day's connection of the Mystical Body to the visible Church pushes against a strong identification of the nonviolent resistance to war implicated by Church teaching with the Church itself. Insofar as the Mystical Body is an anthropological confession before it is an ethical one, the liturgy of the Church (which confesses Christ) may lead to nonviolence, but does not have to. While Day certainly sees nonviolence as the logical outworking of her ecclesiology, the connection is not one of necessity. What are we to make of this strong connection between Christ and the Church in the absence of a corresponding ethic of nonviolent resistance to war, which Day understood as the fulfillment of Christ's mystical body? Yoder, for his part, distinguishes between the "ecumenical movement and the faithful church," freely drawing connections between "church" and the ethic of nonviolence, insofar as the work of God is consistently accompanied by this ethic from the Old Testament to the eschaton. In other words, Christ's tie to the Church is accompanied by certain ethical and hermeneutical commitments for Yoder that are lacking in Day's work. But Day finds good reason for this lack: if Christ's humanity implicates all human existence—with the love of Christ meeting us through all of our loves and affections—nonviolence becomes one way among others that can direct the conscience toward its telos.[140]

This theological difference—which leads Day to frame nonviolent resistance by ecclesiology rather than identify ecclesiology with nonviolence—exposes another significant difference between Day and Yoder as to how and why nonviolence is an ecclesially-necessitated act. For Day and the Catholic Worker movement, nonviolence is an unalterable absolute. However, out of a commitment to the human conscience, she does not argue that non-violence is a necessity for participation in the Mystical Body, insofar as Christ's formation of humanity approaches us most basically through our loves. While I have already raised the question as to whether nonviolence can be as tightly connected to ecclesiology as Yoder depicts it in the previous chapter, Yoder does challenge Day to clarify how much value should be ascribed to the formation of

140. In this sense, Day could name just war bishops as co-members of the Mystical Body of Christ.

conscience, particularly if that conscience leads one to participate in war.[141] If conscience leads a person away from the life of Jesus, Yoder might argue, can it be that trustworthy?

For Day, conscience is a non-negotiable aspect of performing nonviolence; without conscience, one kind of conscription is replaced by another. But we might argue that Day places too much trust in the capacity of the conscience to arrive at a conclusion of nonviolence in the absence of explicit Church teaching on the matter. In an age when "conscience" has become a mantra by which the individual becomes the sovereign judge of moral acts, Day offers a strong alternative—that one's conscience is gifted by God for a *particular* direction. This is not to say that conscience cannot err or that what one takes as the voice of conscience cannot be self-justification. By downplaying conscience in terms of ecclesiological and moral discussions, Yoder presses the question as to whether conscience remains (or has ever been) an appropriate value for ecclesiology; perhaps Christians should speak less strongly of conscience with regards to war and more vigorously of obedience.

Read another way, Day's connection of nonviolence (which is called for by Christ's Mystical body) with conscience emphasizes that nonviolence is ultimately exercised in hope and patience, both with regards to the ones who practice nonviolence (but are not of the Church) and with regards to the prospect of nonviolence in the world. The hope that Day expresses for her own Church—that it might recognize what is embodied within its own teaching but not fully expressed—is similar (though not identical) with that of

141. Interestingly, Day was often accused of elevating nonviolence to the counsels of perfection rather than leaving it as a matter of conscience. See "Day after Day," *Catholic Worker*, May 1942, 1, 4, 7. She responds that though the "precept is the end, the counsels are the means to that end," meaning that nonviolence is one means by which we love our neighbor—a clear "counsel" of Christ. Her willingness to claim nonviolence in this way, while allowing that not everyone will travel this path toward their true end, demonstrates the point I have been making here.

Yoder. Seeing this witness fleshed out in his own church tradition, Yoder wished for it to be an ecumenical possession of all churches. In this way, Yoder and Day find common ground in the hope that nonviolent resistance to war, which witnesses to Christ's work in the world, might be a gift to the Church catholic.

As we move forward, the common ground of nonviolent resistance as witness to Christ's work will prove a useful first step in approaching Stringfellow and Brown, though Yoder and Day disagree concerning if and how nonviolence and ecclesiology relate. In the work of William Stringfellow, to which I will now turn, we find a figure who comes to hold nonviolence as consistent with the renewal of life by the Word of God, as addressed by proper ecclesiology, but who arrives at this conclusion in a much more cautious fashion and with far greater caveats than Day or Yoder. While professing with Yoder and Day that nonviolence is for the sake of all humanity—a humanity over which Christ has claims—Stringfellow retains a greater skepticism concerning the limits and conditions under which nonviolence can be exercised, and even greater skepticism as to whether ecclesiology and nonviolent resistance can be fruitfully partnered.

4

The Church as *Naming* Nonviolence: William Stringfellow, The Powers, and the Word's Renewing Work

In this chapter, I will continue the exploration of the relation between ecclesiology and nonviolence by turning to one of the most enigmatic theologians of his generation, William Stringfellow. Best known as the man Karl Barth singled out (during Barth's trip to America) as the individual who grasped the significance of Barth's work, Stringfellow was an Episcopalian self-trained theologian and a lawyer by trade—read widely in his own day but largely neglected in our own.[1] Like Yoder and Day, Stringfellow maintains a deep

1. For a full description of Stringfellow's life and career, see Anthony Dancer's biography *An Alien in a Strange Land: Theology in the Life of William Stringfellow* (Eugene, OR: Cascade Books, 2011), and Marshall Ron Johnston, "Bombast, Blasphemy, and the Bastard Gospel: William Stringfellow and American Exceptionalism," (unpublished Ph.D. diss., Baylor University, 2007. The encounters between Barth and Stringfellow are recounted in Dancer, pp. 166-182. Barth's affirmation of Stringfellow is found in the foreword to Barth's 1962 lectures in Chicago, published as *Evangelical Theology: An Introduction* (New York: Holt, Reinehart, and Winston,

suspicion of political arrangements that bring churches into close alignment with military and political institutions. And, like Yoder and Day, he understands the work of Christ, witnessed to in the church, as the indispensible reason for thinking about the possibility of nonviolent resistance to war.

However, Stringfellow, differs from our previous figures in two important respects. First, though he wrote extensively on nonviolence as a christologically-authorized act, he did so largely independent of an institutional church setting; a series of clashes with ecclesiastical authorities convinced Stringfellow that church institutions were more interested in maintaining an institutional identity than with providing a credible social witness, resulting in his arguments for nonviolent resistance to war *in spite of* ecclesiastical resources available to him.[2] The second difference is equally important: Stringfellow refuses to make the rejection of violence an ethical non-negotiable. For Stringfellow, nonviolence is not an act that can (like Yoder) be assumed *a priori* as intrinsic to the Christian faith or that can (like Day) be assumed as the true telos of human life. For Stringfellow, nonviolence is an act that can be conceived of only as a response to God's act in one's own time, called for by Christ as an act of resistance to Death, which the church should participate in.

1962), ix. In recent years, popular reception of Stringfellow has been furthered by Anthony Dancer's recent volume, as well as by three volumes of essays either anthologizing Stringfellow's work, or providing critical evaluation and response to his work. During his own life, Stringfellow was a relentless speaker and writer, and the lone layperson invited to respond to Karl Barth during his lectures in Chicago.

2. While holding a number of posts within Episcopal life in his early years, Stringfellow's relationship to Episcopal life was a contentious one. Cf. Andrew W. McThenia, "Introduction: How This Celebration Began," in *Radical Christian and Exemplary Christian*, ed. Andrew W. McThenia (Grand Rapids: William B. Eerdmans Publishing Co., 1995), 14ff. Prior to being drafted into the U.S. Army in 1950, Stringfellow was an Anglican delegate to a variety of international ecumenical organizations such as the World Conference of Christian Youth and the Anglican World Youth Conference. These activities ended for the most part during Stringfellow's university years. In 1959, while living in Harlem, Stringfellow was approached to be a delegate for the Episcopalians to the World Council of Churches, but declined.

In this chapter, I will first discuss the framework that shapes Stringfellow's thinking on both war and the church: the powers of Death and the resistance to Death by the Word of God. For Stringfellow, humanity is ubiquitously approached by the powers and principalities of Death, a state that can only be overcome by dying in Christ and "listening to the Word." As people listen to the Word, they are renewed in Christ and made part of the "community of the resurrection," becoming witnesses to Christ's work. The church, as that visible body who, in their worship and proclamation of the Scriptures name the Word's redemption within the world, is not meant to be a self-sustaining body or an insular institutional communion. In its structures, practices, and institutions, the church exists as it participates in the Word's redeeming work, rejoicing in Christ's triumph over death. For Stringfellow, nonviolent resistance to war can never be commended absolutely, but only in times appropriate to the task of witnessing to the Word's act in the world. While he never commends nonviolence as an intrinsic church practice (like Yoder) or understands it to be universally consistent with tradition (like Day), Stringfellow believes that the proper mode of existence for the church and certain forms of Christian nonviolence are marked in similar ways. More specifically, because certain forms of nonviolence resist Death in tangible forms, they are actions that the church is called to partner with and to name these movements as the redeeming work of God. Participating in God's redemption of creation, the church can never encompass the forms this resistance to death might take but remains of service to the Word's work in the world, participating in and naming nonviolent resistance to war as a form of Christ's resurrecting work for society and itself.

Death, the Powers, and Christ's Work in the World

Stringfellow's writings depend in large part upon his thanatology, his understanding of the way in which Death and its powers have corrupted human existence. In a creation corrupted by Death, the work of Christ comes to us, creating a community of life in the midst of decay, a community which by its ubiquitous nature (centered between church and world) bears witness to the Word of God, who overcomes Death and all of its powers. This conflict between Death and Christ colored Stringfellow's own narration of his own life and of the world around him.[3] He viewed his life as participating directly in this conflict; after receiving his law degree from Harvard University, he chose to take a position as counsel for the East Harlem Protestant Parish, describing this vocational choice later in life as a kind of "mortification," an intentional renunciation of careerism.[4]

Much of Stringfellow's work consists of these kinds of autobiographical expositions and critiques of contemporary society, explicating Death's ongoing influence within the full contours of life and human experience; this writing style stems from his belief that Death's corruption is not an abstract affirmation, but validated in the empirical description of creaturely life.[5] The "powers and

3. For a brief biographical synopsis of Stringfellow, see Johnston, *Bombast*, 33-93.

4. Stringfellow, *A Simplicity of Faith: My Experience in Mourning* (Nashville: Abingdon Press, 1982), 125: "I died to the idea of career and to the whole typical array of mundane calculations, grandiose goals and appropriate schemes to reach them." Stringfellow practiced law on his own, and then in the firm of Ellis, Patton, and Stringfellow until 1962, in Johnston, 45.

5. Stringfellow, *My People is the Enemy* (New York: Holt, Rinehart, and Winston, 1964), 29-30: "The awful and the ubiquitous claim of death is not different for the poor than for other men....but among the poor there are no grounds to rationalize this claim, no way to conceal the claim...no place to escape or evade it." Stringfellow's own lifelong health problems were likewise a constant reminder of Death's influence; in 1950, Stringfellow contracted hepatitis while travelling with the World Student Christian Federation, a condition which led ultimately to the loss of his pancreas in 1968 and to his early death in 1985. Stringfellow details his own health issues and recovery from the 1968 surgery his autobiographical work *A Second Birthday* (Garden City, NY: Doubleday, 1970). Similarly, the impingements of physical death prompted the authoring of *A Simplicity of Faith*, detailing the death of Stringfellow's long-time partner, Anthony Towne.

principalities," which function as the "acolytes of death," exalt death and usher people toward death in existential ways; Death, as the state encompassing all humanity, impinges on the individual body as well as corporate bodies, creating not only individuals defined by death, but institutions and political systems governed by death, creating a kind of thanatopolis, a society founded on and existing as Death. The powers, thus, are those things which threaten to destroy the common life of the world, rather than being idealized concepts which could not be seen in the events of history.[6]

Death rarely confronts humans directly, for even physical decay is described by Stringfellow as a "principality."[7] Rather, Death—an existential state in which humanity persists—approaches and corrupts humanity via an endless series of "powers and principalities" which encompass human existence:

> The separation from life, the bondage to death, the alienation from God which the fall designates is not simply to be accounted for by human sin. The fall is not just the estate in which men reject God and exalt themselves....The fall is also the awareness of men of their estrangement from God, themselves, each other, and all things, and their pathetic search for God or some substitute for God within and outside themselves and each other in the principalities and in the rest of creation.[8]

6. Cf., *An Ethic*, 79: "What is being described and designated is a form of life, a creatureliness, which is potent and mobile and diverse, not static or neat or simply defined by what it may now or then be called." It is in this sense that Stringfellow would sometimes call himself an "empirical theologian."
7. Stringfellow, *A Second Birthday* (Garden City, NY: Doubleday Publishers, 1970), 53, in which pain is described as a "demigod representing death." More than others, pain is "literally a symptom of the advent of death," but still testifies to death in a representative fashion. The proliferation of the powers in Stringfellow's writings—which indeed encompasses a wide range, from financial institutions and sexual attitudes to war and ecclesiastical institutions—has led some to conclude that the powers are in fact "arguably the centerpiece of Stringfellow's theology" (Johnston, 95). See also Walter Wink, "William Stringfellow: Theologian of the Next Millennium, A Review Essay," *Cross Currents* 45, no.2 (Summer 1995): 205-216 for this assessment.
8. Stringfellow, *Free in Obedience* (New York: Seabury Press, 1967), 62. In contrast to Yoder, Stringfellow does not limit "powers" to that which is outside the church, but understands the

The principalities, which are "consigned to death just as much as the men who worship them," serve as conduits for humanity to be delivered unto Death.[9] Taking ubiquitous forms in human society—ranging from the Pentagon to the Olympics to white supremacy—the principalities and powers are creatures with their own personalities and modes of life, meaning that though they involve humanity, they are perpetuated and can exist independent of specific human intentions for them.[10]

The "powers and principalities" function primarily for Stringfellow in two modes: 1) by *undervaluing* humanity's status as created and contingent beings (ideology), and thus denying ourselves as created by and for God, or 2) by *overvaluing* created life (idolatry), thereby forgetting that the world exists not for its own sake, but because of and for God. Both of these modes of operation by the powers, Stringfellow argues, deform creaturely life, and blind us from not only seeing what the world is for, but how to rightly inhabit it. The first way, *ideology*, names the denial of ourselves as created, and thus, as beings contingent upon God.[11] Ranging from ecclesiastical morality to racism, these entities communicate a static view of human

"powers" to be ubiquitous in both church and the world. As I will explain shortly, churches frequently operate as principalities and powers.

9. Ibid., 63.
10. Stringfellow, *An Ethic for Christians and Other Aliens in A Strange Land* (Waco, TX: Word Books, 1973), 78-79. Whereas Yoder viewed the "powers" in terms of created structures which Christians can engage and seek to reform in a limited fashion, Stringfellow viewed the powers as corrupted entities which ultimately supercede and encompass human intentions for them. Mark T. Nation has criticized Stringfellow's stance at this point as too totalizing of human existence, providing no room to distinguish "between greater and lesser evils, greater and lesser approximations to what God desires from us," in "The Vocation of the Church of Jesus the Criminal," 123-124, in *William Stringfellow in Anglo-American Perspective*, ed. Anthony Dancer, (Aldershot: Ashgate Publishers, 2005). What Nation's critique neglects is that Stringfellow is not doing away with moral discernment entirely, but radicalizing the *locus* of moral discernment, that it cannot be done from *a priori* position, a position which is a denial of ourselves as created, contingent beings.
11. Ibid,67. See *Imposters of God: Inquiries into Favorite Idols* (Washington, DC: Witness Books, 1969), 45: "ideology is inherent in every institution, while institutional forms are implied in every ideology." For religion and race as ideology, cf. *Imposters,* 80-87, 106-109.

life which refuses the fluctuations of "empirical" conditions, in a refusal to acknowledge the contingency of all existence upon God.[12]

One of the most common examples of "ideologies"—refusals of God's ongoing valuation of creation—in Stringfellow's early writings was that of nonviolence, labeled as "ideological pacifism." Pacifists, in their *a priori* rejection of violence, presume universal divine favor upon their act, and in doing so, only oppose one principality (war) by participating in another (ideological pacifism):[13]

> The ethics typically concocted from religion or ideology . . . repudiate time and common history as the sphere of ethical concern and political action in multifarious ways. They may focus upon asserted prospects beyond history, outside of familiar time...They may deny the moral significance of time as the era of the Fall and diminish history as the story of the Fall.[14]

The problem with "ideological pacifism" in particular then is that it tempts humanity to deny its creaturehood, by retreating from the contingencies of life, assuming a moral response as knowable apart from the ongoing movement of God in history, assuming an appropriate response before God has called for it in the midst of life.[15]

Whereas ideology *undervalues* created contingency, and tempts humanity to totalizing and abstraction, the second mode of the

12. "Empirical" observation became a key term for Stringfellow, in that one could only speak of God's activity as it played out in the life of the world. To retreat from the events of the world in describing God's work was, for Stringfellow to fall into ideology. Cf., Stringfellow's description of himself as an "empirical theologian" in this sense, in *Second Birthday,* 40ff.
13. *Ethic for Christians*, 132: ". . . what is deficient in traditional pacifism [is] . . . the attempt to ascertain idealistically whether a projected action approximates the will of God. . . . It is a query seeks assurance beforehand of how God will judge a decision or an act."
14. Ibid., 56. As Stringfellow argues, "in this world, the judgment of God remains God's own secret. No creature is privy to it, and the task of social ethics is not to second guess the judgment of God." Cf. *A Second Birthday,* 88–91.
15. Whether in the form of racism, which asks humanity to judge persons in abstraction from their actual existence, or in certain forms of theological judgment which seek to judge a situation *a priori*, the principalities tempt humanity away from their created state toward an atemporal place outside the world.

powers—idolatry—tempts humanity to *overvalue* created contingencies, denying the God who creates and interrupts creaturely discourse.[16] Appearing not only through the activities of human relationships, but also through institutions (such as the Pentagon) and social activities (such as war), the powers of idolatry are penultimate goods which masquerade as ultimate ends, promising absolute social deliverance independent of God's act.[17] One of the most explicit examples of this idolatry for Stringfellow was the Vietnam War, in which Stringfellow saw dramatized "this insatiable appetite for human sacrifice typical of ideological and institutional powers," as men sought to overcome the threat of Communism (an ideology) by trusting in the salvific power of war (an idolatry).[18] In viewing the Vietnam War as an idolatry, and (early on his career) nonviolence as an ideology, Stringfellow illustrates the manner in which the various manifestations of death may conflict with one another at times, but that in the end, the difference between the powers is *only* apparent.[19]

The end result of the principalities and powers' operations in the world, whether in the form of ideology or idolatry, is a proliferation of Death *through* human bodies. As Death proliferates in various forms, and through various activities and institutions, death creates its own kind of sociality, a fully corrupted *politic*, which attempts to

16. *Ethic for Christians*, 82–84.
17. Ibid.
18. Ibid., 92. Through the principality of the media, war spreads a public and demonic claim of "safety, prosperity, virtue, even immortality."
19. For example, in William Stringfellow, *A Private and Public Faith*(Grand Rapids: Eerdmans, 1962), 72, Stringfellow recalled counseling an East Harlem youth named Ramon to join the Marines to avoid jail, an option which would teach Ramon a trade; Stringfellow contended that this counsel was advocacy in the midst of a concrete situation, and thus, Christian action. In *Ethic for Christians*, 89-90, written ten years later, none of this optimism is visible, as Stringfellow sees both the police *and* the military as implicated in the powers. On occasion, there is collusion between powers, but Stringfellow argues this is not because there is coherence or common good shared between the powers, but rather an *ad hoc* opportunity for cooperation.

stand in direct opposition to the work of God in Christ. Because death permeates human existence, Death is made known in and through human autobiographies, which in turn flowers into a corruption of human sociality, forming a humanity fully united in decay.

Because Death ultimately posed a threat to corporate human existence, politics became a paramount issue for Stringfellow's work, in that this issue of human social organization was the ultimate vehicle of both human redemption and death's aggrandizement.[20] As with our individual biographies, so our corporate life (politics) construct either accounts of humanity as being created for God, or as self-aggrandizing creatures.[21] As he wrote:

> The biblical topic *is* politics. The Bible is about the politics of fallen creation and the politics of redemption . . . The Bible expounds with extraordinary versatility . . . the singular issue of salvation—which is to say, the preemptive political issue. It bespeaks the reality of human life consummated in society within time in this world, now and here, as the promise of renewal and fulfillment vouchsafed for all humans and for every nation—for the whole of creation—throughout time.[22]

20. Stringfellow, *Dissenter in A Great Society* (Holt, Reinhart, and Winston, 1966), 131-136. As Stringfellow said during the trial of Philip and Daniel Berrigan, "the State has only one power it can use against human beings: death. The State can persecute you, prosecute you, imprison you, exile you, execute you. All of these mean the same thing. The State can consign you to death," in William Stringfellow, *A Keeper of the Word: Selected Writings of William Stringfellow*, ed. Bill Wylie-Kellerman (Grand Rapids: Wm. B. Eerdmans Publishing Co., 1994), 69.
21. In describing the "credo" of democratic discourse, Stringfellow noted that the 1964 presidential debates: [S]et forth quite specifically a doctrine of man—one, by the way, which it behooves heretics, as well as the true believers, to understand, since those who are not dedicated to it are guilty not of 'merely political differences or mere political mistakes' but of 'a fundamentally and absolutely wrong view of man, his nature and his destiny', in *Dissenter*, 59. Cf., "Watergate and Romans 13," *Christianity and Crisis*, June 11, 1973, 110-112, and "God, Guilt and Goldwater," *The Christian Century*, September 2, 1964, 1079-1083.
22. Stringfellow, *An Ethic*, 14-15. Beginning with 1966's *Dissenter in a Great Society*, his concern for a redeemed sociality turned more explicitly toward politics. Framed as a critique of President Lyndon Johnson's administration policies called the "Great Society," *Dissenter* argued that social forms of death, such as poverty and racism, are not ultimately perpetuated by laws, but primarily through the political processes which creates law; political process—as the creator of laws—reify the conditions of poverty and disorder through the rule of law.

It was through his increasing interest in national politics and the ways that Death takes corporate form that he undertook a trip to Vietnam en route to a speaking engagement in Australia, during which he saw first-hand the devastation made possible by the politics of Death.[23] Rather than existing to facilitate human flourishing, fallen politics and the governments and wars created by them "destroy the witness of human resistance by preemption, by the fabrication of opposition, by a kind of absorption."[24] True politics stood in opposition to Death, and celebrated the redemption of ordinary life and narratives by the Word of God; fallen politics too united humanity, but did so through means designed to accelerate its destruction and decay.[25]

As this point, Stringfellow's vision of creaturely life as populated by powers could be seen as producing a vision of moral paralysis, particularly with regards to war; whether one resists war or participates in it, one ultimately is in the grasp of the powers. But this is only half the picture. As we have seen, creation, though characterized as full of principalities and powers, is not a necessary evil, but a celebrated good, the "medium through which men may love God."[26]

23. Cf., "An American Tragedy," *Christian Living*, January 1967, 32, and *Dissenter*, 80ff. Stringfellow's itinerary of this year is found from Slocum, *Prophet of Justice*, xii. In Stringfellow, *Conscience and Obedience* (Waco, TX: Word Books, 1977), 38, notes that his mature thinking on politics arose as a consequence of Vietnam and Watergate, which "exposed incumbent political authority...as illegitimate."

24. "Must The Stones Cry Out?," *Christianity and Crisis*, October 30, 1972: 237.

25. "Does America Need a Barmen Declaration? ," *Christianity and Crisis*, December 24, 1973, 275: ". . . political authority in America has little need to launch indoctrination or practice much ideological manipulation because the available means, furnished by technology, of transmitting information have transfixing capabilities to paralyze human comprehension." Cf. "Watergate and Romans 13," 110-112; "Technocracy and the Human Witness," *Sojourners* , November 1976, 14-18; "Open Letter to Jimmy Carter," *Sojourners*, October 1976, 7-8. Late in life, Stringfellow would enter the political realm on Block Island, where he and Towne moved in 1967, running for second warden of the island in 1978. Describing his vision of politics as centering around the "self-respect, dignity and scope of the town council and the integrity . . . of the town meeting," it becomes more clear how Stringfellow saw most large-scale politics as essentially dehumanizing, which is to say, leading toward death. Cf. Stringfellow, "Politics on Block Island," *Sojourners* 7 (January 1978): 17-18.

> Men's existence in fallen creation is existence in sin. . . . By giving Himself to men in Creation, God gave men to each other; God gave men community in Creation, and this is shattered when men sever themselves from Him . . . *In Creation, God gives men life; in sin men die.*'[27]

This final line in one of Stringfellow's earliest writings introduces us to the paradox of his soteriology, and indeed, of his theology. Insofar as the Gospel "means that the very life of God is evident in this world, in this life, because Jesus Christ once participated in the common life of men in the history of our world," Christological salvation involves being more deeply embedded into acts which celebrate creaturely life and foster its renewal.[28] As he wrote

> [The Christian] looks like [a sucker] to other men because he is engaged in the wholesale expenditure of his life. He looks like that because he is without caution or prudence in preserving his own life. He looks like that because he is not threatened by the power of death either over his own life or over the rest of the world. He looks like that because he is free to give his life—*to die*—imminently, today, for the sake of anyone or anything at all, even for those or that which seem unworthy of his death, thereby celebrating the One who died for all though none be worthy . . ."[29]

The presence of God and the powers of Death thus coexist within creation, with both Death and the power of the Resurrection confronting through their personal and corporate lives.[30]

26. Stringfellow, *The Life of Worship and the Legal Profession* (New York: New York National Council, 1955), 5.
27. Ibid., 5-6, emphasis mine.
28. Stringfellow, *A Private and Public Faith*, 15.
29. Ibid., 42-43, emphasis mine.
30. ". . . no man confronts and struggle with and surrenders to any of the powers of death—any anxieties—any crisis—without beholding the power and the truth of the Resurrection: the presence of God in history which is greater than any of deaths' threats or temptations and more potent and which endures forever," ibid., 64. This is in part because of Stringfellow understands the "Word of God" as God's agency made manifest in Scripture, but at work in creation as well, such that creation, in its movement toward death, is not something separate from creation sustained by God. Though not worked out in these early works explicitly, Stringfellow's articulation of the Word as the key to resisting death is here in nascent form.

In *Free in Obedience*, Stringfellow most clearly highlights the Christological backing for this thesis. Whereas previous works narrated Death's effects upon contemporary life, *Free* describes the operations of Death in contrast to *Christ's* own life. Arguing that Christ's crucifixion is "a witness to the end of death's power over the world,"[31] and that Christ's conquering of death stands as "pre-eminently the event which brings all of the ordinary issues of existence in this world within the province of the gospel," Stringfellow sees in Christ the basis for any resistance to Death's ubiquity.[32] In earlier writings, he had detailed how various aspects of creaturely life (urbanization, industrialization, industry) were indications of the various *emissaries* of death (powers and principalities); in the conflict with Christ, Death itself come to the forefront.[33]

> [T]he resurrection encompasses and represents all of these particular historic encounters in a single, consummate, and indeed cosmic disclosure of the triumph of Christ over death. The resurrection is

Cf., *The Life of Worship*, 7: "The Christian view of God as Creator is not simply, nor primarily, that of some Originator of things. Christians know God as One who makes and sustains them and all things in this very moment. Men have life...only because God wishes to give it to men. Even fallen creation, even cursed life, even existence in sin....[is] sustained by Him." For the complete corruption of human existence by death, see Stringfellow, *Instead of Death: Inquiries into Favorite Idols* (Washington, DC: Witness Books, 1969), 31: "the Fall is about the milicacy of death's presence within all relationshps in the reality of our present existence and in the history of this world." Apart from Christ, we actively receive death in our activities, such that death does not simply corrupt creaturely activities, but that death is multiplied through our various activities, such as sex, work, relationships, and religion.

In his follow-up volume, *My People is The Enemy*, Stringfellow narrated his years in Harlem in terms of death's intimacy, examining the ways in which death impinged upon the daily existence of Harlem's residents. For example, in writing that "poverty is vulnerability to death in its crudest forms" (6). Stringfellow is not naming poverty *as* death, but a material condition which exemplifies that "all men, in short, live in a history in which every action and omission and abstention is consequentially related to all else that happens everywhere. That is the theology of Adam's Fall and with him, the fall of all men. In history, men live at each other's expense" (29).

31. Stringfellow, *Free in Obedience* (New York: Seabury Press, 1967), 16.
32. Ibid., 16-17.
33. Ibid., 34-36.

> impregnated with all that has gone before; these encounters of Christ with death and its powers in history mean that his triumph over death there shown is offered for men and for the whole world.[34]

Through Death's clash with Christ—the one whom enables a new human existence—the true and naked power of death is revealed. Death and Christological salvation, consequently, play out this struggle in and through bodies of humanity, moving people toward or away from death.[35]

In the same way that Death culminates in a thanatopolis—human participation and collusion in ideology and idolatry which yields death—so human redemption through "listening to the Word of God" yields a corporate resistance to Death in and through the contours of creaturely life.[36] For Stringfellow, the Word impacts "any and every biography," meaning that all persons, as subjects of the Word's operations in history, are "parables of the incarnation," creating pluriform sites of resistance of death appropriate to each individual life because of the Incarnation, "the presence and vitality of the Word of God in common history."[37] Because of the Incarnation,

34. Ibid., 72.

35. Discerning *how* this redemption of our lives is occurring takes place as one reflects upon one's life in creation from a Christological vantage point. For example, as Stringfellow's own health and the health of his longtime partner Anthony Towne began to deteriorate, Stringfellow's writings began to emphasize these aspects of bodily decay as an example of this conflict between death and Christ. In keeping with his description of the Christian conflict in ways which emphasize the bodily terrain of the conflict, Stringfellow calls the clash of Christ and death to be paradigmatic of every person's conflict with death, whether personally or corporately. As Stringfellow describes the significance of this bodily theology in this way, reflecting on his own near-death experience during a 1968 surgical procedure to control his diabetes: "There is nothing whatever in the experience in history of men or nations that is not essentially theological, and the discipline of academics is not to speculate or innovate from some...stance outside on the outside of common experience but to expound and enlighten empirical reality, relating inheritance, memory and the happenings of the past to the contemporary scene, alert for portents of that which is to come in this world," in Stringfellow, *A Second Birthday*, 40–41.

36. *The Life of Worship and the Legal Profession*, 5: "Creation is God giving Himself to men, and the only way men may receive Him is in love, by giving themselves to Him. All that men have by which to love God is the life which He has given them and the dominion which He has offered them over the rest of Creation. Creation is the medium through which men may love God."

the "historic, incarnate activity of the Word of God," the Word of God is known in its "militancy . . . both in cosmic dimensions of space and time and in each and every item of created life, including *your* personhood and *your* biography or mine."[38] This activity of the Word encompasses both personal and corporate aspects in a four-fold designation of the presence of "Word of God": 1) "militant" in the world, 2) Jesus Christ, the incarnate Word, 3) present in Scripture, and 4) present in liturgy.[39]

It is significant to note that for Stringfellow, these loci are *interlocking* loci of the "Word of God"; to "listen to the Word of God" is to listen to the Word in the various arenas in which the Word is present. For example, Scripture and liturgy are described as loci for this "listening," with the Word's presence in human existence and as Jesus Christ (the incarnation of the Word which enables human existence to be "parables of the Word") also described as loci for "listening" to the "Word of God."[40] Scripture, contrary to some

37. *A Simplicity of Faith*, 20: "any biography and everybiography, is inherently theological, in the sense that it contains already—literally by virtue of the Incarnation—the news of the gospel whether or not anyone discerns that. Weare each one of us parables." Cf. Dancer, 74-86, on Stringfellow's understanding of his own biography as a theological disclosure of the Word in his life.

38. *Simplicity of Faith*, 20.

39. Ibid., 21: "We are each one of us parables. . . . This world is the scene where the Word of God is; fallen creation—in all its scope, detail, and diversity—is the milieu in which the Word of God is disclosed and apprehended; Jesus Christ verifies how the Word of God may be beheld by those who have sight and hearing to notice and give heed to the Word of God." On the Word's presence in liturgy, see *Dissenter in a Great Society*, 154: "The liturgy, therefore, wherever it has substance in the Gospel, is a living, political event. The very example of salvation, it is the festival of life which foretells the fulfillment and maturity of all of life for all of time in *this* time. The liturgy *is* social action because it is the characteristic style of life for human beings in this world." Cf., "Liturgy as Political Action," in *A Keeper of the Word*, 123-126.

40. Stringfellow's formulation can be read as responding to a tension in Episcopalian ecclesiology. From their earliest days, Episcopalians have vacillated between a highly liturgical form, divorced from extra-ecclesial concerns (exemplified by John Henry Hobart), and the transformation of society through ecclesial auspices (as exemplified by Vida Scudder). See David Hein and Gardiner H. Shattuck, Jr., *The Episcopalians*, (Westport, CT: Praeger Publishers, 2004), 64-72, 96-99.

Protestant articulations, does not fully encompass the "Word of God," but rather attests *to* the living Word of God.[41]

In other words, the act of "listening to the Word of God"—the root activity of the resistance to death—takes place in polymorphous circumstances, linking together liturgical settings with the rest of society; the Word which Scripture speaks of, Stringfellow argues, "is free and active in this world and Christians can *only* comprehend the Word out of their involvement in this world, as the Bible so redundantly testifies."[42] The Word "militant" in the world, in the depths of our experience, and the Word witnessed to in Scripture and liturgy, are one and the same, meaning that our "listening" in these settings is mutually interpreting and inextricably linked, in a kind of feedback loop between the church and the world. Because the same Word heard in Scripture is at work in the world and in human autobiographies, "the Word cannot be threatened by anything whatever given to men to discover," and that "all these are welcome to Christians as enhancements of the knowledge of the fullness of the Word of God and of the grandeur of men's access to the Word."[43]

The Word of God in this four-fold loci creates resistance to death, not by directing us away from the creation and the death which permeates it, but further *into* creation—in Christ, learning to rightly embrace creaturely existence, both individual and collectively. In Jesus Christ, "there is a radical and integral relationship of all men

41. *Simplicity of Faith*, 21: "Jesus Christ verifies how the Word of God may be beheld by those who have sight and hearing to notice and give heed to the Word of God (cf. John 1:1-14)." It is these kinds of designations of Scripture that have led some to draw connections between Stringfellow and Karl Barth's work, who described Scriptures in similar terms. Cf. Karl Barth, *Evangelical Theology*, 21: "These men are the *biblical witnesses of the Word*, the prophetic men of the Old Testament and the apostolic men of the New." For how Stringfellow understood his own relationship to Barth's theology, see *A Second Birthday*, 151-152.

42. Stringfellow, *Count it All Joy: Reflections on Faith, Doubt and Temptation Seen Through the Letter of James* (Grand Rapids: William B. Eerdmans Publishing Company, 1967), 16, emphasis mine.

43. Ibid. Scripture, according to Stringfellow, "reports the news of the Word of God manifest and militant in the events of this history" (17).

and of all things," meaning in part that those in Christ are not to escape creation, but to enter a *renewed* creation, a creation which is not characterized by "alienation of people from themselves and from one another and from God. "[44]

This Christological reconstitution of human community occurs as we engage the multiple senses of the Word, gathered both in liturgy and "worldly" action. Viewing worship as "the celebration of life in its totality," and the "festival of creation" as an anticipation of history's eschatological consummation, Stringfellow configures the worship of the Word as "incessantly calling for the overturning—or, more literally, the transfiguring—of the incumbent order in society."[45] Resistance to death, enabled by one's "death in Christ," makes one a participant in the renewed humanity, characterized by a renewed autobiography, which culminates in a renewed participation in corporate life:

> The Holy Spirit denotes the living, acting presence and power of the Word of God in the history of this world: the presence and power which lives and acts now in unity and integrity with the works of the Word of God in creation, redemption and judgment, as well as in solidarity and identification with the advent, birth . . . of Jesus Christ in this world.[46]

The interweaving aspects of "Word of God" create, thus, a community of resistance to Death which is centered neither in the liturgical setting *nor* the world, but which is found in *both* liturgical activity and "worldly" activity, as both the creaturely existence of overcoming death and Scripture are aspects of the single Word of God's activity. Rather than envisioning (as with Yoder) a movement

44. *Instead of Death*, 29.

45. *A Second Birthday*, 101. Cf. *Instead of Death*, 123-127, in which Stringfellow argues that those who die in Christ, i.e. those whose lives conform to the Word operative in Christ and the world (as confirmed by the witness of Scripture and liturgy) are those who undergo this "transfiguring" which frees human life from the loss of self produced by death.

46. *Free in Obedience*, 100.

toward participating in the binding/loosing community, or (with Day) a movement toward participation in the Eucharist which speaks of Christ's humanity, Stringfellow views the individual autobiography as disclosing the parameters of the Word's movement and direction, a disclosure which the church in its liturgical life is indispensible to naming. Because Death is a ubiquitous reality, there is not a *locale*—church or world—which is free from Death and the powers; accordingly, there is not a locale—church or world—in which one can solely identify this "community of resistance."

Because the activity of the Word occurs in and through human autobiography, the shape of this redeemed humanity is for Stringfellow to be discerned in an ongoing fashion, never presumed once and for all. There is always the presumption that naming the manner of the Word's redemption is not something which is "captured," but an identity which must be received constantly.[47] Likewise, because the Word who renews human existence is present as the Word within the world, but also within the liturgy and in the Scripture, there is absent a duality of church and world in Stringfellow, complicating any attempt to name a limit to the Word's work.

But while this new humanity is not circumscribed by the liturgy of the church, this new humanity is not possible *apart from* the liturgy, creating a necessary connection between the redemption understood within an individual's life and the redemption proclaimed in the liturgy and Scripture. For Stringfellow, the liturgical identification of Christ as the Word of God is the naming which makes possible

47. This is not, as has been suggested, a kind of "situation ethics" in which moral choices are made appropriate to the existential moment On this suggestion, see Gregory Bezilla,. "William Stringfellow's Theology and Ethics of Eschatological Existence" (M.Div thesis, Emory University, 1998), 63ff. Stringfellow's description of the Word's renewal of humanity sociality is a reorientation of what the moment is, now the occasion of moving the person from death to life rather than an occasion for their further decay.

an explicit naming of what lies implicit elsewhere in the world. This being said, however, because redemption is properly an event inaugurated by the Word, the liturgy must follow where the Word is leading, narrating the Word's work in the world according to how the Word has been witnessed to according to the Scriptures and not according to what God must do.

If we are to understand how nonviolent resistance to war—as an act of resistance to Death—is to be understood, we must thus first understand that the church which can rightly name nonviolence is one which is "a redeemed principality," a body which is in its constitution prepared to name God's work outside the liturgical setting in new and surprising ways. Stringfellow's relationship with his own Episcopalian tradition was more combative than either Yoder or Day, and as such, was far less optimistic that church institutions or traditions could be allies to a proper theological understanding of Christ's work in the world. But as we see already, to name the work of God in the world cannot ultimately be done *without* the church, insofar as the church—in its proclamations, celebrations, and unity—provides the interpretative key to naming the redemptive work of the Word in the world.

Ecclesiology: Existing by the Word for the Sake of the World

As I have argued already, the "listening to the Word" that constitutes the church occurs both inside and outside the liturgical setting. The church's liturgy and worship (one of the loci of the Word's presence in the world) is that space which makes explicit what is already true about the Word's activity in the world. For the institutions of the church to not fall into "idolatry" (behaving as one of the powers), these aspects of the church must be described in terms of their contingency upon the free movement of the Word, who freely sustains this emerging community of redemption. Without this character, churches will find themselves operating as principalities, opposing those acts of the Word of God that were emerging all around them, such as nonviolent resistance to Vietnam.

As a body created as an "event" of the Word, any institutions of the church which facilitate the church's gathering cannot see themselves as self-authorized, but as responsive to God's work in and through human lives, attending to these personal contours of the Word's appearance. As seen in Stringfellow's descriptions of church institutions (such as liturgical acts and institutions of authority). In this capacity—in exhibiting the renewing Word in their mode of existence—the church is able to properly name the Word's renewing work in creation. My argument here is that this description of the church connects to Stringfellow's nonviolence, in that Stringfellow's description of ecclesiology and nonviolence bear similar contours, contours which Stringfellow seems to go unmined in his own writings.[48]

The Church and the "Word of God"

Early in his career, Stringfellow defined "church" in a substantively a-procedural way: "Wherever and whenever men know Christ as the One who restores Creation, there is the Church. If we recall that in giving Himself to men, God gives men to each other, gives men community in Creation, then we can see that the gift of Christ is the restoration of community. In history, on earth, that community is the Church."[49] Aspects of this definition from his early work resonate

48. On the writings of the Episcopal General Convention and House of Bishops on war, cf. Allan M. Parrant, "On War, Peace, and the Use of Force," in *The Crisis in Moral Teaching in the Episcopal Church*, ed. Timothy Sedgwick and Philip Turner, 94-118 (Harrisburg, PA: Morehouse Publishing, 1992), as well as in the history of the Episcopal Peace Fellowship in Nathaniel W. Pierce and Paul L. Ward, *The Voice of Conscience: A Loud and Unusual Noise?* (Charlestown, MA: Charles River Publishing, 1989).

49. *Life of Worship*, 8-9.

with his later, more detailed work on the powers. First, "church" is designated by way of Christ's activity, not vice versa; the knowledge of Christ as the restorer of the created world designates where the body of the Church exists. Subsequently, the relationship between persons in the Church is one which is established by the work of this redeeming Word which, as we have seen, occurs in and through human autobiography and history as well as in liturgy and Scripture.

In short, "church"—in both its existence and in its relations—is driven by the actualism of the redemptive work of Christ. Such a definition, far from negating liturgical activity, rather orders liturgical life toward the church's specific vocation of witness within the totality of creation. As seen within his thanatology, the liturgy is one but one of the Word's renewing works, operating in tandem with the other arenas of Christ's work. As he remarked as early as 1957

> The church evident as the congregation is named *event* to show a difference between a definition of 'the idea of church' and an affirmation of that which actually takes place whenever the church is constituted. This attempt is not to discuss an abstraction but to describe a happening; not to speak theoretically but existentially. The church as event is always now and new. The church comes into being in response to the summons of God in the present moment and place. The response of our ancestors is not surety for us.[50]

Naming the body of the church as "event" and "new" calls for a persistent "listening" for the Word instead of reliance upon church tradition. In the same way that a Christian exists *qua* Christian in their contingency upon the Word's redeeming activity, so the gathered body of the church exists *qua* church in this mode.[51]

50. Stringfellow, "The Christian Lawyer as Churchman," *Christian Scholar* 40 (1957), 211.
51. As Stringfellow puts it in *A Second Birthday*, 42–43, denying the church as event "assumes that God was only empirically active a very long time ago, but that now editors have to elaborately transpose the biblical saga in order to make sense of it in terms of present circumstances. This

This understanding of the church as an "event" ordered toward witness in turn influenced how Stringfellow understood the institutions and practices of the church. Worship, for example, is "the way restoration and reconciliation are shown forth...a description of the event of restoration."[52] Likewise, while Stringfellow describes the presence of God in the liturgical acts of the Lord's Supper, baptism, and preaching, the church's full existence cannot be limited to these aspects, as Christians live "scattered in the world," continuing worship in their daily lives.[53] "Church" persists in the individual acts of a Christian's creaturely life which conform to the central confession of liturgical worship: that God has restored and is restoring the world.[54] Within this divine economy, liturgical activities of worship are not superior, but, as I have suggested, state *explicitly* what is the case already within other acts of the Word in human lives and history, making liturgy "revelatory" of what is the case within the world.

Speaking of the liturgy as that which makes visible the "restoration and reconciliation" which is being wrought by the Word in autobiography and history is one thing, but this is different than saying that the liturgy *establishes* that reconciliation. Mark D. Chapman has described Stringfellow's theology as a kind of "politics of liturgy," similar to the British Socialist reformers of Anglican

approach holds that God is an absentee from the modern scene; it envisions God as alive but truant. It is hard to decide which of these perversions is more scandalous."

52. *Life of Worship*, 11-12. Cf., "The Christian Lawyer," 211-213. By contrast, seeing the liturgical acts of the church as *containing* God's activity (in radical distinction from the rest of creation) reinstates a kind of feudalism, in "The Mission of the Church in the Decadent Society," *The Episcopal Theological School Journal* 8 (1962): 3-8. Dancer, in *An Alien in A Strange Land*, 137, argues that "the focus of his ecclesiology...is here concerned to balance the internal life of the church with its external life in the world" does not seem to be entirely right, insofar as Stringfellow is not so much concerned with balance as he is how both "internal" and "external" life are both oriented toward their renewal by the Word.

53. *Life of Worship*, 13.

54. Ibid., 14. In this way, the celebration of Communion "is the real dimension of the Christian experience of work," unintelligible apart from labor in the world.

life. Casting Stringfellow in the line of F.D. Maurice, writes that "sacramental activity in the world is thus a witness of the renewal of creation which flows beyond the sanctuary and the narrowly religious life into life in the wider world."[55] While this comparison is useful, this view supposes that there is a priority of liturgical activity which precedes the life of the world, whereas for Stringfellow, the Word appears both in liturgical life and "worldly" life, without the clear priority of direction as Chapman supposes; Chapman, by Stringfellow's reasoning, assumes that in the extra-liturgical world, "God is yet to be discovered."[56]

Following Christopher Rowland's interpretation, Stringfellow's theology is rather an *apocalyptic* one, as Christ's work is manifested in history, unconstrained by either church or world, and effecting the renewal of humanity in both.[57] This is not meant to create a kind of ecclesial relativism for Stringfellow, but rather to confess that, if creaturely life is what is redeemed by Christ's life, this redemption has

55. Mark D. Chapman, "William Stringfellow and the Politics of Liturgy," in *William Stringfellow in Anglo-American Perspective*, 156. Likewise, James F. Griffiss, "A Reluctant Anglican Griffiss," in Slocum, ed. *Prophet of Justice, Prophet of Life*, 40–57, has helpfully located Stringfellow within his Episcopalian heritage, as one drawing upon a tradition beginning with Thomas Hooker. Beginning with Hooker, Griffiss identifies a theological lineage in which the Incarnation of Christ is the foundation of both ecclesial and political order. Anglican theologians of the 19th century, such as F.D. Maurice, held that the Incarnation reveals the social order of all human beings, in a kind of "hallowing" of human society such that divine justice was to be advocated by the church on behalf of the church. For the history of Anglican socialists, see Bernard Kent Markwell, *The Anglican Life: Radical Social Reformers in the Church of England and the Protestant Episcopal Church, 1846-1954* (Brooklyn, NW: Carlson Publishing, 1991). Stringfellow certainly follows in this vein, seeing the presence of the Word as foundational for any ecclesiastical or civil order, but differs from the liturgical theologies of Anglican reformers such as James O.S. Huntington. Rather than flowing from church to world, as in the case of Maurice and Huntington, the liturgy of the church was grounded not in an ecclesial "center," but in the presence of the Word in *both* church and world.

56. *Private and Public Faith*, 17.

57. Christopher Rowland has described this hermeneutic as an "apocalyptic hermeneutic," in which "faith breaks out of the linear conceptions of time and confounds sequential doctrine of history . . . [encompassing] all things as in a single moment," in "William Stringfellow's Apocalpytic Hermeneutics," in *William Stringfellow in Anglo-American Perspective*, 140. Cf., Stringfellow, *An Ethic*, 152.

both ecclesial and non-ecclesial contours, both of which contribute equally in Stringfellow's estimation to the Christian's understanding of "the Word." For Stringfellow, the redeeming and unifying Word—present through Scripture, liturgy, autobiographies, and militant in the world in Christ—cannot be spoken of in a way which fractures God's divine life into a church/world dichotomy, or in a way which names in advance what the Word's redemption will consist of.[58]

But apart from these acts of liturgical confession which provide institutional visibility to the church, the church remains simply an *idea* and not, as Stringfellow will call it, "a *redeemed* principality." For the church to exist institutionally, it must do so as contingent upon the movement of the Word, and not as a self-defined totality, as the various institutions of the "powers" do. Because Stringfellow locates the work of the Word in the liturgical setting as well as within individual lives, naming some of the contours of how new community celebrates the Word in its ecumenical labors, its liturgy, and in its polity is of no small concern, in that this is in part how Christians are able to name the work of the Word beyond the liturgy.[59]

58. *Free in Obedience*, 113: "There are these problems which entice and tempt the Church and the members of the Church: to legislate the gospel; to equate obedience to God's freedom with loyalty to the church institutions; to adulterate the Word of God by exaggeration of the importance of the Church in the economy of salvation; to make the witness of Christ himself contingent upon the Church . . . The issue is the Church God instead of worshipping God in service to the world."

59. Stringfellow's ecclesiological presuppositions does not fundamentally change over the course of his life; throughout his writings, his work on the various aspects of the church's institutional life remains fundamentally oriented toward the church's contingency upon the Word of God. Dancer, *An Alien*, identifies a shift in Stringfellow's work such that Stringfellow becomes more *optimistic* about the institutional church in his later life by comparison. Cf., Dancer, 137-138n. 14.

Church as Redeemed Principality of Witness

Stringfellow's writing on ecumenism and ecclesiastical structures dates back at least to Stringfellow's visit to Oslo in 1947, as an American representative to the World Conference of Christian Youth, while still an undergraduate at Bates College.[60] In following years, Stringfellow continued working overseas, learning about European Christianity while speaking for the World Student Christian Federation.[61] As Anthony Dancer observes, in these early works, Stringfellow is not interested in ecumenism for the sake of ecumenism; rather, "the unity of which [ecumenism] is an expression is the basis for faith; all faith is necessarily political . . . and the primary context for faith is in the world . . ."[62] In other words, the church's unity is a vehicle by which it makes explicit the unity which all Creation is called to in Christ.[63]

Describing the secret of "Christian unity" as one which exists "in *this* world, where Christ lives," Stringfellow argued that church unity exists as the churches "live in this world for which Christ died." Church unity, contingent upon the Word, comes as churches join together with the activity of the Word in the world: "[The Christian] must live in this world not for his own sake, and not for the sake of the churches, and not for God's sake, but for the sake of the world.

60. Dancer, 44–48. During 1949-1950, Stringfellow attended the London School of Economics (LSE), writing on the work of William Temple, an Anglican theologian best known for his work on the relation between church and civil society.

61. A number of unpublished papers point to Stringefellow not being interested in ecumenism for its own sake, but in ecumenism as church unity related to political life, in Dancer, *An Alien*, 51.

62. Ibid., 52.

63. Like Mark Chapman, Dancer takes the movement to be *from* liturgy *to* extra-ecclesial life, in that the prior ecumenicity of the church lays the groundwork for involvement in politics. As I have been arguing, however, if the Word is present both in liturgy *and* militant in the world, Stringfellow's 1954 statement that "politics is the ordering of life by men in society...the gospel is politics" is not one of *movement* from the liturgy to the world, but of simultaneous identification. See Dancer, *An Alien*, 53. Ecumenism, thus, becomes the church's means of articulating the presence of the Word in all of creation, making visible in the church's unity that which remains invisible in the divided world.

That is to say, he must live in this world, where Christ lives: he must live in this world *in* Christ."[64] Instead of cooperating in "internal maintenance, in constructing and preserving a cumbersome, self-serving, officious, self-indulgent ecclesiology," Stringfellow calls for the Protestant churches to find their unity by celebrating Christ's work in the world, and naming it in their own worship.[65] As we have seen, to understand the work of the Word is to recognize it in its full range: autobiographically, christologically, liturgically, and historically. In being "to a great extent separated from the world, afraid of the world," churches were not only estranged from Christ, but from one another, insofar as the unity among churches lay not in aligning institutions, but in mutually celebrating the Word.[66] Arguing that the "rudiment of mission is knowledge of the city because the truth and grace of the Incarnation encompass in God's care all that is the city," involvement in the world and ecumenism are dependent upon each other, in that both church relations and missions remain oriented by the Word's work.[67]

The unity of the church in its mission, thus, reflects the reconciliation of Christ to the world:

> The unity of the Church of Christ which is the gift of God is the same unity revealed in the world in Christ Himself, that is, man reconciled to God and, within that unity, reconciled within Himself, with all men and with all things in the whole of creation. This is the unity which the

64. Stringfellow, "The Secret of Christian Unity," *The Christian Century*, September 13, 1961: 1074.
65. Ibid., 1074.
66. Ibid., 1074–75.
67. Stringfellow, "The Church in the City," *Theology Today* 20, no.2 (July 1963): 146. Cf., Stringfellow's review of Paul Ramsey's *Christian Ethics and the Sit-In*, in "Too Little, Too Late, and too Lily-White," *The Christian Scholar* 45, no.1 (Spring 1962): 78-80. Seeing the work of the Faith and Order Commission of the World Council of Churches as largely "redundant," he glimpsed hope in proposals which would "confront the technological sciences...and at the same time explore the works of the demonic powers in the world," in Stringfellow, "Ecumenicity and Entomology: New Church Problem," *The Christian Century* 81, no. 41 (October 7, 1964): 1240.

> Church is given and which the Church embodies on behalf of the world which has no unity at all.[68]

In light of the diversity of churches, the desire for a "super church" is secondary compared to an "organic union of all who are baptized professing the same Biblical and Apostolic faith."[69] This "organic union" involved loss of certain institutional trappings such as property, but these dispossessions were intrinsic to the church's recognition that its unity with the Word and with other church is found in common mission.[70]

This ecclesiological vision underlay his understanding of the church's internal life as well. In the setting of gathered worship—the reading of Scripture and the celebration of the Eucharist—the worshippers were to look for "the discernment of the same Word of God in the common life of the world," such that the unnamed acts of redemption in the world and the explicitly named life of worship confirmed one another.[71] The very Word of God, worshipped through and disclosed in the liturgy, "is *hidden* in the ordinary life of these boys in gang society and in the violence of the streets which part of their everyday existence."[72] With salvation "the event in which a man utterly and unequivocally confronts the presence and power of death in and over his own existence," the sacraments are likewise for the sake of uniting the church to the world, where people find their salvation.[73] Baptism was not "a ceremony for naming a

68. Stringfellow, "The Unity of the Church as the Witness of the Church," *Anglican Theological Review* 46, no. 4 (October 1964): 395. Cf., *Free in Obedience*, 104: "How shall the nation . . . know what it means to be a society under God, a true community of reconciliation, if there is no visible witness in the existence and life of the Church as the exemplary holy nation to behold?"
69. Stringfellow, "The Unity of the Church," 396.
70. Ibid., 398.
71. *Private and Public Faith*, 57.
72. Ibid., 61, emphasis mine.
73. Stringfellow, "Evangelism and Conversion," *International Journal of Religious Education* 40, no. 3 (November 1963): 7.

child," but "the public proclamation to the world by the Church . . . in the power of God to raise the dead and of the care of God that this child . . . be saved from death," an opportunity for the gathered church to reconsecrate itself to the common task incumbent on it as those called to Christ.[74]

The liturgy internal to the church's life, in other words, "is a theatrical form of the ethical witness of Christians in this world."[75] The churches, if they are to be the *explicit* witnesses to God's work, illuminating the hidden witness in the world, must reject the temptation to "seek first the preservation of the Church or the conservation of the possessions, reputation, and power of the institutions of the Church," but rather "leave all such things to God's disposal, and thus, free from this most worldly anxiety...to celebrate the presence of the Word of God in the world."[76]

This understanding of the liturgy and sacraments—as facilitating and making explicit the work of the Word in the world—underscores Stringfellow's contentious relationship with church authorities, such as in his legal defense of bishops James A. Pike and William Wendt against charges of heresy.[77] In their narration of the heresy trials of

74. *Private and Public Faith*, 66-67. Cf., *Instead of Death*, 110: "Baptism is the assurance—accepted, enacted, verified, and represented by Christians—of the unity of *all humanity* in Christ. The baptized are the people in history consecrated to the unity humans receive in the worship of God." See also "Liturgy as Political Event," 1575. Stringfellow wrote similarly on various church practices, including discernment within the church body politic, in *An Ethic for Christians*, 138-140.

75. Stringfellow, "Liturgy as Political Event," 1574.

76. *Free in Obedience*, 116.

77. Stringfellow's first job with the East Harlem Protestant Parish lasted only fifteen months. Claiming that his "loyalty to Christ" was in conflict with "participation in the group ministry and it is conceived and constituted," Stringfellow saw the institutional aspects of the EHPP to be characterized less by ministry and listening to the Word than internal politics. Cf., Dancer, 80-81. Pike was brought up on heresy charges by House of Bishops in Wheeling, West Virginia in 1966, ostensibly for denials of the doctrines of the Trinity and incarnation of Christ as irrelevant and "nonessential doctrinal statements." Stringfellow's involvement with Bishop Pike is recorded in two volumes co-authored with Anthony Towne, *The Bishop Pike Affair* (New York: Harper and Row, 1967), and *The Death and Life of Bishop Pike* (Garden City, NY: Doubleday, 1976). For Stringfellow's involvement in defending William Wendt, see Johnston,

Pike, Stringfellow and Towne say little on the charges of heresy Pike faced, instead raising the suspicion that Pike was not truly on trial for his theological views, but for his involvement in the Civil Rights movement and Vietnam.[78] The legal charges, interestingly, contain no mention of Pike's involvement in social activism, but for Towne and Stringfellow, the censuring of Pike was an "obvious, ominous portent" of the Episcopalian church's rejection of involvement in social issues.[79] Concluding that there was, amidst the council of bishops, an intimate connection between heresy charges and progressive social witness, Pike's censuring was taken by Stringfellow to be the result of an act of conscience by Pike, pointing the church toward its vocation in the world.[80]

In sum, Stringfellow's vision of the church was of a church which, as a *redeemed* principality, could make use of structure and order for ends suitable to the church's calling to listen to the Word.[81] When existing as a "principality," ecclesial institutions affected people in the same manner as non-ecclesial principalities: diverting them

86–89, and "The Bishops at O'Hare: Mischief and a Mighty Curse," *Christianity and Crisis* 34, September 16, 1974, 195–96.

78. *Bishop Pike*, 25–26, 186–94.

79. Ibid., 194.

80. Ibid., 193–94. Similarly, in Stringfellow's defense of Bishop William Wendt, we find Stringfellow more concerned with the church's witness to the Word in the world, than in proper polity. Cf., "Bishops at O'Hare," 195. As he had observed in the Bishop Pike trial, polity in and of itself is not an assurance of the church's fidelity, but actually had the potential to perpetuate the church's *infidelity.* Wendt had ordained 11 women to the priesthood in July 1974, prompting a meeting of the Episcopal House of Bishops to bring up heresy charges against Wendt. The House of Bishops, ruling against the ordination, according to Stringfellow, acted in a paternalistic fashion, excluding the women in question from the proceedings, in a "poignant and terrible defamation" (196). Stringfellow continues his comments in "An Open Letter to the Presiding Bishop," *The Witness* 63, (January 1980): 10–11. I do not take this to mean that Stringfellow is unconcerned with Chalcedonian orthodoxy, but rather, that orthodox faith—characterized by faithful response to the Word—cannot be measured by verbal assent to traditional formulae.

81. Cf., *Free in Obedience*, 78-88, for Stringfellow's critique of the church as slow to act and witness on issues of race and nationalism, previously identified as two of the preeminent powers. Throughout his career, Stringfellow wrote of the manner in which the church, despite the fundamental witness of the Word given to it, had given itself over to the principalities.

from creaturely life and toward Death.[82] When the church accepts, however, that it is called into existence by the Holy Spirit, and that it is freed from being among the "powers," then it is able to exist as a holy nation, enabled to live "in solidarity and identification with the advent, birth, ministry, death, descent, resurrection, and Lordship of Jesus Christ in this world."[83]

One could read this as a kind of anti-institutionalism, but to reject the church's nature as an institution was to err in *under*determining the church in in the same manner that zealous fidelity to church institutions *over*determined the church in its institutionality.[84] The church's capacity to be an institution was not in question for Stringfellow, but rather what *kind* of institution:

> I do not denigrate institutionalism as such in the Church. I see, specifically in the account of Pentecost, that the Church's peculiar vocation is as an institution—as the exemplary principality—as the holy nation. So ideas of a non-institutional church or a deinstitutionalized church or underinstitutionalized church seem to me to be as nebulous as the Greek philosophy from which such ideas come and contrary to the biblical precedent. That does not temper my critique of the inherited churchly institutions . . . The Church is called into being in freedom from that ethic of survival and where renewal or reformation in the Church happens for real, that very freedom is being exercised, and the Church is viable and faithful.[85]

Far from negating the significance of liturgy and the sacraments, Stringfellow argued that it was "from this hidden company within

82. Ibid., 98.

83. Ibid., 100.

84. *Second Birthday*, 147. Stringfellow's own history embodied this struggle with the powers within the institutions of the church, legally representing those who had found themselves in opposition to the various structures with Episcopal life. In 1970, having retreated to Block Island, Stringfellow saw himself as having been "rejected by the ecclesiastical establishment of the Episcopal Church," with various Episcopal seminaries withdrawing their invitations for him to speak in the wake of his defense of Bishop Pike, as well as being removed as a representative to the Faith and Order Commission, in *Second Birthday*, 145–47.

85. Ibid., 147–48.

the churches that [renewal of the Church] will come."[86] The church, in its consistent communication of a Gospel, passed down through the Scriptures, liturgy, and traditions, cannot cease as an institution without losing the very means by which it makes known the explicit nature of the Word's activity. Insofar as "principalities" facilitate human organization, it is not possible be rid of them, either with regards to the fallen powers or the church as a kind of "principality." The church—as a renewed form of human organization ordered toward worship and witness—functions as a redeemed principality when it recognizes its existence as an "event" sustained by the Word, joins with the Word's work in the world, and names creation accordingly.

The Church and Nonviolent Resistance: An Analogy of Existence

Terming the relation between liturgical activity and social action as the "orthodoxy of radical involvement," Stringfellow understood the reconciliation spoken of clearly in the liturgy as of a single piece as that effected by the Word outside the liturgy.[87] In this way, the institutions and practices which sustain "church" were not simply the event of liturgy, but those acts and entities which witnessed to the Word's renewal of humanity. As such, conceiving of a relationship *between* ecclesiology and nonviolence is perhaps less appropriate for Stringfellow than describing how both the nature of the church and a certain kind of nonviolent resistance to war (of similar orientation and form as that of the church) are both made possible by the ubiquitous Word of God.

86. Ibid., 153–54.

87. Cf. William Stringfellow, transcript from "A Conversation with William Stringfellow on the Ethics of Resistance," an interview for KEED, Portland, Oregon, interviewer Father Edgar M. Tainton , taped October 18, 1968, 2. Box 35, William Stringfellow Papers, #4438, Department of Manuscripts andUniversity Archives, Cornell University Library. Cited in Johnston, 251.

But why does Stringfellow not make this connection in his writing? In large part, I suspect this is because Stringfellow's writings about war and about ecclesiology are chronologically separate; following his move to Block Island from Harlem with his partner Anthony Towne in 1967, a move accompanied by both a falling out with the EPHC and his defense of Bishop Pike against the Episcopal Church, Stringfellow writes little about either ecclesiology or his own churchgoing, and begins to write extensively about resistance to war.[88] This historical reason aside, it would appear that his concerns for both nonviolence (as a form of resistance to death), and the church (the body gathered in celebration of the Word's triumph over Death) possess a number of similar features which substantiate this connection. Both are described as contingent upon the movement of the Word, with both ideological nonviolence and ritualistic religion as presumptions of the Word of God's free movement and free judgment. And (as we shall see shortly) both church and a properly theological nonviolence are celebrations of the resistance to death. It would appear that—given the common basis for the church and this ethic—Stringfellow simply did not follow through the implications of his own thought.

In fact, Stringfellow gave time and energy to many anti-war movements, including ecclesially-based ones such as the Episcopal Peace Fellowship (EPF), speaking at their 1979 meeting.[89] Stringfellow's reticence to *unequivocally* advocate nonviolence in all times and places is due, (as we have already seen) to the manner

88. *A Simplicity of Faith*, 101-103. Stringfellow describes going on occasion to St. Ann's Church on the island, which was revived by Stringfellow and others but, much to Stringfellow's dismay, became associated with the diocese of Rhode Island as soon as it had been revived. As Stringfellow notes, "We do not do Bible study any more; we do not seriously consider the mission of the Church in the world, including block Island. . . . We are into raising money, which we will likely spend to embellish the social life of Episcopalians and their kindred in the summer colony" (102).

89. "The Witness of a Remnant," delivered before the Episcopal Peace Fellowship in 1979, but only published in, *The Witness* 72 (1989), 21, 23.

in which many arguments for nonviolence becomes "ideological," abstract judgments on what is good for human life, independent of time and space (a critique which he levied against particular aspects of the church-as-institution). Across his writings, Stringfellow changed his mind on the practice of nonviolence, always cautious to note that if nonviolent resistance is to be faithful to the Word, it must operate not so much as an *absolute* ethic, but as an ethic which listens to the Word, one which names itself according to the work of Christ and acts provisionally, as a consequence of listening to the Word in this time and this place.

Nonviolence: The Resistance to Death

As we have seen, one of the consequences of Stringfellow's vision of resistance to death is that resistance must be negotiated *as* one fully "listens to the Word" and not *a priori* (as "ideologies" do). Because of this presupposition, Stringfellow slowly turned toward commending nonviolence as a consequence of "listening to the Word" in America during the Vietnam War Era, despite his critiques early in his writings of "ideological pacifism." In contrast to Day and Yoder, this was not a practice which Stringfellow was able to commend universally; Stringfellow was perfectly willing to concede that resisting the powers of Death could involve a *rejection* of nonviolence at times, insofar as the redeeming work of the Word may be accompanied by war. And though, like Day, Stringfellow sees Christ's incarnation as implicating all of human existence, he does not, like Day, view the nonviolence of Christ as normative for all humanity. Rather, nonviolent resistance to war was viewed as the appropriate means of bearing witness to Christ's renewal of human life *during that time*.

In this section, I will trace how he arrived at a qualified form of nonviolence and how this coheres to his ecclesiology, in two steps. First, I will outline his early arguments against nonviolence, establishing what nonviolence *cannot* mean. Specifically, nonviolence cannot oppose the emergence of a truly human politic; if the Word is operative among humanity in a way which renews human life, then nonviolence must contribute to the genuine promotion of creaturely life. After this, I will describe what a ecclesiologically-named nonviolent resistance to war *can* look like for Stringfellow. Following his visit to Vietnam in 1966 and through his friendship with Daniel Berrigan, Stringfellow found a way to articulate nonviolence as a practice which is the consequence of "listening to the Word," and significantly, one which coheres to how he understands the church rightly existing.

Nonviolence: Caveats and Prohibitions

In approaching Stringfellow's work on war and nonviolence, three tendencies must be avoided. First, we must not approach him as if he were not open toward nonviolence.[90] While true that Stringfellow saw war as one of the means by which the powers operate determinately upon human life, the claim that Stringfellow was "no pacifist" can be a misleading description, as Stringfellow wrote at length about his understanding of nonviolence as one of those means by which the powers of death were resisted, while arguing that not *every* form of nonviolence properly bears witness to the Word's redemption of humanity.[91]

90. Stanley Hauerwas at times exhibits this tendency, writing, "no pacifist himself, Stringfellow saw the worship of war through the power of the modern nation-state clearly as one of the most determinative signs of the perversion of the powers, yet he identified the violence of war as but one of the "strategems of the demonic power that aim at "the dehumanization of human life" in *Dispatches from the Front: Theological Engagements with the Secular* (Durham, NC: Duke University Press, 1994), 111.

Conversely, Stringfellow cannot be read as a pacifist of the absolutist persuasion. Whatever changes occurred within his thinking on the possibility of nonviolence later in his life, his position on nonviolence does not approach anything akin to principled nonviolence. Walter Wink suggests as such, on the basis of conversations with Stringfellow prior to his death in 1985: "[Stringfellow] had moved to a more principled embrace of nonviolence, not as an abstract moral absolute, but as the unavoidable logic of his own understanding of the dominion and ubiquity of death. And that is, in fact, the logic of his entire enterprise."[92] Wink is correct to assert that Stringfellow's late-in-life embrace of nonviolence was commensurate with his opposition to death. But to say that this was "unavoidable logic" violates Stringfellow's emphasis on "listening to the Word," making an idol of one's own moral reasoning.

Finally, we cannot argue that his nonviolence was the calculated result of failed just war thinking, the ethical runner-up to the vanishing possibility of a just war.[93] Stringfellow's writings do follow certain just-war trajectories, particularly in his concern for proper political authority. But for Stringfellow, violence initiated by national entities was indicative of the *failure* of a political entity.[94] Any claim by a government to be "just" in its warmaking is a capitulation to the "necessary" logic of death.[95]

91. Cf., Stringfellow, *Ethic for Christians*, 145–48.
92. Walter Wink, "Stringfellow on the Powers," in *Radical Christian, Exemplary Lawyer: Honoring William* Stringfellow, ed. Andrew W. McThenia (GrandRapids: Eerdmans, 1995), 30.
93. See Edward McGlynn Gaffney, Jr., "The Challenge of Peace in an Age of Desert Storm Troopers," in *Radical Christian*, 148: "[Stringfellow's] perspective gave much sharper focus and urgency to their efforts to speak about the Vietnam War in the usual categories of the just war theory, which calls for the balancing of the various evils that are inherent in military violence"
94. Cf., *Conscience and Obedience*, 38: "the opposition (notably that of confessing Christians) to the war and to the war enterprise in Southeast Asia during the late nineteen sixties upheld the position that the criminal policy and unconstitutional conduct of the war exposed incumbent political authority . . . as illegitimate."
95. Ibid., 40–41.

To reiterate Stringfellow's position from a 1966 essay

> I am not an ideological pacifist, nor do I believe that a Christian may never be involved in war. I affirm the Christians who fought in the anti-Nazi underground, among many other instances that might be cited. I am only saying that how a particular war is regarded is a matter only disclosed in God's own judgment and Christians are not called upon to second guess that judgment.[96]

Because Christians remain beholden to the Word of God, called to listen to the Word in each and every situation, participation in war cannot be ruled out. In commenting on Bonhoeffer's involvement with the *Abwehr*, Stringfellow argued that

> Bonhoeffer's witness has helped to expose the simplicity of ideological pacifism as an answer to the question of whether there can ever been Christian involvement in explicit violence. Just as there were among the first century confessing Christians those who identified with the Jewish zealots in the advocacy of violent tactics against the Roman State, so Bonhoeffer's ethics undo the hypothetical imperatives of doctrinaire or pietistic pacifism.[97]

What is to be avoided in thinking about resistance to war is an *ideological* nonviolence which is not contingent upon the Word who

96. Stringfellow, "The Case Against Christendom and The Case Against Pierre Berton," in *The Restless Church: A Response to the Comfortable Pew*, ed. William Kilbourn (Philadelphia: J.P. Lippincott Company, 1966), 15. Cf., "Harlem, Rebellion, and Resurrection, *Christian Century*, December 11, 1970, 1348.

97. *An Ethic*, 132. I would argue that this is in some ways a misreading of Bonhoeffer's pacifism. On the one hand, Stringfellow is correct to assert that nonviolence for Bonhoeffer always had to take a concrete form. On the other hand, however, Bonhoeffer's stance could hardly be equated with that of the "zealots" of Jesus' day. Rather, Bonhoeffer saw his own involvement in the *Abwehr* plot to assassinate Hitler as part of the church's call to be a suffering presence in the world, to the point of taking on guilt on behalf of others. Cf. Larry Rasmussen, *Dietrich Bonhoeffer: Reality and Resistance* (Louisville: Westminster John Knox, 2005), 170–73. Disputing this read of Bonhoeffer's involvement is the recently published *Bonhoeffer the Assassin? Challenging the Myth, Recovering His Call to Peacemaking*, Mark Thiessen Nation, Anthony G. Siegrist, and Daniel P. Umbel (Grand Rapids: Baker Books, 2013).

moves and sustains the world, determining nonviolence as an *a priori* mode of social engagement.

His early writings on nonviolence during the Civil Rights movement bear this out. The advocacy of nonviolence by whites was in his view pre-empting an emerging Black political voice, and predetermining reconciliation in a way which favored existing social arrangements. Calling Martin Luther King Jr. "the best friend white Americans have ever had,"[98] Stringfellow saw nonviolent resistance in the Civil Rights struggle distracting the movement from tactics which might empirically lead to a new order, such as economic boycotts and sanctions.[99]

Stringfellow likewise wrote approvingly of the role of violence in social change in various places, calling riots in Selma and Watts "violence of despair," and one of the only ways to confront ethics of acquisition.[100] The self-immolations of Vietnam protesters were similarly affirmed as acts of bodily resistance to the powers, dramatically portraying frustration, helplessness, and resistance.[101] The "martyrdoms" of these protesters were, in Stringfellow's estimation, a "surrender to death in adherence to a cause thought to be of greater moral significance than the life sacrificed," testifying to "the absolution of men from the worship of death, which is precisely the meaning for men of the Resurrection of Christ."[102] The spontaneous violence of the riots and the gruesome self-immolations stood as twin signs of judgment upon corrupted national politics; a society which was "engaged in self-immolation" by idolatrously

98. *My People is the Enemy*, 141.
99. Ibid., 140.
100. Stringfellow, "The Violence of Despair," *Notre Dame Lawyer* 40 (1965): 528. A similar position is seen in Stringfellow's view of the violence in the "undisciplined, chaotic"1966 Watts Riots, describing the violence of the riots as the mirror image to others' apathetic withdrawal from the Watts neighborhood. See Stringfellow, "The Ethics of Violence," *Cross Beat*, March 1966: 3-6.
101. *Dissenter in a Great Society*, 81-82.
102. Ibid., 86.

valuing property over people cannot help but *produce* immolations and violence.[103]

While violence was affirmed as meaningful protest option for Stringfellow, the modes of violent protest are described as intrinsically *negative* acts, expressing either despair, or as the condemnation of an existing politic.[104] Though these acts are envisioned as a first step, which would "emancipate whites from the prison of their own complacency and paternalism" or move society toward a "demythologizing of the Great Society," violence is not described by Stringfellow as an act which can sustain or generate humane politics.[105] In fact, whenever violence is used for the *construction* of political life, Stringfellow argued, it perpetuates an unbiblical mythology

> If America goes to war, it is in the name of securing peace, and not for conquest or aggrandizement. If the U.S. Marines occupy a Latin American capital, it is for the sake of safeguarding the self-determination of the Latin Americans...It is an ambiguous universe that this mythology propounds, in which God rules with the United States as His favorite surrogate, and in which what is right always triumphs and therefore, what does in fact triumph must be right. Theologically, of course, such a crude view is ridiculously unbiblical.[106]

103. Ibid., 87. One could say that their resistance conformed to the ways the prophetic judgment of God is rendered in Scripture, in that prophetic utterances of judgment in the Old Testament were bodily performances. Cf. Thomas W. Overholt, "Seeing is Believing: The Social Setting of Prophetic Acts of Power," *Journal for the Study of the Old Testament* 23 (1982), 3-31. For an analysis of the performative nature of violence during Vietnam, see Joel Rhodes, *The Voice of Violence: Performative Violence as Protest in the Vietnam Era* (Westport, CT: Praeger, 2001).
104. "The Great Society as a Myth," *Dialog* 5, no.4 (Autumn 1966): 252–57. At best, violence directed against a great "blasphemy" of poverty can hope to be "absolved" by social programs such as President Johnson's "Great Society" (257).
105. "Great Society," 257. Cf., *Dissenter in a Great Society*, 121–22, in which Stringfellow remarks that a "day of wrath" may be coming in which blacks come after whites. In that day, Stringfellow remarks that it will be incumbent upon white Christians to not resist violence, that "the Cross means the gift of love even to one's own enemy—even to the one who would take one's life." (122).
106. "Great Society," 254.

As the Vietnam War became more problematic for American political life, with Stringfellow's analysis turning toward war as the rising shape of Death in American life, Stringfellow began to reconsider nonviolent resistance as a theologically consistent response to war consistent with the form of life exhibited by the true church. It is to these writings which we will now turn.

Nonviolence and the Word's Renewal of Humanity

In *Dissenter in a Great Society*, written in early 1966, Stringfellow first publically broached the question of whether nonviolent protest could be affirmed as a witness to a renewed politic. Despite his earlier qualms about nonviolence, he saw the peace movement against Vietnam as a stark contrast to "the militarization of the police," designed to quash dissent to the government. Whereas the United States government sought to equate unified political life with a lack of dissent, nonviolent protest witnessed to the possibility of a politics characterized by dissent and diversity of opinion.[107]

As the Vietnam War escalated in the mid-1960s, the war became the most prominent example of Death's principalities for Stringfellow, and thus demanded a response which would bear witness to what Christian worship spoke of explicitly.[108] Through

107. On this contrast, cf., *Dissenter in a Great Society*, 76–77. As Stringfellow noted, "That is why I am grateful for *every* movement of protest which has a serious purpose, whether I happen to concur with a particular protest or not," ibid., 79. It was with Stringfellow's *The Bishop Pike Affair*—his first book after his trip to Vietnam—that he begins to suggest nonviolent protest as an act which witnesses of the Word's activity in the world.William Stringfellow and Anthony Towne, *The Bishop Pike Affair: Scandals of Conscience and Heresy, Relevance and Solemnity in the Contemporary Church* (New York: Harper and Row, 1967) reflects this transition from issues of racism to issues of war. The book, which chronicles the heresy trials of Episcopal bishop James Pike, focuses largely on the relationship between social action and faith, asserting in short that Pike's trial was occasioned by Pike's desire to engage the issues of his day, seeing orthodoxy as related to social involvement rather than simply creedal affirmations. The majority of the book deals with Pike's stand on racial issues, suggesting that the immanent issue of the Vietnam War as the next issue which will engulf the Episcopal Church (194).

108. "The Demonic in American Society," *Christianity and Crisis*, September 29, 1969, 244–47 (245).

a multi-pronged approach by which citizens to either *directly* contributed to the war (through conscription and punishment of draft protesters) or *indirectly* (through educational facilities supporting war efforts), Stringfellow saw society being militarized; in its comprehensive approach, the principality of war was orienting all human society toward military productions which "assaults, dispirits, defeats, and destroys human life."[109]

The theological problem then was that, through war, "the surrogates of death" are enabling the "moral power" of death to be more prominent in both bodily and political life.[110] Whereas with the riots and the Civil Rights Movement, he had seen violence as a tool to open a space for political change, violence in the hands of the state had become monopolized for sustaining the status quo.[111]

In 1966, a trip to Vietnam "to observe, to listen and hopefully, to learn," unexpectedly "converted [Stringfellow] to radical opposition to the American war there."[112] Through observing troop movements and the Vietnamese people first-hand, Stringfellow came to the conclusion that the war in Vietnam was operating in the ideological manner in which he had initially critiqued nonviolence, namely, by presuming divine favor

> It is, for Americans, gruesomely dramatized in Vietnam, where the initial involvement and the subsequent escalations were so vainglorious, so certain of the commendation of God's judgment upon the nation,

109. Ibid., 247. Comparison with the work of Michel Foucault's work on the ways in which disciplinary power forms bodily actions, behaviors, and mindsets are instructive here. Cf. Michel Foucault, *Suveiller et Punir*, (Paris: Gallimard, 1975), trans. Alan Sheridan and reprinted as *Discipline and Punish*, (New York: Vintage Books, 1977).

110. "Why is Novak So Uptight?," *Christianity and Crisis* 30, November 30, 1970, 259.

111. "The Law, the Church, and the Needs of Society," *Proceedings of the Thirty-Second Annual convention of the Canon Law Society of America* (1970): 50: "It is a measure of the illegitimacy of the States' action in America today that official violence would seek to capture and confine the very citizens who have an influence to deter or mitigate the unofficial violence in this land."

112. *A Second Birthday*, 37, 40. As one who described his approach as "empirical," observing what the Word was doing in the world, such first-hand observation of the war provided a basis for opposition which ideology could not.

> so assertedly righteous that, now, to extricate the country's troops and wealth from the misadventure not only taxes the credibility of the nation but also ridicules the probity of God.[113]

But the nonviolent opposition to the war which Stringfellow had observed prior to his trip to Vietnam often lacked an explicitly Christian base.[114]

With the work of Daniel and Philip Berrigan, Stringfellow's mind began to change. Stringfellow's association with the Berrigans dated back at least to1965, prior to the Berrigans' rise to national prominence in 1968, when the Berrigans were involved in the burning of draft files with homemade napalm, in Catonsville, Maryland.[115] Following the Catonsville event, the Berrigans were tried on the charges of destruction of government property and interference with the Selective Service Act, and convicted;[116] rather than go to prison, however, Daniel Berrigan went underground,

113. Ibid., 87.
114. While "the Christian pacifist movement has been reactivated through the protests against the war," he noted that the churches as a whole "have been timid, tardy and vacuous in their reactions to this most gruesome war," in "An American Tragedy," *Christian Living* , January 1967, 32. Stringfellow's assessment of a lack of Christian nonviolent responses to war most likely reflects an ignorance of what movements were actually underway at that time. It was not until 1965 that a national organization of clergy opposed to Vietnam emerged, known as CALCAV (Clergy and Laity Concerned about Vietnam), and headed by Robert McAfee Brown. For a history of CALCAV, see Mitchell Hall, *Because of the Their Faith: CALCAV and Religious Opposition to the Vietnam War* (New York: Columbia University Press, 1990). But as we have seen with Yoder and Day already, American Christianity had a long history of nonviolence prior to Stringfellow. For a critical history of four of the most prominent national pacifist organizations (all of which date back to before the First World War), see Guenter Lewy, *Peace and Revolution: The Moral Crisis of American Pacifism* (Grand Rapids: W.B. Eerdmans Pub. Co, 1988).
115. In his elegy to Stringfellow, Daniel Berrigan provides no date for their initial meeting in "To Celebrate the Death and Life of William Stringfellow," *Religion and Intellectual Life* 2, no. 4 (Summer 1985): 71–74, simply saying that his friendship "dates notoriously from 1970." However, in 1965, Stringfellow wrote the introduction to Daniel Berrigan, *They Call Us Dead Men: Reflections on Life and Conscience* (New York: Macmillan Company, 1965), 11–13.
116. Stringfellow, *Suspect Tenderness: The Ethics of the Berrigan Witness* (New York: Holt, Reinhart and Winston, 1971), 117–18.

visiting Stringfellow and Towne's home on Block Island on numerous occasions prior to his arrest there on August 11, 1970.[117]

In many ways, Berrigan's approach was perfectly suited to usher Stringfellow into an affirmation of nonviolent resistance as consistent with his ecclesiology. As seen, resistance to death for Stringfellow is not escaping the world, but fully *embracing* the world as the location in which one dies in Christ and "listens to the Word"; Berrigan, likewise, articulated nonviolent resistance to war as "a kind of life outside the law of Death itself" which participates in Jesus' own life, describing nonviolence as a consequential kind of act which negates death and witnesses to new life.[118] In contrast to "death as a kind of universal military service," which corrupts God's intention for life, Berrigan argued that the nonviolent way of Jesus "preferred to suffer violence . . . rather than to inflict it on others."[119] Like Stringfellow, Berrigan was less concerned with the "conventional ethics" but rather with "how he and the others could most effectively perpetuate their witness against the war, their ministry for peace."[120] And while Stringfellow had complained that much nonviolence had been non-Christian in its adoption of Gandhian strategems, Daniel Berrigan had plotted to appeal to the Pope in the wake of the action, in order to draw the Church universal more directly into the struggle against the war.[121]

For Stringfellow, the conflict between the power of a militarized society and the Word of God in the world was displayed no place

117. Ibid. Stringfellow and Towne, subsequent to Daniel Berrigan's re-arrest, were charged with harboring a fugitive, though the charges were later dropped.

118. Ibid., 5. Cf., 51, Stringfellow's description of Berrigan's position: "The power of death is powerless in the face of the nonviolent intransigence of Christ."

119. Ibid., 6.

120. Ibid., 21.

121. Ibid., 22. Cf., ibid., 50: "Dan had met often with groups concerned to gather. These gatherings had been loosely in the form of what Christians like to call retreats. But the ingathering had been more ambitious than is customary within the caution of Christian tradition. The Body of Christ had been defined so exhaustively as to lack exclusions. Whoever breathed was welcome."

more clearly than in the clash between the United States government and the nonviolent witness of Daniel and Philip Berrigan. The treatment of the Berrigan brothers by the authorities was for Stringfellow exemplary of the government's attitude toward anyone who would attempt to mitigate the exercise of violence and Death.[122] The Berrigans' witness was for Stringfellow emblematic of the approach which the Church should embody in such times: confronting emissaries of death which endangered creaturely life through tactics which specifically counter the ability of the principality to perpetuate death[123]

> I am persuaded as a Christian that resort to violence to topple the idol of death in the state and in society invariably results in idolatry of death in some refurbished form. This is, in truth, the central theological issue of our time. It is the point at which ethics and eschatology meet, for if the practice of violence, even in the name of revolution, is hopeless, the practice of nonviolence, even where it seems unavailing, represents a most extraordinary hope.[124]

In sum, as a sign of the Word's work in the world, the nonviolence of the Berrigans witnesses to a Christian existence which counters the power of Death. Stringfellow's description of the Berrigans' act as "nonviolent" requires remembering that, for Stringfellow, violence is that which speaks of death (as in the case of the "violence of despair"), or that which moves people toward death (as in the case of the draft and the militarization of society). In other words, the involvement of Christians in resistance to death in ways which promote humanization in opposition to the dehumanization death, is, by

122. Ibid., 83–84.

123. Ibid., 51. Stringfellow specifically looks to the Berrigans' burning of draft cards as this kind of effective counter to the draft, one of the principalities of death. While the Church need not emulate the specific tactics of the Berrigans, Stringfellow thought that it should follow their lead in confronting the "illegitimacy in the State."

124. Stringfellow, "Harlem, Rebellion and Resurrection," *Christian Century* 87, no. 45 (November 11, 1970): 1348.

definition, not violent.[125] Whereas for Dorothy Day, the Catonsville action diverged from traditional nonviolence, in that nonviolence for her was part of a personalist vision leading to the formation of persons of conscience, for Stringfellow, the Catonsville action was the exemplification of nonviolence because of its negation of death's ability to extend into more corners of human life, by resisting the draft and destroying draft mechanisms.[126]

Following the Berrigan's arrest at Stringfellow's home, Stringfellow continued this argument, naming the nonviolent witness of the Berrigans as descriptive of "the resurrection in a political context," in contrast to the violence of the state, whose only sanction is Death.[127] The resurrection and the nonviolence of the resurrection community are affronts to the war-making State, in that "the resurrection exposes the subservience of the State to death as the moral purpose of the society which the State purports to rule." The Catonsville action, having taking care that their action not cause "violence or any harm to human beings," was done in opposition to

125. As Stringfellow would put it, "violence is the undoing of Creation," the clashing between the work of God and the work of fallen humanity. Stringfellow,"Must the Stones Cry Out?," *Christianity and Crisis*, October 30, 1972: 234. Stringfellow is able to name Daniel Berrigan's arson as a "nonviolent" act, in that the destruction of draft cards involved both the freedom of potential draftees away from death, and in doing so, did not destroy persons. Cf. Stringfellow and Town, *Suspect Tenderness*, 75: . . . "the Berrigan brothers . . . [had taken] effective precautions against their action causing violence or any harm to human beings . . ." Cf. Stringfellow, "The Acts of the Apostles (Continued)," *Christian Century* 98, no. 11 (April 1, 1981): 341-342, and Stringfellow, "The State, The Church and the Reality of Conscience," *IDOC Internazionale* 31, (September 11, 1971): 19–26.

126. One could also make the argument that, in negating the institutions which *de*-humanized society, Stringfellow's approach also emphasizes a kind of personalist attention analogous to Day.

127. *Suspect Tenderness*, 73. Cf., 61–64 for Stringfellow's sermon on Jesus as criminal, in October 1969, with the recently convicted Daniel Berrigan serving as the liturgist at the service. Linking Barabbas with violent revolutionaries such as the Weathermen, Stringfellow called the violent form of revolt "unrevolutionary" in this sermon, in that violent protest generates death rather than resisting it. By contrast, the revolution of Christ "is constantly welcoming the gift of human life, for himself and for all men, by exposing, opposing and overturning all that betrays, entraps, or attempts to kill human life," with militarization of national life as the occasion by which the truly Christian revolution can be named.

the death exemplified by war, with those participating in the action were subsequently persecuted by death.[128]

Tactically savvy in its execution, using forms which Day and Yoder were both unconformable with, Stringfellow's nonviolent resistance to the war was articulated as what would be appropriate to listening to the Word in *that* time, and with *that* place in view:

> Tactics cannot be severed from ethics, and imitation of the enemy is the most common way in which ideology has been confounded, idealism corrupted, and revolutions rendered futile. The Christian perseveres in nonviolent actions of protest and resistance—shunning whatever increases the work of death—in the hope of thereby calling into being new forms of life in society.[129]

These "new forms of life in society," seen in hope, were the undergirding justification for nonviolence, in that nonviolence bears witness to the renewal of world by the Word, seeking to preserve those aspects of creaturely life which allow for humanity to flourish:

> We persevere, as Christians, and, simply as human beings, in nonviolence. We do so whether or not the witness is understood or distinguished as such by the political authorities, and whether or not any revolutionaries advocating violence it effective. We do so because nonviolence has become the *only* way in America, today, to express hope for human life in society, and transcending that, to anticipate an eschatological hope.[130]

Through the nonviolent witness of the Berrigans, "an astonishing ecumenical community" had emerged as a witness to Christ's judgment of the world, though unnoticed by many church

128. Ibid., 75–76: "To fail or refuse to act against [the power of death incarnate in the State] amounts to an abdication of one's humanness, a renunciation of the gift of one's own life, as well as a rejection of the lives of other human beings . . . In the face of that the only way no matter how the State judges or what the State does—is to live in the authority over death which the resurrection is."
129. Ibid., 83–84.
130. Ibid., 111.

authorities. The Berrigans, through their nonviolent witness, Stringfellow argued, had been "in our midst improvising the Church," bearing witness to a new community—"a community of resurrection"—founded in resistance to a "common jeopardy . . . in order to live in a common hope as human beings."[131]

This statement by Stringfellow—that the Church is improvised in the form of this "community of resurrection" committed to the opposition of Death—turns us back to Stringfellow's ecclesiology. For nonviolence to be fully Christian, it must not simply bear witness to individual narratives, but to the formation of a people visible, in part, through the worship of the gathered church. As a form of action which 1) bears witness to the renewing work of the Word in the world, 2) refuses to be self-referrential, 3) operates in ways appropriate to the task of witness, and 4) yields judgment on the rightness of its form before the free and renewing Word, nonviolent resistance to war becomes the perfect analogue to Stringfellow's ecclesiology. As the church bore out "listening to the Word" in liturgical and institutional forms which were appropriate to the free Word who calls for the church out of death, so a nonviolence which recognizes its proper modality in light of the Word's work in society could be commended as well. These acts together for Stringfellow cohered as a single act of "listening to the Word," beholding and witnessing to the renewing work of God in the manifold contours of life.

To say that the church 'names' this nonviolent resistance does not mean that the church—as seen in Stringfellow's experience—is to take charge of it, or to circumscribe it. Insofar as the church is circumscribed by the activity of the Word and not vice versa, so nonviolent resistance to war is an act which the church *participates*

131. *Suspect Tenderness*, 113.

in, but does not claim ownership of. This being said, the church is called to name nonviolent resistance as an act analogous to its own constitution: witnessing, hopeful, outwardly-turned, and following the Word's lead. Insofar as the church attends to is character as the servant of the Word, having been redeemed by the Word, and formed by the Scriptures, the church remains able to name the Word's work in the totality of creation.

Conclusion

In the work of William Stringfellow, we find one whose theological vision helps us to see the ways in which resistance to war can easily be a mirror to the pathology which it seeks to resist. By describing creation as impinged upon by the powers of Death, Stringfellow offers a way to see how—if the church is to offer a witness against war which coheres to its best insights—both the church and its ethic must be chastened in their vision. To be of the church (and to resist war) for Stringfellow are bound together by the conviction that the world is populated by principalities and powers, and that the church—in its institutions and in its witness—is to see itself as offering a vision of redeemed humanity, a community of the resurrection.

Insofar as the Word of God is listened to in the liturgy, history, autobiographies, and Scripture, the church—while called to a certain mode of witness—is *not* called to controlling the direction that witness might take. As Stringfellow argued, to predetermine the direction which God might call God's people to act is to perpetuate the power of ideology, stating in advance what God will do. The church is called, in adherence to the Word, not to control the direction of the Word, but rather to join in with that work, to celebrate, and—as I have suggested—*name* it as the work of the Word. This last point, for Stringfellow, is critical, in that naming the work of God is a statement by the church that it cannot determine what the work of the Word is, but rather follows *after* it, describing the Word's work in the world according to Scripture.

Stringfellow's careful acceptance of nonviolence—enabled by the self-same Word as churchly existence—proves to be a challenging conception when laid over against the work of Day and Yoder. In contrast to Day and Yoder, Stringfellow refused to say that nonviolence is absolute, but a consequence of listening to the Word within the world, an act appropriate to resisting the idolatry of war. And as such, Stringfellow—as seen in his relationship with the Berrigans—is able to places with regards to his advocacy for nonviolent resistance which were unavailable to either Mennonite or Catholic traditions. Insofar as institutional concerns were prioritized over social witness, Stringfellow saw his own ecclesial traditions as defaulting on their call to listen to the Word, leaving the door open for him to exceed traditional Episcopalian insights.

In considering how to draw this framework into conversation with the figures already described then, Stringfellow's ambivalence toward the liturgical setting—either *as* the witness or *framing* the witness—becomes more of an issue. Because the basis of the church and the basis for nonviolent resistance to war are one and the same (the Word's movement), there is not for Stringfellow a stable foreground which can be assumed as with Yoder or Day; church tradition, to recall Stringfellow's words, "can be of no surety to us." What is a virtue for Stringfellow—the contingent nature of the church upon the Word—becomes a liability when establishing a dialogue among Christian traditions, in that not even Stringfellow's own tradition (as formative as it is for his own thinking) can be assumed; for Stringfellow, one's own thinking and tradition can easily morph into an ideology when left unexamined.

For Stringfellow, of course, the question of church unity is not found in formulations of tradition, but in "the orthodoxy of radical action," meaning that church union occurs when and where churches join together in celebration of the Word's redemption of the world, as an "event" and not a possession. To this, Day and Yoder would press the question of whether this sufficient: to what degree can one *name* the Word's work without first assuming some veracity of vocabulary given by the tradition? Stringfellow does not argue for a de-institutionalized or disembodied church—as this would be to reinscribe ideology into our thinking of church—but he does not grant such groundedness in the language of the tradition, willing to exceed the language and practice of the tradition without precedent. The willingness to improvise upon theological tradition is itself, of course, not without precedent, as seen in the work of Dorothy Day, but for Stringfellow, to truly "listen to the Word," one must be willing to risk the loss of the tradition's language itself in pursuit of the Word's empirical redemption.

The question of how to approach the goods of tradition will be taken up again in the book's conclusion, but for now, we will move to examine our final figure, Robert McAfee Brown. One of the seminal figures in the founding of CALCAV—an ecumenical organization committed to advocating against the Vietnam War—Brown was likewise committed to the church's involvement as a body of witness, but in a different mode than the figures considered thus far. Whereas Yoder, Day, and Stringfellow had much more *ad hoc* and tenuous relationships with governing bodies, Brown chose to work more directly with governing bodies, to bring ecclesial insights more directly to bear upon public policy. Brown's work, more than the previous figures, saw nonviolence as not simply a moral presumption of the churches, but as a possibility for public policy. It is to Brown's work that we now turn.

5

The Church *Supporting* Nonviolence: Robert McAfee Brown, CALCAV, and Worldly Ecumenicity

In this chapter, we turn to a fourth articulation of the relationship between ecclesiology and nonviolent resistance to war: church as supporting nonviolence. As the Vietnam War continued to unfold, the longstanding dissent of Yoder, Day, and Stringfellow was joined by a chorus of other voices; by 1965, the smaller protests of Catholics and Mennonites were joined by much larger Christian groups.[1] As the attention of more American churches turned from internal struggles over racial equality to questions of foreign policy and war, national groups such as the Student Nonviolent Coordinating

1. It is important to note that clerical protests against nuclear warfare occurred before this; in the early 1950s, the National Committee for a Sane Nuclear Policy (SANE) was formed, and the Federal Council of the Churches of Christ made statements on "The Christian Conscience and Weapons of Mass Destruction," See Michael B. Friedland, *Lift Up Your Voice Like a Trumpet: White Clergy and the Civil Rights and Antiwar Movements 1954–1973* (Chapel Hill: University of North Carolina Press, 1998), 142ff.

Committee (SNCC) and the National Council of Churches (NCC) began to issue statements and mobilize support for the burgeoning antiwar movement.[2]

Whereas clergy support for racial equality could claim a more straightforward rationale from Scripture, clergy support against involvement in the Vietnam War proved to be a much more difficult nut to crack.[3] Despite low clergy involvement overall, a new ecumenical witness against Vietnam began to emerge, coalescing Christians across denominational lines—the Clergymen's Emergency Committee for Vietnam (CEC). This new movement, later known as Clergy and Laity Concerned about Vietnam (CALCAV), became a key voice in bringing an ecumenical church voice to bear on issues long addressed by other pockets of American Christians.

In this chapter, I will focus on one of the key figures in CALCAV, Robert McAfee Brown, who connects the ecumenical life of the churches to their common witness against the war. Like Stringfellow, Brown would not describe himself as a pacifist for reasons that I will soon detail. Brown also found himself compelled (like Stringfellow) to oppose the war in Vietnam, marshaling support of the ecumenical church for policies and societal actions that would end the war without the use of violence. Through his own writings and through

2. See SNCC, "Student Nonviolent Coordinating Committee Position Paper: On Vietnam," (position statement, The Sixties Project, 1993), http://www2.iath.virginia.edu/sixties/HTML_docs/Resources/Primary/Manifestos/SNCC_VN.html. On the activities of the NCC (National Council of Churches), see Jill K. Gill, *Embattled Ecumenism: The National Council of Churches, the Vietnam War, and the Trials of the Protestant Left* (Dekalb, IL: Northern Illinois University Press, 2011).

3. The reasons behind low clergy involvement in opposition to Vietnam (by some estimates as low as 5 percent) remain difficult to generalize. See Richard John Neuhaus, "The War, the Churches, and Civil Religion," *Annals of the American Academy of Political and Social Science* 387 (January 1970): 135–42. Most denominations, however, retained groups that registered official opposition to Vietnam regardless of clergy participation rates. See also Michael B. Friedland, "Breaking Silence: Churches and Opposition to the Vietnam War, 1964–1975," vol. 3 of *The Cambridge History of Religions in America*, 1st ed., ed. Stephen J. Stein (Cambridge: Cambridge University Press, 2012), 170–86.

his work with CALCAV, Brown articulatea a strong relationship between the church's unity and the nonviolent, though not pacifist, witness of the church.

Brown's work opens up an area left relatively unexplored by the previous thinkers. In what ways can an ecclesially-framed witness against war find allegiance with public policy or non-Christian forms of resistance? In the Vietnam context as well as in situations today, many protests and responses to war are offered independently of the congregational setting and apart from theological language. In connecting the ecumenical movement to the larger *oikumene* (household) of human life, Brown offers a compelling, though not entirely unproblematic, vision of the church's participation in public, intraorganizational, and non-fideist forms of advocacy against war. In terms of the larger project of this book, bringing Brown's work into conversation with Yoder, Day, and Stringfellow begs the question concerning how ecclesiology informs nonviolent witness against war in relation to public policy, not by its direct action but by its support of public sector actions.[4] In contrast to the previous figures—whose particular denominational ecclesiologies frame their resistance to war—Brown presents us with an argument for how the nature of Protestant ecclesiology more broadly connects to a nonviolent, ecumenical witness in times of war.

Brown, the son of a Presbyterian minister, came of age on the American East Coast and was educated at Amherst College, Union Theological Seminary, and Oxford University. With teachers such as Henry Fosdick, Reinhold Niebuhr, and Paul Tillich, Brown was steeped in theological liberalism, convinced that if theology was

4. This dimension of Brown's thought remains largely marginalized within studies on his work. For example, in the *Spiritual Masters* series published by Orbis Books, the volume devoted to Brown's writings makes no mention of his ecumenical work in the introduction, nor are any of Brown's ecumenically-oriented works included in the volume. See Paul Crowley, ed., *Robert McAfee Brown: Spiritual and Prophetic Writings* (Maryknoll, NY: Orbis Books, 2013).

to address public life, it must be willing to support secular approximations of the church's truths in support of human life.[5] Reflecting certain tenets of Reinhold Niebuhr's thought, Brown argues that churches cannot presume a direct line between the ethics of Christ and life in the world; churches are not called to directly implement their confessional vision but to partner with society in provisional and *ad hoc* ways, looking toward the common good and watching for the ways in which God's appearance may be hidden and refracted in history.

Brown was a theological polymath, writing extensively on ecumenism, liberation theology, theological language, ecclesiology, and ethics. However, his primary contribution to our discussion comes from his argument that the church does not so much directly provide an alternative to war as it does embed itself ecumenically within a broader coalition of witnesses against war. In other words, the end of Christian social witness is the church's offer of practical political and material support to broad-based nonviolent movements and public policies that offer nonviolent alternatives to war more than it is merely framing or embodying nonviolent resistance.

Ecclesiology: Christ, the Protestant Church and the End of Ecumenical Witness

As I will detail, Brown's vision of the relationship between ecclesiology and nonviolence turns on his description of the church's vocation as an ecumenically-oriented body. Like Stringfellow, Brown travelled tirelessly both as an observer for the Presbyterian church and as a participant in a number of the twentieth century's

5. For Brown's account of his formative years at Amherst College and Union, see *Reflections over the Long Haul: A Memoir* (Louisville: Westminster John Knox, 2005), particularly 1–80. For a shorter synopsis of Brown's life, see Linda Glenn, "Robert McAfee Brown: Presbyterian, Theologian, Activist," *American Presbyterian* 72 (1994): 49–59; Paul Crowley, introduction to Crowley, *Robert McAfee Brown,* 1–17.

most important ecumenical discussions, including Vatican II and the 1968 World Council of Churches meeting in Uppsala. Before exploring Brown's ecumenical ecclesiology—and in particular, how Brown orders the ecumenical life of the churches toward engagement with the world—I will briefly narrate the ways in which Brown's ecclesiology is deeply shaped by two influences: Reinhold Niebuhr and P.T. Forsyth.

Reinhold Niebuhr, who preached Brown's ordination sermon and represents a prominent influence during Brown's seminary career, would have been an imposing figure to any seminarian at Union Theological Seminary between 1943 and 1945.[6] For Brown, who came to Union after completing a thesis on the Quaker understanding of pacifism, the challenge of Niebuhr and longtime Union professor John C. Bennett to Brown's social ethics was nothing short of life-altering. As Brown writes, Niebuhr's writings undermined any form of pacifism that would have left Brown with "clean hands and a pure heart," while denying the luxury of pacifism to those who had no choice as to whether or not to go to war.[7]

This challenge to Brown's pacifism includes the fruit of a deeper theological inheritance from Niebuhr: the rejection of an ecclesiology that preserves its moral purity at the expense of its social engagement.[8] In place of the forms of witness that Brown believed emphasized the moral purity of the witnessing body, he adopted an understanding of ecclesiology that is much more embedded within society—a willingness to shoulder blame in order to minister to one's neighbor. Reflecting on his decision to become a Navy chaplain

6. For an analysis of Niebuhr's tenure at Union Seminary, and particularly the intersection of his work with Tillich's during that time, see Ronald H. Stone, *Politics and Faith: Reinhold Niebuhr and Paul Tillich at Union Seminary in New York* (Macon, GA: Mercer University Press, 2012).

7. Brown, *Reflections*, 38–39. Brown frequently draws upon Niebuhr's work, as in "To the Defense of Reinhold Niebuhr," *Christian Century* (January 30, 1963): 142–43.

8. Brown, *Reflections*, 39–40

during the Second World War, Brown displays the Christological roots inherent in this vision of the church:

> My response centered on where God is to be found in that evil world. My answer: God was to be found in the midst of all the evil—not apart from it. What is it like for God to be situated in the midst? We have a picture of what God is like, a picture of a man hanging on a cross. . . . The picture tells us that God asks nothing that God will not also endure. So God is in the foxhole, in the Jeep. God is in the bomber screeching down in flames . . . God is a vulnerable God, sharing the human predicament with us.[9]

For Niebuhr, descriptions of the church are inseparable from an account of history that emphasizes both the presence of the church in history and the disjunction of historical agency from eschatological perfection.[10] Though Niebuhr's vision of history is permeated by a kind of tragedy in which ecclesial performances are frustrated by the limits of human action, churches are not left wringing their hands, unable to minister.[11] Khurram Hussein argues that while Niebuhr's moral realism acknowledges the limits of human acts, it also assumes a kind of moral freedom in which humans are capable of transcending their historical finitude by envisioning and enacting alternatives to presently insurmountable problems.[12] I will return to Brown's understanding of war and peace shortly, but here, it is important to note that this ecclesiology links together situations of intimate concern for Christian witness and the church's own form. To paraphrase Jennifer McBride, Christian solidarity with the world

9. Ibid., 41.
10. As Ruth L. Smith argues, Niebuhr's vision of history bears within it a tension, in that history is described as that which forms and limits human agency but also that which is devalued in light of transcendence, in "Reinhold Niebuhr and History: The Elusive Liberal Critique," *Horizons* 15 (Fall 1988): 283–98.
11. Khurram Hussain, "Tragedy and History in Reinhold Niebuhr's Thought," *American Journal of Theology and Philosophy* 31 (2010): 147–59.
12. Ibid., 155–56. See also Robin Lovin, *Reinhold Niebhur and Christian Realism* (Cambridge: Cambridge University Press, 1995).

means embracing the frailties of history in which the church forsakes its own moral purity and internal sanctity in the pursuit of solidarity with suffering.[13]

Though Brown adopts his mentor's ecclesiological vision, he rejects Niebuhr's vision of history's tragedy; according to Brown, the church looks to history "not as a meaningless, tragic jumble of events, but the arena in which God is at work."[14] Though he agrees with Niebuhr that the church's perfection is ultimately eschatological, Brown retains a more positive evaluation of God's direct involvement in history—and thus, the church's role within history—than Niebuhr would often grant.[15] Holding that Christ's work is present not only as a critical apparatus over against historical agency but also as a providential force within history, Brown transposes Niebuhr's prophetic ecclesiology into history, to the extent that Niebuhr might have seen it as a return to a liberal ecclesiology. For Brown, insofar as "the race set out before [the church]" is one of witness in history, Christians are free (as Niebuhr argues) to make use of more local forms of witness (giving to the needy) and more national forms of agency (political power).[16] Unlike Niebuhr, history (in all of its dimensions) is to be taken seriously as the arena of God's ongoing work, insofar as Christians follow the risen Christ, who sacramentally infuses history.[17]

13. Jennifer McBride, *The Church for the World: A Theology of Public Witness* (Oxford: Oxford University Press, 2011), 14–19.
14. Brown, "Eschatological Hope and Social Responsibility," *Christianity and Crisis* 13 (1953): 146–49.
15. For Niebuhr, the church cannot claim moral purity for itself because it participates in a fallen history that cannot fully embody the ideals of Christ prior to the eschaton. On this, see Reinhold Niebuhr, *Moral Man and Immoral Society: A Study in Ethics and Politics* (New York: Charles Scribner's Sons, 1935); *An Interpretation of Christian Ethics* (Louisville: Westminster John Knox, 2013), 101–37; *Faith and History: A Comparison of Christian and Modern Views of History* (New York: Charles Scribner's Sons, 1949). On the paradox of Niebuhr's view of history, see Arne Rasmussen, "'The Curious Fact That . . . the Lord Always Puts Us on the Just Side': Reinhold Niebuhr, America and Christian Realism," *Studia Theologica* 66 (2012): 41–61.
16. Brown, "Eschatological Hope," 148.

Brown is able to adopt Niebuhr's critical ecclesiology of a more providential vision of history (without slipping back into the liberalism criticized by Niebhur), I suggest, because of the Christology which he marries to Niebuhr's social analysis. Whereas Niebuhr could be read as seeing in Christ only an embodiment of an eschatological logic—an "impossible possibility" that could not be manifested within time and space—Brown sees Christ as the One who overcomes the gap between history and eternity, invading history with an alien Gospel capable of disrupting history's injustices.[18] Brown found this Christology in the work of P.T. Forsyth, whose work Brown discovered during doctoral work at Columbia following his graduation from Union and service in the Navy.

As the subject of Brown's doctoral work, P.T. Forsyth holds to the strong doctrine of sin found in Niebuhr, but Brown believes that Forstyth corrects the one-sidedness of these "neo-orthodox" theologies that, having distinguished God from humanity, do not adequately reconnect the infinite God to finite creation.[19] While agreeing with Niebuhr's distinction between God and the world, Forsyth (a "Barthian before Barth") emphasizes the manner in which the grace of God through Christ initiates an actuality of God's work in the world, such that the distinction between God and the world

17. Ibid., 149.
18. Niebuhr, *An Interpretation*, 58. Brown reads a positive—rather than simply formal—Christology throughout Niebuhr's corpus, in "Defense," 143. This is in contrast to the more recent claim by Stanley Hauerwas that Niebuhr's Christology is more formal than substantive, in Hauerwas, *With the Grain of the Universe: The Church's Witness and Natural Theology* (Grand Rapids: Brazos, 2001), 124–31. Part of this dual reading of Niebuhr can be attributed to the sources being mined; Brown draws from the *Nature and Destiny of Man,* 2 vols.(Louisville: Westminster John Knox, 1996) and *Beyond Tragedy* (New York: Charles Scribner's Sons, 1938) in his defense of Niebuhr's Christology, while Hauerwas reads Niebuhr predominately in light of *An Interpretation* (though he also draws from *Nature and Destiny* to a lesser degree).
19. Brown, *P.T. Forsyth: Prophet for Today* (Philadelphia: Westminster, 1952), 11.

is preserved but is also overcome through Christ's work, infusing history with a christologically-meaningful character.[20]

Forsyth's theology is rooted in an encounter between God and humanity that can only be provisionally put into language, theological or otherwise. Again, the difficulty of using language to express this encounter is central to a theology that prioritizes divine agency. In Brown's description, Forsyth asserts that Christology and christological redemption cannot be proved by language or argument but only revealed in and through the experience of redemption, to which witnesses then attest.[21] This encounter of the living God and humanity is one of "the union of wills," making the Gospel not simply an eschatological possibility but a transformative actuality in the world; likewise, faith is an ongoing and self-involving affair that can never claim to definitively encapsulate the significance of Christ and Christ's work.

Made known in the proclamation of the Scriptures in the church, Christ "gives a vantage point from which to see all else"; the world, which stands "redeemed by the power of Word," is the calling of the church, and the church is the starting point of Christ's redemptive work in creation but not the end of that work.[22] Having been redeemed in Christ, the world is "freely raising questions that only the gospel can answer." Far from being a neo-liberal affirmation of history, Forsyth sees history's validity as the consequence of christological work.[23]

Because of the distinction between God and creation (maintained in the Incarnation) as well as the distinction between the church's experience of Christ and the language used to express it, Forsyth argues that Christian witness occurs not by repeating Christ but by

20. Ibid., 33–45.
21. Ibid., 73.
22. Ibid., 54.
23. Ibid., 61.

living and ministering *in light of* Christ. The moral key to this witness is not that Christians are required to duplicate Christ's ethics but to inhabit a theological existence that calls for recurrently novel forms of witness consistent with, though not identical to, Christ's own life. In Brown's words, the teachings of Christ are "part of the revelation, but they are not the whole revelation . . . We cannot distill out of Jesus' teaching any sort of final social blueprint."[24] For the early Christians, Christ made "new men, not a series of ethical aphorisms"—freed in a way that always attended to God's work in history.[25] Thus, Forsyth notes that making the "new life" of the Gospel visible in the world means changing the economic and political order to deal with previously unseen systemic sins that now oppose the free theological existence found in Christ, not simply issuing forth moral platitudes.[26]

With Niebuhr, Forsyth maintains that creation suffers from grave effects of sin, but unlike Niebuhr, he asserts that a Christology "invasive" to history is not ontologically limited by sin. As such, history can be understood as the arena of God's activity, calling for Christians to enact provisional witness for the Kingdom of God in the language, vocations, and structures available to them in keeping with Christ's ongoing act in history.[27] For Forsyth (and thus for Brown), nothing can be more deeply christological than living out a life of constructive criticism of the world in service to God. Insofar as time is the vehicle of God's revelation, history is taken up as the indispensible backdrop of God's work, a time in which Christians act in witness to Christ's work.[28] In this framework, the church remains the proclaimer of the Gospel, encountering Christ in and through the sacraments and the Word and proceeding in faith from the

24. Ibid., 119. As Brown says, "The Christian lives in Christ, rather than like Christ" (114).
25. Ibid., 120.
26. Ibid., 122–25.
27. Ibid., 127.
28. Ibid., 136ff.

church into the world under the guidance of the Spirit. The church's encounter with Christ enables it to enter the world as Christ's agents, "not to provide schemes but to remake men, and give them the power and motivation by which to develop social schemes."[29] This, Brown argues, is the church's catholic heart—not a common polity but a common proclamation of Christ's work in history.[30]

The influence of the gathered church's liturgy and confession upon society will "be largely indirect," given the task of "[providing] the principles upon the basis of which crises can be met and also to provide the men who can make skillful and intelligent use of the principles" by elucidating the deepest christological ground of creation that allows Christians to meet history's questions enabled by Christ's work. Brown writes that Forsyth's truism "contains within it a great lesson for contemporary Protestantism."[31]

The claim that the church's political advocacy—in both act and word—takes on a different form once it enters into public discourse is, for Brown, the upshot of Forsyth's Christology. Forsyth's understanding of the redemptive work of Christ as experiential, rooted in an I-Thou encounter of God and humanity, demands a corresponding distinction between the experience of grace and the language used to describe and bear witness to it.[32] The relation of encounter between God and humanity, which does not collapse the God-creation distinction, is borne out in an approach to witness; in the same ways that Christians cannot conflate theological language with the existential encounter with God, so Christians cannot conflate the life of the church (the place of confessional language)

29. Ibid., 168. See also Brown, "When the Church Speaks Out," *Christianity and Crisis* 14, no. 3 (1954): 17–19.
30. Brown, *P.T. Forsyth*, 163–65.
31. Ibid. 167.
32. Ibid., 49. By noting the differences between first-order dogmatic claims and theology—what Brown calls "a further step toward the tentative"—he distinguishes between Scripture's authoritative testimony and the language that describes the Christian journey of faith (ibid., 46).

with their lives of witness in the world (the place of political judgment). Called into the world for the sake of the Kingdom of God, Christians enter into the world aware that churchly language and confession—though not abandoned—cannot be used without conflating God and creation.

These central ecclesiological motifs of Forsyth's thought—the Christological renewal of history and the subsequent missional nature of the church—become key notes within Brown's own thinking. As Brown learned well from Niebuhr, this reformation of society amidst the difficulty of history cannot be properly undertaken by Christians unless they remember that they live in Christ but not identical with Christ, such that their language and acts are formed by Christ but will most often take the form of provisional alliances and broad-based public engagements.[33]

These intertwining concerns of ecclesial life and political activism began to take shape for Brown upon his graduation from Columbia when he briefly took a position at Macalester College and subsequently began to campaign for the Catholic Eugene McCarthy (much to the chagrin of his Protestant colleagues).[34] For Brown, the public opposition to McCarthy on the basis of his Catholicism was indicative that (in Forsyth's terms) not only had the orientation of Christians toward common witness in history been lost within Protestant life but artificial theological divisions separated Protestants and Catholics in their common call to action on behalf of the Kingdom of God. As Brown commented later, "My entrance into ecumenism—the problems of restoring a divided church—was

33. Reflecting on his work on the congressional campaign for Eugene McCarthy, Brown notes that Christian theology's contribution to political judgment reminds "us constantly that all men are sinners. . . . that all men are created in the image of God . . . Let the political neophyte be reminded that everything stands under the judgment of God and that no final and unconditioned loyalties can be given to any candidate or political party or party platform," in Brown, "Confessions of a Political Neophyte," *Christianity and Crisis* 12 (1953): 189.

34. Brown, *Reflections*, 75–79.

through the door of politics. That is a reality that has been full of special meaning throughout the rest of my life, and because of the coming together of those two strands, I refuse to believe that religion and politics can be separated from one another."[35] In 1953, Brown returned to Union Seminary as the Auburn Assistant Professor of Systematic Theology, marking a new era in which he began to bring his ecclesiology to bear on burgeoning public problems, including militarization. From this point forward, Brown asserts that the reunion of the divided church is integral to the church's mission.

The Road to an Ecumenical Ecclesiology: History, Dialogue, and Common Witness

Upon moving to Union Seminary in 1953, Brown's writings turned increasingly to ecclesiology and eventually to intramural dialogue with Catholicism.[36] In light of his experience at Macalester, he found it insufficient to think of "Protestant" as an insular tradition but rather one that is irreducibly related to Roman Catholicism in the divine economy. For Brown, ecclesiological formation is the indispensible presupposition for thinking about Christ's work in the world, insofar as Christians are shaped to be participants in God's work in history through their lives in the church. However, Brown had yet to fully work out how, for Protestants, an ecclesial witness is irreducibly an

35. Ibid., 78.
36. For an overview of the trajectory of Brown's ecumenical writings, see John T. Carmody, "The Development of Robert McAfee Brown's Ecumenical Thought," *Religion in Life* 43 (1974): 283–93. Dominating Brown's writing, the theme of ecumenism has scarcely been explored in the secondary literature on Brown, which focuses more on Brown's post-Vietnam work involving liberation theology. As I have noted throughout this book, the division of a theologian from their social witness is a common tendency in the secondary literature on other figures as well. The festschrift for Brown contains no essays on Brown's ecumenism, see Denise Lardner Carmody and John Tully Carmody, ed., *The Future of Prophetic Christianity* (Maryknoll, NY: Orbis Books, 1993). Likewise, the edited collection *Robert McAfee Brown: Spiritual and Prophetic Writings*, ed. Paul Crowley (Maryknoll, NY: Orbis Books, 2013) contains no selections from any of Brown's ecumenical or ecclesiological writings.

ecumenical one. During this time, in which he served as both an official participant in the World Council of Churches and an observer at the Second Vatican Council, Brown began to link together the need for ecumenical discussion with the context in which unified Christian confession is borne out: social action.

After moving to Union from Macalester, Brown's first ecclesiological writings are concerned primarily with explicating a fully Protestant doctrine of the church, with only occasional concern for ecumenism. For Brown, the contemporary church stands in direct continuity with Scripture, insofar as the Scriptures describe the ongoing drama of the Holy Spirit (of which the contemporary church is part), creating a revolutionary situation for today's church.[37] During this time, a question is raised that will haunt his ecclesiology: the nature of the church vis-à-vis tradition. As we have seen with Day, tradition contains valuable resources, but it also has the potential to be selective in terms of the implications of a Christian social witness. However, as Brown claims, if the church is fundamentally the body that encounters Christ—in light of that encounter formed toward witness—the riches of tradition are an open question. Far from being an academic exercise, the question of how much weight to give the witness of previous generations hypothetically creates a problem for an ecclesiology fundamentally narrated as the existential encounter of God and humanity.

As a witness to the Spirit's past work, tradition is a gift to the churches for Brown, forming and informing them in the "principles" by which they should act. However, the church still tends to conflate the wisdom of the past with God's present act. Insofar as Brown describes the Spirit's work as one that grasps the individual in an existential encounter of faith, there remains an uneasy relationship

37. Brown, *The Bible Speaks to You* (Philadelphia: Westminster, 1955), 72. See also Brown, *The Significance of the Church* (Philadelphia: Westminster, 1956), 43–44.

between the traditions that accompany the act of faith and the act of faith itself. Because the Spirit's work is primarily through the life of the regenerated individual (and only derivatively through the institutions and practices in which a person participates), the church can never assume to have fully actualized the moral principles of Scripture in institutional or traditional form. Moral deliberation by the church—formed by the principles of Scripture—enters into contextual deliberation concerning what a Christian moral witness means today, insofar as the encounter of Christ is an ongoing act that tradition can explicate but not replicate. In the same way that the ongoing encounter and person is the basis for thinking about the church's place within the world, so this encounter forms the basis for thinking about the value of liturgical life.[38]

Though it draws upon tradition, the church finds its sacramental outworking not simply in its celebrations of worship but "as it concerns itself in love with the lives of men."[39] The church's sacraments of bread, wine, and water are "enactments of the gospel," dramatizing the Word made flesh. In participation with one another in these elements, Brown writes that we take part in a service that "underlines the significance of our everyday lives" in which the people of God are called to serve their neighbors.[40] Put differently, the church's sacramental celebration of its status as "holy" and "one," (signified in bread, wine, and water) is inseparable from its unified social witness, with the sacraments acting as a foretaste of the church's vocation to the world. To the extent that the church is ordered

38. The ongoing reception of the "Word made flesh" in history presents new and ongoing challenges to the church that cannot be answered in terms of Biblicism, nor by appeals to tradition. As Scripture indicates, the response of Christians involves "community ethics," that emerge from their common lived life, in Brown, *Bible Speaks to You*, 244ff.

39. Brown, *Significance of the Church*, 50.

40. Ibid., 73–74.

toward the world, any assessment of ecclesiology—Protestant or Catholic—must have that witness as its backdrop.

Unsurprisingly, Brown's early forays into Protestant-Catholic dialogues identify the issues of social influence and witness as areas (on the popular level) most readily dividing Protestants and Catholics.[41] In Brown's half of *An American Dialogue*, co-authored with Catholic Gustave Weigel, he raises questions concerning traditionally divisive ecumenical issues such as Mariology, the authority of the Pope, and the nature of Tradition. Yet, what permeates Brown's analysis of ecumenical division is the persistent Protestant conception of Catholics as inattentive to issues of social inequity; for example, the Leonine Catholic approach is described as being open to the marginalization of non-Catholics in the attempt to create a more just social order.[42]

In emphasizing the way in which social witness inhibits ecumenical unity, Brown is not simply moving toward a purely pragmatic ecumenism that glosses over significant theological differences or that asks Catholics to "stop being Catholic."[43] For Brown, denominations do not represent "historical phenomenon incidental to the full ordering of the Gospel"; since we approach God and the world as historical beings, denominations and traditions cannot simply be bypassed en route to common action and confession.[44] That being said, ecumenism cannot avoid the ways in which liturgical unity (common worship and prayer) are linked with

41. Robert McAfee Brown and Gustave Weigel, *An American Dialogue: A Protestant Looks at Catholicism and a Catholic Looks at Protestantism* (Garden City, NY: Doubleday, 1960).
42. Ibid., 57. The issue of religious freedom emerges repeatedly in light of statements by leading Catholics in the 1940s who advocated prudential denial of religious freedom to non-Catholics in places where Catholics constituted the majority. See *Civiltà Cattolica*, April 3, 1948, cited in *American Dialogue*, 56–57. See also John Bennett, *Christians and the State* (New York: Charles Scribner's Sons, 1958), 105ff; and particularly John Courtney Murray, *Religious Liberty: Catholic Struggles with Pluralism* (Louisville: Westminster John Knox, 1993).
43. Brown, "That All May Be One," *Christianity and Crisis* 12 (1952): 59–62.
44. Brown, "The Emerging Ecumenical Complex," *Theology Today* 20 (1964): 530–31.

common acts of witness such as joint practices of feeding the poor and surrendering political visions that would oppress another branch of the Christian family.[45]

This proposal, which links together the church's *internal* confessional unity with unified external and public witness, is not surprising given the links that Brown has already drawn between the life of worship and the life in the world in Protestant ecclesiology. In his early work, Brown notes that the most prophetic movements of the church are likewise some of the most ecumenical in their orientation toward "a fresh discovery of the Gospel"—by which Brown means they recover the Gospel as an encounter of faith between God and humanity, in Christ, led historically to joint social action.[46] Once this common core of the Gospel is named—as faith in and through Christ worked out and witnessed to in the world—issues such as Mariology and papal authority can be productively discussed.[47]

Similar remarks permeate Brown's report from the Second Vatican Council—that the "prophetic concern of the bishops for the state of the world" will, with their Protestant counterparts, lead to "mutual contrition and a mutual forgiveness, [and] a willingness for both partners to walk along a new path together, not quite sure where it will lead, but willing to walk with a certain amount of risk because of the assurance that the Holy Spirit is taking the lead."[48] Such

45. Brown and Weigel, *American Dialogue*, 113.

46. See Brown, *Significance of the Church,* 94–95. Interestingly, Brown cites the East Harlem Protestant Parish (where William Stringfellow was employed during this period) as an example of prophetic Protestantism. As we have seen, Stringfellow had a much different evaluation of the EHPP than Brown.

47. Brown and Weigel, *American Dialogue*, 122–23. As Brown notes in his *Observer in Rome: A Protestant Report on the Vatican Council* (Garden City, NY: Doubleday, 1964), 173: "I do not think there is a single thing the Council can do that will have more *immediate* effect in bettering Catholic-Protestant relations than a forthright and unambiguous statement favoring full religious liberty for all." This movement by the Catholic Church was seen as an act of good faith inviting further discussion of theological differences (*Observor in Rome,* 174; italics mine).

48. Brown, *Observer in Rome*, 249.

partnerships with Protestants are not replacements for difficult ecumenical dialogue but, potentially, could be a common witness that bears out a proleptic unity between "separated brethren" and a foretaste of deeper unity. Though Christians remain divided on issues of sacrament and ministry, "there are other matters about which Christians on the road to unity should be able to say something that Christians going their separate ways cannot."[49] Though ecumenism is commonly considered to work from doctrine to social witness, ecumenism could conceivably work in the opposite direction. In Brown's estimation, unity in Mariology is possible, though further off than the immediate possibility that Christians can unify in their witness against racism, anti-Semitism, and nuclear war.[50]

During the ecumenical discussions of the 1960s, it became increasingly clear to Brown that the approach he considered to be the Protestant solution to ecumenism was not being taken by the modern ecumenical movement, which had typically bracketed concerns of social witness from dialogues relating to dogmatic concerns; both Vatican II's *Mater et Magistra* and the World Council of Churches were guilty on this point.[51] In viewing dogmatic concerns as separate from social witness, both Catholics and Protestants had come to view the missional nature of the church as adjunct to ecclesiology—the

49. Brown, "The Road to Unity," *Christianity and Crisis* 21 (October 30, 1961): 179.

50. Ibid., 179. See also Brown, "Jews, Christians, and Human Beings," *Christianity and Crisis* 22, vol. 7 (April 30, 1962): 62. Brown's assessment of Vatican II on ecumenism was favorable in this respect, in that it explicitly couches intrafraternal arguments about doctrine against ongoing common action in areas of famine, poverty, and economics, in Brown, *The Ecumenical Revolution* (Garden City, NY: Doubleday, 1967), 308ff.

51. On *Mater et Magistra*, see Brown, "An American Protestant View," *Cross Currents* 12, no. 2 (Spring 1962): 236. While it reiterates the teaching of Leo XIII—with a particular eye toward contemporary issues of wages, economic development, and remuneration—*Mater et Magistra* does so without consideration of these acts as opportunities for ecumenical partnership. Though they address the common good in passing, para. 102, 146, and 151 of *Mater et Magistra* do not make reference to joining with Protestants in these ventures. See John XXIII, *Mater et Magistra* [Encyclical on Christianity and Social Progress], Vatican Website, May 15, 1961, http://www.vatican.va/holy_father/john_xxiii/encyclicals/documents/hf_j-xxiii_enc_15051961_mater_en.html.

social witness of Christians as an addition to ecclesiology, rather than as an intrinsic property of it. The internal debates over proper polity within both Catholic and Protestant traditions had thus, in Brown's estimation, led to a misunderstanding of both ecumenism and the internal dynamics of ecclesiology.[52]

As represented by the World Council of Churches, the modern ecumenical movement began at the 1910 Edinburgh meeting of the World Conference of Missionary Societies out of the recognition that fraternal divisions on the mission field were limiting any church's effectiveness. Divided into two major areas—Faith and Order (which discusses intrafraternal doctrinal divisions) and Life and Work (which focuses on social, political, and ethical issues)—the World Council of Churches (WCC) began to discuss the themes in separate working groups, bringing them together at the major world assemblies. But though both issues of doctrinal and ethical significance were given attention at the assemblies, the concerns of Faith and Order received the lion's share of attention, according to Brown.[53]

By not seeing the proper form of Christ's sacramental mediation and the Christian's social witness as part of the same cloth (as Brown did), both Protestant and Catholic participants in these discussions misunderstood the theological economy within which the sacraments are placed, dividing the initiatory work of the sacraments from their witness in the world. As we have seen in Brown's work, because the work of God in Christ occurs in faith outworked in the world, liturgical life cannot be thought of as an entirely different species than worldly life, meaning that the "what" of dogma and liturgy cannot be considered apart from the "what" of the ecumenical mission—the redemption of humanity in Christ.[54]

52. Brown argues that the polemical debates of the Reformation seldom resonate with the thousands of churches emerging in the developing world. See Brown, *Significance of the Church*, 94.

53. Brown, "Uppsala: An Informal Report," *Journal of Ecumenical Studies* 5 (1968): 636.

In the years following Vatican II, Brown began to observe a shift in the attention of ecumenical discussions as they turned more and more toward "common ventures for the sake of the world" and created a new era of "secular ecumenism"—not only among Christians but with Jewish and secular groups as well.[55] The WCC meeting of 1966 signaled "the beginning of a new era in ecumenism" in which churches began turning their focus outward again, reconnecting mission to the internal life of the church in such a way that ecumenical discussions of inward unity could not take place apart from considerations of how best to bear witness to Christ in the midst of the challenges of the 1960s.[56]

Brown's move from Union Seminary to Stanford in 1962 accompanies the shift in his writing, as he began to move away from writing only on the proper internal conditions of the Protestant church and toward an ecclesiology interlaced with ecumenical witness. His new appointment in the Religious Studies department took him out of a confessional setting and placed him amidst secular colleagues with whom he found common cause in civil rights and war.[57] Describing his relocation from Union to Stanford as a move "from Jerusalem to Athens," Brown found himself forced to consider the true nature of ecumenism as witness to the world.[58] For Brown,

54. Brown, *Significance of the Church,* 88–90. As Brown writes, it remains a perennial temptation that "faith acting in love is secured and is replaced by moral codes. . . . The church becomes so intent to preserve its own way of doing things. . . . that it fails to notice its way of doing things is not reaching people" (89–90). Brown went so far as to suggest that "mission" be described as one of the marks of the church, in "True and False Witness: Architecture and the Church," *Theology Today* 23 (1967): 521–37. This argument has been echoed by John Flett as a proper reading of Karl Barth's theology of mission in John Flett, *The Witness of God: The Trinity,* Missio Dei, *Karl Barth, and the Nature of Christian Community* (Grand Rapids: Eerdmans, 2010).

55. Brown, *Ecumenical Revolution,* 309–10. Brown also names this as a kind of "practical ecumenism" (311). We will use both terms going forward to describe this trend.

56. Brown, "Uppsala," 638.

57. Brown, *Reflections over the Long Haul,* 115–22. During this time, Brown became increasingly involved with the Freedom Rides of the Civil Rights movement as well with the growing shadow of the Vietnam War. See Brown, "Further Reflections on Freedom Riding," *Christianity and Crisis* 21 (August 7, 1961): 146–47. See also *Reflections,* 92–105.

the catholicity of the church is worked out inseparably from its common confession of the transformative grace of God being worked out in the world, a world already borne by the redemption of Christ. Because of this, the "full ordering of the Gospel" also involves a corresponding willingness to see ecumenism as working not only *on behalf* of the world but *with* the world. I will now turn to this further expansion of Brown's ecumenical ecclesiology.

Expanding the Household of the Gospel: Inhabiting the World and the Pseudonyms of God

As an ecumenical observer and participant, Brown contends that Protestantism holds the promise of an ecclesial catholicity that brings together polity and mission; the Protestant insistence of God's persistent judgment ofthe church's confession and language allows the church to appropriately connect its internal language to witness—the former being distinct from, and yet ordered toward, the latter. By first recognizing the tendency to idolatry in their own structures and doctrine ("the falsehood in our truth"), Protestants are, in principle, well placed to orient themselves out to the world without fear of compromising inviolable doctrinal language or confession, especially since the church has little at stake in preserving its own language as such.[59] Though it is proper to affirm that God's grace comes to us through the bread and cup, we should not be surprised if God chooses to approach us in other ways that we might see as lowly.[60] Insofar as God's grace—attested to in Scripture, sermon, and sacrament—directs us to the person of Jesus Christ

58. Brown, "A Campaign on Many Fronts," *Christian Century* 82 (1965): 577–79.

59. Brown, *The Spirit of Protestantism* (Oxford: Oxford University Press, 1961), 44–47.

60. Ibid., 58ff. For Brown, the presence of grace apart from the sacraments is not a rejection of tradition in favor of some vague "mystery" but rather a full affirmation of the otherness of God, who is able to approach us in surprising ways. The rejection of idolatry central to Protestant theology goes hand in hand with a penitent approach to Scripture that recognizes our limits as readers and an openness to God's continual movement (ibid., 79–80).

(presented to us by the Holy Spirit), we should not be surprised that these signs appear in society as the work of the Holy Spirit, who not only enables the questions of the world but also calls the church into an eccentric existence.[61]

By the mid-1960s, Brown began to tease out the implications of an ecumenically-voiced Christianity, while abandoning neither his writing on the Protestant vision of the church nor his ecumenical discussions. Ordered toward its mission to the world, Brown's vision of ecumenical Christianity attends to the theological economy intrinsic to such a venture. For Brown, this missional impulse toward the world had always been (stereotypes aside) the intent of the Reformation: to move the one church toward a unified mission.[62] However, to fully grasp the missional intention of Reformation theology, one must understand that *ecumenical* for Brown does not simply mean intra-church unity but an intra-church unity with society: "There is a second basic meaning of ecumenical, which stresses not only the unity of the church, but also the worldwide *mission* of the church. Not only must the church throughout the *oikoumene* be one, but the one church must go forth in mission to the whole *oikoumene*."[63] In other words, the full sense of the term *ecumenical* implicates the church's unity with the household of the world. For the Reformers, renewing the catholicity of the *communion sanctorum* through a renewed understanding of the Gospel was meant to be the first step toward unity with the world.[64]

61. Ibid., 77–79.
62. Brown, "Reformation Then and Now—A Reformed Perspective," *Lutheran World* 14 (1967): 33–42. As Brown writes, "to say that the Reformation did in fact rend Christendom asunder is not to say that this was either the intention or the necessary consequence of the Reformation impulse" (ibid., 34).
63. Ibid., 34, italics original.
64. Ibid., 37.

In a similar way, while the liturgy (as the "work of the people") pertains to those acts that communicate the church's internally unified worship of the same Christ, it is not complete if it does not bring forth a church-world union:

> *Leitourgia*, liturgy, is what people do wherever they are, and it is a linguistic catastrophe that it has come by us to be associated only with what people do in church. No, liturgy is fulfilling jury duty, playing center field in Candlestick Park, singing praise, washing diapers, counseling the sick, making love, designing buildings, reading Holy Scripture, checking footnotes. *Leitourgia,* properly understood, therefore is a way of describing the wholeness, the oneness, the indissolubility of all life.[65]

The materiality of the Eucharist—the sowing, harvesting, and baking of bread that is joined with the presence of Christ at the table—speaks most powerfully to this meaning of liturgy, "since God uses the earth to communicate his presence to us, all that is of the earth must be of our immediate concern."[66] Continuing the Reformation today, Brown argues, consists of nothing less than continuing this missional impulse of the Reformation in what he describes as "secular ecumenism"—joint Christian action for the sake of and with the secular order.[67]

As the Vietnam War continued to unfold, the suggestion that war represents an "emergency situation" for divided Christianity was raised, asking not for a sidelining of traditional ecumenical concerns as represented by the Faith and Order commission but for a renewed understanding of how the church's common mission put issues of Faith and Order into proper perspective.[68] As Brown notes, "unity is a sham until it includes full sacramental unity," which does necessarily

65. Brown, "True and False Witness," 527.
66. Ibid., 528.
67. Brown, "Reformation Then and Now," 40.
68. Brown, *Ecumenical Revolution*, 342.

mean that liturgical and sacramental unity need to be achieved prior to a secular ecumenism.[69]

I will soon describe Brown's ecumenical work with Clergy and Laity Concerned About Vietnam (CALCAV)—the most visible expression of Brown's commitment to the relation between ecclesiological ecumenicity and mission for the sake of the world.[70] However, before the ecumenical movement against the Vietnam War can be explored, a question must be put to Brown's work thus far: In what way is cooperation in extra-ecclesial social struggles the extension of intra-Christian unity? On the one hand, Brown is quite explicit that church and world are not interchangeable terms, though they are related in common human struggles. On the other hand, Christian missional commitments to the common good of creation are intrinsic to both a proper ecclesiology and the divine economy of salvation.

For Brown, the solution is not simply to perform as though "this-is-that," equating the extra-ecclesial goods of social justice with the internal ecclesial goods of justification, an exchange that diminishes the church to nothing more than a social service agency.[71] Rather, Brown's solution is to follow the trajectory already seen in his early work on P.T. Forsyth: affirming the free work of God in Christ means a willingness to see God at work in pseudonymous ways within creation. In terms of how action with the world is an extension of Brown's secular ecumenism—the united church's social witness—the payoff can be summed up in this way: joining with

69. Ibid., 344.

70. CALCAV did operate alone in this venture. See Gill, *Embattled Ecumenism*,for a detailed account of not only the NCC but also a summary of other ecumenical movements in protest of the Vietnam War.

71. Brown, "Discoveries and Dangers," *Christian Century* 87 (1970): 44: "The danger in my *political changes* is, of course, always the danger of reducing the faith to a humanistic ethic . . . My temptation, which besets ethicists as well, will be to forget the dimensions of life not covered by ethics," emphasis mine.

the world for the common good does not require instrumentalizing doctrine for the ends of social action but affirming that ecumenical action by the Church will find allies in that missional work because, outside the church, the same God who calls the church into mission is at work in hidden ways.

Theology, Brown writes, is an act of gratitude through which we receive life's good from God and confess our appreciation by being involved with that goodness.[72] Rather than rejecting a specifically christological (and thus, ecclesial) center for theology, this center calls for a more deeply christological conviction that God has revealed God's self as the one who is for us, calling to the church from surprising venues.[73] Following the words of Vatican II, Brown understood that listening to the various social renewal movements of the world is akin to hearing the voice of God in the voice of the times—not as a rejection of a christological center but as its ecstatic logic: a participation in a christologically-endowed creation that extends beyond human (and ecclesial) control.[74]

Discerning these pseudonyms of God involves following the narrative of Scripture, which describes how God does not simply usealternate means (besides the Law and the prophets) to speak the Word and to enact the will of God, but that God is present in these means. Seen supremely in Christ—who was rejected as the Word of God by his own contemporaries—this pattern points to the manner in which God's act appears in ways that exceed our expectations concerning the means available to God for revelation, without denying or eclipsing previous acts of God.[75] Far from closing

72. Brown, *The Pseudonyms of God* (Louisville: Westminster, 1972), 17. See also Brown, "Theology as an Act of Gratitude," *Union Seminary Quarterly Review* 16 (1960): 83–95.

73. Brown, *Pseudonyms of God*, 35.

74. Ibid., 37. To be sure, Brown's assertion of God's pseudonymity is not simply an emergency "fix." Exercised when the church fails in its vocation to be for the sake of the world, the grace of God raises up others to prompt the church into action, though this seems to be a state in which the church forever finds itself (ibid., 35).

down this pseudonymity, the Christological center of God's revelation continues to proliferate it; Christ is described polyphonically in Scripture as clown, rebel, Lord, and social offense (among many other images).[76] With each proliferated image, our vision of the christological scope of communication grows wider as Scripture discloses manifold ways by which the Triune God can be seen by the church in creation.

As we can see in God's use of the Assyrians, Babylonians, and natural events in the Old Testament, "God can use whatever he choose, whatever means are at hand . . . in order to communicate his will to his people."[77] Rather than being a remnant of God's act in the Old Testament, God's expansive speech is intrinsic to grace as the free act of God, spoken by a free God. Modern pseudonyms are manifold in the modern world, Brown argues, and many such pseudonyms were raised up in response to the church's failure to meet the most pressing issue of the early 1970s—the Vietnam War.[78] Case in point: by the early 1970s, various protest movements were gathering, but the churches had little to no representation among the leadership of the movements or presence in the demonstrations.[79]

Left unspoken in this explication of the church's collaboration with society in response to the pseudonymous work of God is what to make of the non-ecclesial actors through whom the Holy Spirit works. Whereas Day's theology of natural loves motivates these actors, Brown's account rests more fully upon the assumption that the various advocates against Vietnam act out of an encounter with the grace of God, the Holy Spirit. Because of Christ's work, all

75. Ibid., 86–87.
76. Ibid., 87–94.
77. Ibid., 76.
78. On the biblical justification for pseudonyms, see ibid., 73–76.
79. Ibid., 62. Brown writes of the Christian support present to him in prison after his arrest for his involvement with the Civil Rights movement (ibid., 167–72).

persons are assumed into a Christic existence to the extent that people encounter Christ in existential ways that they may or may not recognize as necessarily religious.[80] Though not voiced in theological language, a person's opposition to war is a participation in the Spirit's work for a unified creation.

In this sense, the secular ecumenism of the church meets the world on a ground prepared for them both by a common Christological existence. Without knowing that it is taking part in one of God's pseudonyms, the world participates in these movements through an existential journey, a self-involved grasping of faith made possible by Christ's work. Theologically, this approach is not without its dangers for Brown; as Christians enters the public square, they communicate the faith without the benefit of theological language and risk linguistically diminishing the difference between church and world.[81] For the Christian, offering one's theological goods in service to the world is intrinsic to a self-involved life of faith—a life that risks one's idols and one's words in seeking more faithfully after God in Christ.[82] We see at this point the depth of Brown's claim that Protestantism continues to hold the key not only to "secular ecumenism," but to a theology concerning how the world and the church can cooperate together, without abandoning the Gospel's centrality: apart from the Gospel, the church cannot interpret God's movement within the world, nor does it have the courage to join with God.[83] By the

80. This can be read either as an extension of Forsyth's teaching or perhaps as an influence of Tillich, who remained influential in Brown's thinking even though he was not always cited. Brown elucidates the practicalities of this approach most clearly in terms of how one approaches teaching theology in a confessional context versus a more secular venue such as Stanford. See Brown, "Teaching Theology in a University Setting," *Union Seminary Quarterly Review* 22 (1967): 357–65.

81. Brown, "A Campaign on Many Fronts," 578–79.

82. For Brown, who offered religious studies classes in the midst of a non-confessional university, how best to communicate the faith without transforming "the classroom into a chapel and the lectern into a pulpit," remained a constant struggle, in Brown, "Teaching Theology in a University Setting," 363. For Brown's most comprehensive statement on the existential life of faith, see Brown, *Is Faith Obsolete?* (Philadelphia: Westminster, 1974).

same token, just as the Gospel helps to inform and define the world, "the world helps to inform and define the gospel," insofar as God's pseudonymous activity is that which makes possible the church's mission and that toward which the church's mission is ordered.[84]

Nonviolence: Ecumenical Contextuality and Public Action

As we have seen, Brown held that the church's ecumenical unity (which Protestantism provides to the church catholic) is intimately connected to the church's ecumenical witness. However, this witness is not simply *to* the world but joins *with* the world, insofar as the same Christ whom the church proclaims authorizes history as significant and valued. As I begin to describe Brown's involvement with CALCAV and how CALCAV worked for the sake of the wider household of society, it will be important to examine the ways in which Brown's attention to the ecumenical nature of the church's witness both enables and limits his advocacy for nonviolence.

As noted in the introduction, discussing Brown in this context must bear in mind that Brown's later work exhibits ambivalence on the question of nonviolence, as he would move more decisively toward liberation theology and, consequently, become more open to the possibility of violence in service to liberation. In what I will now describe, the seeds of Brown's later work can be seen: that any ecumenically-voiced response to war could not ignore issues of class and race within the *oikumene* of the church—particularly the effects that class and race have on ethics. Consisting of both privileged and

83. Brown, "Is Ecumenism Reversing Our Roles?," *Journal of Ecumenical Studies* 7, no. 4 (1970): 783–85.

84. Brown, "Discoveries and Dangers," *Christian Century* 87, no. 2 (January 1970): 40–45. In the future, Brown saw theology becoming more inductive than deductive—a service to the world's questions in a kind of renewed *diakonia* parallel to his expansive understanding of the church's service to the *oikumene*. See Brown, "Theology and the Gospel: Reflections on Theological Method," in *Theology and Church in Times of Change: Essays in Honor of John Bennett Coleman*, ed. Edward LeRoy Long and Robert T. Handy (Philadelphia: Westminster, 1970), 15–33.

oppressed congregations, the body of Christ cannot pretend that the same ethical options are equally available to all parts of the church.[85]

Insofar as the ecumenical church of Brown's time consisted of church bodies that could afford to exercise a nonviolent witness without serious reprisal and oppressed churches in Latin America and Vietnam for whom nonviolence was more costly in both material and physical terms, Brown recognized that the contextual value of violence could not be ignored if the ecumenical movement sincerely valued the range of the church in its response to war.

This being said, Brown also understood the refusal of violence as an integral component to an ecumenical witness. By acknowledging that portions of the church cannot readily turn to nonviolence because of their social powerlessness, the ecumenical church is pressed to consider the ways in which the powerful—who can readily enact a nonviolent witness without loss—must do so on behalf of the weak in a way that does not perpetuate violence elsewhere. In sum, Brown's ecumenical ecclesiology frames his nonviolent advocacy as follows: nonviolent resistance to war is a vocation that the strong can exercise on behalf of weaker partners—a vocation which the churches are called to use in support of policy proposals to benefit the wider *oikumene* of the world.

The Contextuality of Violence and the Ecumenical Church

Influenced by Niebuhr, Brown emphasizes that theology is worked out from within the maelstrom of history, which, as we shall see, complicates Brown's position on nonviolence.[86] As he notes in his memoir, the arguments of nuclear pacifism—that the means of war

85. Brown, *Theology in a New Key: Responding to Liberation Themes* (Philadelphia: Westminster, 1978), 13–15. As Derek Alan Woodard-Lehman argues, in "Body Politics and the Politics of Bodies: Racism and Hauerwasian Theopolitics," *Journal of Religious Ethics* 36 (2008): 295–320, avoiding questions of race in favor of a corporate unified witness tends to turn the church into a "raceless" venture, thus replicating racial prejudices of society within the church's unified body.

far outstrip our ability to manage them—are compelling; more contemporary wars in Grenada, Panama, and Iraq would push him to the point of naming war as "intrinsically evil."[87] However, this does not represent a strict pacifist position for Brown, who allows for the possibility of self-defense by an oppressed minority over against an overwhelming opponent.[88]

As we have already seen in Brown's ecumenical writings, one of his predominant themes centers on his attention to the complexities of the social contexts of the ecumenical partners, particularly in terms of the power differentials that influence these discussions. At the great conciliar gatherings of the twentieth century—gatherings such as the Second Vatican Council and Uppsala, which ostensibly spoke on behalf of worldwide communions—European and American delegates outnumbered the emerging world by nearly two to one.[89]

The results of this disproportionality in ecumenical gatherings means that problems affecting under-represented areas of the world were discussed without consideration of how doctrinal and social stances taken by the WCC would play out in these underrepresented areas. In a particularly poignant example, Brown notes that a resolution drafted by American delegates at Uppsala concerning racism argued for the political self-determination of African-Americans. In response to this proposal, a delegate from South Africa noted that while the proposal by the Americans was well-meaning, the logic of the proposal typified the apartheid that his country had been laboring under and that, in South Africa, "self-determination"

86. Brown describes how chaplaincy—as a presence within the military—offers not an absolution of military norms but a subversion of it, undermining Naval segregation codes during worship and relativizing assumptions about the normativity of death by messages of the resurrection, in Brown, *Reflections*, 53–58.

87. Ibid., 62.

88. Ibid.

89. Brown, "Uppsala: An Informal Report," 644–51.

meant a systematic marginalization of people of color from the political process.[90]

The presence of groups who had previously been "the victims of our exploitation" began to pose an important question in those meetings to the ecumenical church's ability to simply renounce violence univocally.[91] If a truly ecumenical witness were to appear, the concerns of certain groups, particularly those representing the emergent voice of Latin American liberation theology, cannot be dismissed as aberrant, insofar as their struggle for liberation could not in principle renounce violence so easily as their North American and European counterparts.[92]

For Brown, Latin American thinkers such as Don Helder Camara pose a potent challenge to the simple rejection of war, just as they had for Day and Yoder. As Camara points out, violence *by* a society emerges from the violence *within* a society, with war being the most destructive instance of a much more complex spiral of violence.[93] Thus the key issue to consider is not whether nonviolence is preferable to violence in an abstract sense but whether power—leveraged at a local level toward the end of an equitable society—requires violence.[94] Brown notes that the refusal of violence

90. Ibid., 647.
91. Ibid., 660.
92. Brown finds liberation theology to be engaged in an alternate, albeit novel, reading of the tradition that is no different in principle than what the Reformation had done in the sixteenth century. See Brown, "The Uses of the Past," *Theology Today* 31 (1974): 104–13. Brown began this line of reasoning several years before in "Tradition as a Protestant Problem," *Theology Today* 17 (1961): 430–54, in which he writes that "no one is trying to be honest. Everyone claims to be hearing the Word of God. But the indisputable fact of the matter is that Lutherans, Presbyterians, sectarians, liberals, conservatives. . . . southern Afrikaners, Indonesians and Congolese all read the same Scripture and all hear different things . . . It can be explained only by recognizing that Protestants do not rely on *sola Scriptura* in quite the unambiguous way that Reformation Sunday sermons would suggest" (441).
93. Brown, *Religion and Violence*, 2nd ed (Philadelphia: Westminster, 1987), 8–10.
94. Ibid., 32. For Niebuhr, the exercise of power cannot be distanced from the use of force, in "Pacifism and the Use of Force," in *Love and Justice: Selections from the Shorter Writings of Reinhold Niebuhr*, ed. D.B. Robertson (Louisville: Westminster John Knox, 1957). For criticism

is a complex question; we must ask not only whether the measured exercise of force and violence will produce an equitable (and by extension, a non-warring) society but also whether our responses to war and violence do not simply defer the actuality of violence to another location. In particular, Brown worries that the refusal to go to war ensures that someone without the means to resist will go instead.[95]

Nonviolence emerged as a political option primarily for Christians in the context of the privileged West; therefore, Brown believed that Christians needed to be slow to assume that nonviolence, as seen in the witness of Martin Luther King, Jr., could be applicable to all contexts and circumstances. While acts such as refusing to go to war, participating in protest marches, and burning draft cards might create a persuasive witness to the government and prevent further violence in America, Brown was persuaded in the wake of Uppsala "to acknowledge that in some situations nonviolence seems a luxury the destitute cannot afford."[96] Because the voices seeking nonviolence throughout the church emerge from both the American context—where nonviolence is not only desirable but preferable—and more "revolutionary settings," the ecumenical church cannot negate the use of violence entirely, either in instrumental or social forms.

This ecumenical acknowledgment of legitimate moral reasoning in traditionally underrepresented areas such as Latin America is significant for Brown in three interrelated ways. First, acknowledging the Latin American ambivalence toward violence pushes the ecumenical church to hear the full range of its member's voices and to view the quandaries of others as their own, deepening

concerning the pacifist distinction of power from force, see Paul Ramsey, "The Uses of Power," in *The Just War: Force and Political Responsibility* (New York: Charles Scribner's Sons, 1968), 3–19.

95. Brown, *Religion and Violence*, 38.

96. Brown, "Discoveries and Dangers," 44.

ecumenical relations in both a moral and pastoral sense. Second, in listening to the Latin American churches, the WCC was pressed to more deeply examine the relation between war and other forms of structural violence—to move beyond a "pacifism of witness" and embrace an advocacy designed to change the unjust structures of society that produce war.[97] As Brown argues:

> The immediate need, while we still have a democratic process, while we still have instruments of protest, is not for martyrs but for statesmen. We need to do more than get on record. We need to do more than salve our consciences. We need to change our nation's policy. *Protest must be for the sake of persuasion*, for the sake of swelling the ranks of those who feel this monstrous war must end.[98]

Third and finally, listening to the Latin American churches pressed the WCC toward a more concrete and contextual approach to theology. As we have seen with Brown, the work of the Spirit propels Christians to witness in a diversity of concrete situations; the process of understanding the conditions of bearing witness to Christ's peaceable work and to the unity of the church must include speaking in ad hoccontextual forms.

For Brown, an ecumenically-rooted witness against war emphasizes the purity of moral witness less than the empirical ways in which the tactic of nonviolence can lead to the consideration of the deeper social issues that produce war, as well as the ways in which nonviolence can be productively expressed without furthering the suffering of its members. In the American scene (particularly, the white American church), nonviolence remains a tactic, not because it secures the moral purity of the agent but because violence remains—despite its utility in the short run—"morally evil and tactically counter-productive," as well as "pragmatically effective in

97. Ibid., 77–79.
98. Brown, *Pseudonyms of God*, 190.

the long run."[99] Nonviolence can be utilized by churches who can socially and economically afford it, in that through the use of creative dissent, churches stand as witnesses to order in the face of established forms of disorder, becoming communities of subversion who side with victims of violence for the sake of a renewed society.[100]

In contrast to Yoder and Day, the question of the moral validity of nonviolence (as a means to an end, given to the ecumenical church to work toward the establishment of a just society) is a secondary concern for Brown. The rejection of violence in war or in the reordering of society should be exercised by the ecumenical church in places of strength (such as the United States) for the sake of more just relations with societies that cannot exercise that option (such as Honduras or Vietnam). When possible, the church's influence should be leveraged in nonviolent fashion for the sake of others. However, the ecumenical unity of the global church requires a commitment to solidarity with the weakest members of the communion, such that the enactment of nonviolence is done on behalf of the suffering. This approach of internal ecclesial solidarity, as we have already seen, extends externally as the *oikumene* of the church joined together with the *oikumene* of the world in pursuit of a common peace.

Brown recognized that calls for a simple withdrawal of troops had silenced more complex issues, such as the implications of a cease-fire on the Vietnamese. As the public became more concerned with ending involvement in the Vietnam War, Brown noted that the "Vietnamization" of the War—the transfer of responsibility for the conflict to the South Vietnam army—was the same kind of myopic policy that he had seen permeating WCC discussions. By removing itself from the Vietnam crisis prior to its end, the United States

99. Brown, *Religion and Violence*, 81.
100. Ibid., 92–94.

simply transferred the responsibility for the pursuit of peace to the Vietnamese:

> To speak as plainly as possible, the policy strikes me as *de facto* a racist policy. Mr. Nixon's assumption is that the American people will tolerate the killing and maiming of an indefinite number of dark-skinned Asians, but that we will not tolerate the killing and maiming of white Americans. Thus while he talks about "winding down the war," he in fact increases the perimeter of the war.[101]

In other words, a political solution that provided social peace was being pursued at the expense of a minority voice, namely, people of color. Brown, whose work on ecumenism embodies the antithesis of this approach, was already aware of the ways that political advocacy by large bodies—whether the United State or the global church—could sometimes offer solutions that bore more heavily on disenfranchised members of that body.[102] For the ecumenical church to engage in questions of social policy, it had to first address these issues within its own life, attending to its own inequities in order to be able to offer better political possibilities to a society consisting of both the strong, who could reject violence without suffering loss, and the weak, for whom violence might be a valid option for survival.

Secular Ecumenism, Public Policy, and Nonviolence

Though unpersuaded by the arguments of James Douglass and other "absolute pacifists," Brown saw the absolutists' refusal of violence—in light of war's inability to address underlying causes of racial inequity, governmental disconnect from the will of the people, and self-serving intentions—as "the most hardheaded and realistic position imaginable

101. Brown, "Dead Policy, Revived Conscience," *Church and Society* 61 (1971): 16–17.

102. Though more pronounced in Brown's later work on liberation theology, this approach played a significant role in Brown's reflections on how the ecumenical movement could approach the question of nonviolence with respect to the Vietnam War.

when one looks at war as the most obvious example of violence."[103] In part, Brown supported nonviolent protest during Vietnam because he did not think the conflict in Vietnam met just war criteria—criteria that Brown understood to be less and less credible.[104]

In arriving at his opposition to Vietnam, however, Brown sought to do more than end a war; as we have seen in his ecumenical discussions, he also wanted to draw attention to the micro-violences that sustain a culture of war for the long-term benefit of both the ecumenical church and society. In this sense, Brown's opposition of war is both similar to Yoder, Day, and Stringfellow and profoundly dissimilar. Whereas Yoder and Day—in different ways—saw the communion of the church as providing an alternative configuration of human society, Brown's work points toward a reconstructed common life in which the church participates in, supporting proposals that sustain this common life. Insofar as God's Spirit acts with anticipation in pseudonymous ways, the calling of the church is not to lead the way but to join with and offer public support in ways consistent with its ecumenical character.

We see this approach in various ways prior to Brown's joining with CALCAV. For example, in a time when absolute pacifism and absolute commitment to war constituted legal norms, Brown repeatedly wrote in support of selective conscientious objection, understanding it as a way for the populace to make discriminations between just and unjust wars, without forcing them to conform to an ethic that opposed participation in civic life.[105] In other words, selective conscientious objection provides a secular application of the

103. Brown, "Dead Policy, Revived Conscience," 26.

104. Entering the Second World War to stem German aggression, for example, is approved, while the obliterative bombing of German civilians is condemned, in Brown, *Religion and Violence*, 20.

105. Brown, "The Catholic Bishops and the Draft," *Christianity and Crisis* 28 (1969): 328–29; "Revision of Selective Service," *Christianity and Crisis* 27 (1968): 322–23; "The WCC and Selective Objection," *Christianity and Crisis* 28 (1968): 195–96.

insights from the debates raging within the WCC; the discovery of a *via media* to the divisive issue of violence within the ecumenical church provides the basis for Brown's proposals in the wider society.

Brown's political activities independent of CALCAV continued to emphasize finding broad-based coalition responses that were modeled on his ecumenical work. Insofar as traditional modes of resistance tend toward dividing American polity, Brown sought an approach beyond the traditional protest march.

> Can we develop a style of "civil disobedience for squares" by which people who retain some credibility within Middle America can act in ways that would force the others to ask: "If people like that are risking that much, shouldn't I rethink where I stand?" Is it too utopian to hope that some church bodies might at last be willing to say, and then enact, an unequivocal "No" to the war by actively urging their youth not to fight, divesting their portfolios of war-related investments and specifically supporting lobbies pushing for total troop withdrawal and the cutting of funds for other military actions in Southeast Asia?[106]

To be sure, Brown was not averse to participating in more traditionally radical activities, such as speaking at rallies where students turned in their draft cards or blocking the doors of draft boards.[107] But through the work of CALCAV, a new mode of engaging the war presented itself. Because CALCAV focused more on proposals and public policy for ending the war in Vietnam, they approached cessation of hostilities—and thus, the question of the appropriateness of nonviolence—as a matter of public policy, which was ecclesially-informed but enacted by extra-ecclesial entities. For Brown, traditional and more progressive modes of nonviolence, as seen with the Berrigans, were less an absolute model than a "sign"

106. Brown, "What Can We Do?," *Christianity and Crisis* 30 (1971): 293–95. Interestingly, Brown offers these comments after outlining the traditional roads of working through the system—nonviolent protest, withdrawal, and violent rebellion.
107. Brown, "On The Steps of the Federal Building," *Social Progress* 58 (1968): 43–45.

of the kinds of creative thinking needed in response to Vietnam.[108] While appreciative of the Berrigans' work, Brown faults them for contributing to a discourse that understood nonviolence as simply being "not violent" rather than allowing nonviolence to birth new options.[109] While the Berrigans' witness had stirred "white middle-class America" to nonviolent action, their promotion of nonviolence could not be taken as a model so much as a sign of what creative resistance should aim for in order to generate "new centers of support."[110]

Building on the proposition that a common social witness is the extension of an ecumenical ecclesiology, CALCAV began in 1966 as the National Emergency Committee of Clergy Concerned about Vietnam through the initiative of William Sloane Coffin, Abraham Joshua Heschel, and Richard Neuhaus.[111] A number of other national groups opposing Vietnam predated CALCAV, and other ecumenical bodies such as the National Council of Churches (NCC) had issued statements in opposition to Vietnam. However, CALCAV was unique because it sought neither to be a doctrinal body that simply issued a statement about Vietnam (such as the NCC) nor a purely activist body (such as the Fellowship of Reconciliation), nor even a body that emerged from a particular tradition (such as the Catholic

108. Brown, "The Berrigans: Signs or Models?," in *The Berrigans*, ed. William Van-Etten Casey (Avon Paperback, 1972): 60–70.

109. Ibid., 66.

110. Ibid., 66, 68. Brown would take this approach with regards to the question of military chaplaincy, contending that military chaplaincy could persist as a viable form of witness against the war for Christians only if chaplains were able to exercise a prophetic role in their vocation, in Brown, "Military Chaplaincy as Ministry" in *Military Chaplains: From a Religious Military to a Military Religion*, ed. Harvey Cox (New York: American Report, 1973), 143.

111. Mitchel K. Hall, *Because of Their Faith: CALCAV and Religious Opposition to the Vietnam War* (New York: Columbia University Press, 1990), 4–15. Daniel Berrigan is also named as a founding member, though by this time, Berrgian had been directed to South America, ostensibly as a result of his involvement with Vietnam. For analysis of Berrigan's life and thought, see James L. Marsh and Anna Brown, ed. *Faith, Resistance, and the Future: Daniel Berrigan's Challenge to Catholic Social Thought* (New York: Fordham University Press, 2013).

Worker); CALCAV's mission was to give an intentionally ecumenical voice to governmental entities on an issue affecting all churches.

The movement was not meant to replace denominational life or serve as an alternative to other groups, but to be, in Brown's words, "complementary" to other actions.[112] As an ecumenical body, CALCAV self-consciously sought out proposals for witness that did not play to either end of the political spectrum, refusing to advocate specific tactics of nonviolent resistance or a purely negotiated settlement and choosing to formally remain independent of other antiwar movements.[113] Building ties with religiously oriented groups put CALCAV in a difficult position, since religious movements were by far the least represented among Vietnam dissenters. Brown understood this not only as a theological decision but also a pragmatic one to represent "the American middle class" where "votes are found, and it is from here that must come the kind of pressure that can make a difference."[114]

As I noted concerning Brown's ecumenical work, Brown was keenly aware of his social location as a white, middle-class American Christian, but he did not necessarily consider this to be a detriment. As a part of a broad-based ecumenical coalition that included not only the middle-class but also the poor—and of a church that included not only the marginalized but the privileged as well—Brown saw that his position of privilege could be a strategic asset to be leveraged on behalf of the marginalized and the poor, in the same way that churches of privilege were called to act on behalf of poorer churches

112. Hall, *Because of Their Faith*, 22: "All of us, in effect, had one foot in CALCAV and the other foot in our denominational or . . . secular activist groups."

113. Ibid., 33. In an attempt to give a Catholic voice to the movement, Hall details CALCAV secretary Richard Fernandez's attempts to involve members of the Catholic bishops, to little avail. At the time, Richard John Neuhaus was a Lutheran pastor, though he would later be received into the Catholic Church in 1990.

114. Ibid., 49.

(which he writes about in his ecumenical discussions). This being said, CALCAV's self-conscious middle-class location did not prevent Brown and other members from being involved in actions often associated with more radical groups, such as protest marches, demonstrations, and turning in draft cards.[115]

Their tactical solidarity of civil disobedience (including draft avoidance) was not a move away from the churches and synagogues that formed their base but an attempt to reinvigorate conversation and discussion within these groups.[116] As Mitchell Hall argues, CALCAV's persistent attention to church bodies and the ways in which their civil disobedience was ordered toward public conversations and public policy enabled the group to have the ear of Congressional members in a way that eluded many of their contemporaries.[117]

In Brown's own writings for CALCAV, we see how his ecumenical discussions on nonviolence influence his policy recommendations; his co-authored book—*Vietnam: Crisis of Conscience*—with Abraham Heschel and Michael Novak will help illustrate this.[118] Brown's contribution, "An Appeal to the Churches and Synagogues," names four levels of involvement critical to articulating concern for Vietnam: political, social, economic, and congregational—all of which were critical in order to "reconcile across chasms of misunderstanding and hostility . . . *within* a nation."[119] Insofar as religion is a "corporate affair between the individual, God, and the neighbor," churches cannot escape either their calling to one another or their calling to the common good,

115. Ibid., 54–55.
116. Ibid., 60–61.
117. Ibid., 65ff.
118. Robert McAfee Brown, Abraham J. Heschel, and Michael Novak, *Vietnam: Crisis of Conscience* (New York: Herder and Herder, 1967).
119. Ibid., 62. Italics mine.

which requires churches to facilitate political reconciliation and to speak "in the name of their communities" to common concerns.[120] As the issue affecting the *oikumene* of the world, Vietnam requires the voices of the church speaking into the common inhabited world.[121] With the *need* to speak established, the question again turns to *how* this speech will happen. While Brown is content to speak in a dogmatic voice in his other writings, his proposals—offered by the ecumenical church on behalf of the world—freely adopt the voice of public proposals; as such, they appeal not only to a doctrine of the *imago Dei* but to the distance between stated aims of the war and the ends and means being used to prosecute the war.[122]

By using this dual voice for both church and government, I do not think Brown is arguing for a translation of theological goods because—as I have described already—to speak in the idioms of public policy is to respond faithfully to the pseudonymous action of God operating providentially in history. However, this entails offering political challenges, solutions, and criticism as members of the common *oikumene* and speaking on behalf of others within God's world. The role that a critical voice takes in public policy—such as challenging an unjust war—is essential in order to counter a Whig vision of history that attempts to "play Providence not only for themselves but for the far future."[123] Rather, churches are to affirm "God as the father of all men. . . . and a belief that God has planted his image in all men" and to offer actions in a pragmatic voice that policymakers can hear; lacking the ear of policymakers, they are to "initiate a public outcry so loud and so clear that it cannot be ignored."[124] In order to speak in a voice credible to lawmakers and

120. Ibid., 62–64.
121. Ibid., 64.
122. Ibid., 68–69.
123. Ibid., 64.
124. Ibid., 87–88.

attractive to "a broad base of support," Brown acknowledges that proposals less "prophetic than the purists would espouse" would have to be put forward.[125]

Keeping this in mind, Brown's contributions to the CALCAV-sponsored *Vietnam: Crisis of Conscience* read as a proposal for nonviolence as public policy, formed by his prior deliberations of the role of nonviolence within ecumenical discussions. Whereas other proposals (such as those offered by the NCC) emphasize a negotiated settlement for peace, Brown's begins with the supposition that the United States should "unconditionally . . . cease the bombing of North Vietnam."[126] This must be the first movement, Brown writes, not because nonviolence has moral priority over other forms of force but because "the United States, as the stronger nation, has the obligation and the opportunity to take that initiative." Analogous to his view that Christians of privilege can engage in nonviolence since they have little to lose, America—as the stronger partner in the conflict—must take the first step by ceasing its use of force toward the end of a peace settlement.[127] With the space created by this movement, "we will have to use all the diplomatic resources at our disposal to explore and re-explore every hint and clue that may appear," reiterating that nonviolence rightly exists within a larger economy of persuasion, used properly toward ends of order and not simply for the sake of a moral stance.[128] With de-escalation in place, any call to "accept the Vietcong at the negotiation table as a partner in its own right" would be credible.[129]

In short, Brown's work in bringing together various theological traditions foreshadows the hope that Brown had for public policy.

125. Ibid., 89.
126. Ibid., 90.
127. Ibid.
128. Ibid.
129. Ibid., 92.

Through a presumptive cessation of hostilities—*without* the promise of reciprocation by the Vietcong—Brown saw a multi-step process unfolding that would not only lead to negotiations between the United States and VietCong forces but would also draw together "the resources of any and all international organizations in the search for peace."[130] At one level, this is simply wise policy; at another level, it mirrors what Brown had already advocated with regards to the church in its own dealings with violence: insofar as the church could join together as a unified body in the pursuit of peace—prior to any promise of reciprocation by the government—it would find a broad-based body of willing participants who all had a stake in the common life of society.

The churches, operating in a mode of "secular ecumenism," would not only find new avenues for building its own internal unity but would facilitate external unity by joining together through the use of nonviolent means in a common pursuit of peace. In an analogous way, the United States—should it choose to preemptively disarm itself—would find a cessation of conflict and would be joined by a community of goodwill who offered additional resources to end the war.

Brown realizes that the rejection of violence in favor of nonviolence is not and has never been an exclusively Christian prerogative; thus, to make it a distinctive plank of Christian faith and practice not only limits the church's entrance into the single *oikumene* of creation but also forecloses the church's opportunity to identify the various pseudonyms under which the Spirit of God might be at work. In his exploration of the guises under which God has worked historically, Brown devotes nearly a third of the book to Vietnam, under the assumption that this conflict might be a decisive moment

130. Ibid., 93.

in the Church's history—not only in terms of its internal unity but in its common action on behalf of God's creation.

Conclusion

For Brown, the internal shape of ecumenical life provides both the form and method by which the unified church can speak into public life and is able to join with God's pseudonymous work for the sake of all creation. By emphasizing the ways in which nonviolence can be the vocation of the strong for the sake of the weak—attentive to the various social locations that comprise the single *oikumene* of the church—the ecumenical church can join with the analogous work of God already present in various guises throughout the *oikumene* of the world.

In viewing secular ecumenism (joint social action undertaken by the various branches of the church) as an act that benefits the world and provides an *entrée* into ecumenical dialogue, Brown offers a thoroughgoing vision of how the church's vocation to be "one" is furthered by its mission to the world as it aids the world. Whereas the previous proposals draw primarily from one denominational ecclesiological tradition, the strength of Brown's proposal lies in what he takes to be the heart of Protestant thought and the property of the church catholic: the christological call of the church to be one in its mission and worship.

By couching nonviolence within a concern for how the nonviolent opposition to Vietnam furthers both the church's unity and the common good, the link between ecclesiology and nonviolence appears more tenuous in two ways. First, as a Presbyterian, Brown is concerned that churchly goods not be transposed into a blueprint of the church's witness. As such, any direct application of Jesus' words in the Sermon on the Mount is too simple; Christians, directed and gifted by the Spirit, must pass first through the way in which God—the giver of creation and providential Lord of history—calls Christians to witness to their Lord in the depths of history in their particular age. Emphasizing the way in which the church provides principles by which Christians operate in the world, Jesus' call to be peacemaker cannot be equated, for example, with the straightforward calling to never pick up arms in defense of one's neighbor or to halt a conflict. In the case of Vietnam, Brown does not propose total disarmament but simply a unilateral cease-fire; such a proposal does not mean that arms cannot be picked up at a different time.

The ecumenical context of Brown's proposal initially proves to be a second level of slackening between nonviolent resistance to war and the church. Brown's vision of nonviolence within this matrix diverges significantly from Yoder and Day in that the church does not have the luxury of choosing nonviolence as one option among others—in the same way that the church is not permitted to choose its neighbors or its concrete call to witness. For Brown, countries, persons, and indeed churches in situations of deep structural oppression must be allowed the option of violence, if only for a season, as a consequence of their context. In those times, churches with the luxury of choice—who can choose to respond through the laying down of arms and to leverage social change without revolutions or guns—must do so, if only as witnesses within a larger body. The freedom of the church to respond in nonviolence, ecumenically speaking, is also its burden; it is called to persuade bastions of power without the use of force and to hold open the option of nonviolence for churches without that present option unto a better day. Brown saw the vocation of the American church—as common inheritors of the *oikumene* of the world with the Vietnamese—in this way: to call for the laying down of arms and to resist unlawful acts by nonviolence for the sake of persuading the American government to cease hostilities.

In addition to furthering the sake of the church's unity with the world, the effects of this action would hopefully be an occasion to foster the church's internal unity as well. As Brown put it, because faith is posed in the present tense as an existential response to the Gospel, ecumenicity—both in terms of dialogue and the nature of the church's common action—can rightly be framed as a matter of induction, moving from the life of faith to doctrinal unity.[131] As with the medieval scholastics who proposed a distinction between the *ordo essendi* and the *ordo congnoscendi*, the way to a unity concerning arguments of being, doctrine, and ontology may very well occur through the hard work of common action.[132] By beginning with ethics and moving to theology, we move through the love of humanity to the love of God. The love of one's neighbor prompts us to ask questions concerning why the neighbor is loved, how to love the neighbor, the relation of love between persons established in Christ, and the fellowship of God granted to humanity in the love of the neighbor.[133]

This issue of Vietnam "must be forced on the conscience of the churches and synagogues, so that together they can force it on the conscience of the nation." This work must "be done ecumenically," beginning with an act of secular ecumenism, which was Brown's way in ecumenical discussions and would, in time, lead to other discussions.

> While Christians and Jews disagree about the significance of a first-century Jew, they do not disagree about the significance of a twentieth-century Vietnamese. While Catholics and Protestants disagree about the

131. Brown, "Theology and Church in Times of Change," 27.
132. Ibid., 27–28.
133. Ibid., 28.

> authority of the voice emanating from the See of Peter, they do not disagree about the importance of heeding that voice when it pleads with our President to end the devastation of which our nation is guilty. Catholics, Protestants, and Jews represent different theological traditions, but they all embody the shared tradition of a common humanity, united in anguish and increasingly in outrage, and from that tradition they can already speak as one.[134]

Thus, Brown's proposal views nonviolence within an ecumenical economy that takes precedence over nonviolence's absolute nature. What Brown's nonviolence loses in its absolute nature, however, it gains in scope. By pointing beyond the church's own action to the way in which the ecumenical church joins with public policy and other groups in society as co-laborers under the guidance of the one Spirit of God, Brown's appeal finds a national platform for implementation. By viewing common action as the way in which the ecumenical church answers God's pseudonymous work en route to deeper ecumenical discussions, Brown is able to envision common labors on behalf of the world as the context within which churches bear witness to their neighbors and learn to love their estranged Christian neighbors, with nonviolence serving as a means to that end. I argue that, through his subordination of violence to the questions of political ends and ecumenical unity, Brown broaches a question that has been laying beneath the surface of the previous accounts: To what degree is nonviolent resistance intrinsic to an ecclesiological witness against war, and to what degree is it instrumental?

In Brown's thinking, the act of nonviolent resistance is subordinate to the concerns of the ecclesial and worldly *oikumene*. As we have seen, this does not negate nonviolent modes of resistance to war; insofar as a church is able to make use of this act en route to its vocation of unity with other churches and the world, the rejection

134. Ibid., 98.

of violence remains a live option. In contrast to Yoder (for whom nonviolence constitutes an ethical act that indicates who God is) or Day (for whom nonviolence signifies the telos of human life), nonviolence does not have a theologically mediating function for Brown. As such, it can be drawn upon as appropriate to the church's social location but not as an absolute for church identity (Yoder) or as an indication of a properly ordered moral life (Day).

Conversely, the challenge that Day and Yoder (and Stringfellow to a lesser degree) pose to Brown's work is twofold. First, by emphasizing the ecumenical orientation and nature of the church, Brown's work is almost tradition-free. Though he represents the Presbyterians in ecumenical discussions across several decades, Brown's descriptions of ecclesiology tend toward being more generically Protestant than being informed by the particular contours of a denomination, as with Yoder or Stringfellow. By relating nonviolence to such a general ecclesial context, Brown's work lacks traditioned moorings—moorings that enable Day and Yoder to argue that nonviolence is not dependent upon its historical efficacy. For Brown, this means that if the refusal of war is an ecclesiologically and historically available option, only then could it be theologically viable, but not vice versa. In Brown's estimation, a socially-oppressed congregation cannot be expected to make use of an ethic that continues to enable its social oppression.

Second, Yoder, Day, and Stringfellow view nonviolent resistance to war as not only historically possible but as a mediating aspect of ecclesiological existence. For Yoder, nonviolent resistance names the way that Christ is known to be God as well as the way that church is known as God's. For Day, this act names one of the acts of mercy by which people are directed toward the Church. For Stringfellow, this act—properly considered—bears the same contours as proper ecclesiology. For Brown, however, faith may or may not be manifest in this act, depending on the church's place in history. While informed by a commitment to ecumenism, the refusal of war does not intrinsically mediate an aspect of that commitment.

This does not mean that we should reject Brown's work, insofar as Brown's commitments to the church—speaking with one voice in the world for the sake of all creation— provide a powerful framework for thinking about the purpose of ecumenism: the church exists for mission and that mission is intrinsically related to the church's unity. In a certain sense, however, the work of ecumenical unity cannot exist apart from the specifically traditioned projects of Yoder, Day, and Stringfellow. As we turn now to the conclusion, we will explore more explicitly what we are to make of these varied ecclesiological relationships to nonviolent resistance to war.

Conclusion

As our exploration of nonviolent resistance to war and the ways in which it relates to the church comes to a close, two things should be clear. First, ecclesiology frames, forms, and relates to nonviolence in manifold ways, emerging in a variety of forms. In an age of a divided church, we could expect nothing less than plurality, but as I indicated at the onset, the presence of multiple forms is not a reason to lament but rather an opportunity for the churches to recognize the limits of their own witness and to receive the work of the Spirit from elsewhere. Second, nonviolence (as exercised by any one of these communions) is insufficient in terms of its capacity to meet the challenges posed by war. I suggest that the outworkings of witness from one tradition can be coupled with the witness of others as churches begin to recognize the ecclesial life of other traditions and the ways in which they are accompanied by works of the Spirit.

Two basic aims have accompanied me throughout this book. First, I wanted to show the various ways in which nonviolent resistance—as described by four major opponents of the Vietnam War—has been understood as both an individual act of conscience and an act that is formed, framed, and related to ecclesiology. As I have suggested, the call of Christ is not simply to bear witness *against* war but also to bear witness *to* a new alternative form of life made known through the reconciling work of Christ. The articulation of this reconciliation is informed in no small way by a doctrine of the church, insofar as the act of witness in the New Testament is deeply intertwined with what the people of God have been called to be—a new body.

As my first task, I then set out to distinguish among these various articulations. Too often, when the terms *nonviolence* and *ecclesiology* are paired, the immediate impulse is to begin and end the discussion with Yoder's argument of the church as the embodiment of God's peace—or, as I have put it, the church *as* the witness against war. In these case studies, I have shown that while Yoder provides one way of configuring the relationship between ecclesiology and nonviolence, his way is not the only way. As I have argued, Yoder's work remains silent on a variety of aspects of the witness against war that other figures do address, such as the role of virtue formation (Day), the church's failure in witness (Stringfellow), and the ecumenical nature of ecclesial nonviolence (Brown).

If Christian nonviolence is to have a future rooted in the church, it behooves us to be honest about both the promise and the shortcomings of each of these proposals. Accomplishing this task requires that distinctions be drawn between these ecclesiologies: the Catholic way is not the Mennonite way is not the way of the Episcopalians or the Presbyterians. Were I to continue this book ad infinitum, any number of other figures from the Methodist, Eastern Orthodox, or (my own) Baptist traditions—such as Martin Luther King Jr. or Clarence Jordan—could be added to the conversation. However, if nonviolence proceeds as a work of the Spirit within a particular communion—bearing witness to the reconciliation of Christ—the presuppositions of a Baptist ecclesiology will result in a form of witness that is not identical with that of a Roman Catholic or a Mennonite. After drawing these distinctions, I asserted that these acts of witness are not dissimilar either.

Having distinguished between the different ways in which Christian witness against war proceeds, my second aim was to explore how these proposals might be drawn back together. As I argued , if we understand the church to be grounded in the work of the Holy Spirit, who draws the church into the world for the sake of witness, we could further say that the analogous works of witness present via various ecclesial traditions are not entirely dissimilar but rather the fruit of one Spirit. Dietrich Bonhoeffer's early work presents us with a powerful way to conceive of this unity—as churches grounded in their time and place by the work of the Spirit, who grows and nourishes in multiplicity and unity. The narration of these divergent formations of ecclesiology and nonviolence should not lead us to think that these formations are mutually exclusive. Rather, if these churches are born of the same Spirit, then the presence of analogical works of witness against war should lead us to consider the ways in which ecumenical unity is the logical companion to these common works of nonviolent witness against war.

In conclusion, two sets of questions that require more explication underlie the discussions of this book. First, in what sense are these various explications of nonviolence—born out of the Spirit's work within a congregation—indications of the church's unity? Does this claim mean that common actions emerging from divergent church traditions are sufficient to call the church unified? If so, what are we to make of intrachurch unity between these churches in cases where resistance to war is not evident? Second, can these works be seen as compatible works of the Spirit, given that divergent ecclesial presuppositions form each proposal? Does calling these common works of the Spirit ultimately diminish the role that ecclesiology plays in the formation of these acts? Each of these questions deserves a book of its own, but in what follows, I will sketch out answers in the hope that what has been presented in this book may further the church universal's unity in its witness against war.

Ecumenicity and Witness

The first question we must answer is what to make of the various forms of nonviolence described in the previous chapters, particularly when held up against the call of the church to be as one. In certain respects, Brown's work broaches this topic by refusing to see the tasks of witness and confession as utterly separate. Insofar as the church's confession and the church's witness are not two distinct acts but inseparable threads in the same ecclesial cloth, discussions of ecumenical confession and ecumenical witness impinge upon one another. To be the body of Christ is to acknowledge that the church is gathered by the Spirit as the witness to God in Christ, both in its life together and in diaspora throughout society.

Brown's formula, however, is not universally held within these discussions of nonviolence and its relationship to ecumenism. If one argues for an equivocation between practice and confession—put differently, that one's theological confession is only borne out *as* practice—then a unity in nonviolent witness is *de facto* a unity of theological confession.[1] While I do not wish to separate these two aspects (confession and action) of the church's existence, I find it problematic to view them as interchangeable. The common complaint by advocates against war is that proclamations of confessional unity, such as seen in the World Council of Churches, have had little bearing on its common external witness. However, if we reverse this problem by locating the church's unity in its

1. Such an approach runs beneath Craig M. Watts's statement that "only a nonviolent church can be united adequately in order to witness to Jesus as Lord that the world might believe," in Watts, "Church Unity and the Necessity of Nonviolence," *Journal of Ecumenical Studies* 39 (2002): 368–75. See also Miroslav Volf, *Exclusion and Embrace: A Theological Exploration of Identity, Otherness, and Reconciliation* (Nashville: Abingdon, 1996), 54ff.

external actions, without consideration of the disunity of worship and confession, we would simply repeat the problem in a different way.

In short, identifying a common action such as nonviolent resistance to war is not sufficient for comprehensive church unity since any number of common issues of polity, worship, liturgy, confession, and practice remain divided. For example, Catholics and Baptists who join together in a common witness against war cannot circumvent the fact that these two bodies do not share a common Eucharistic meal.[2] In suggesting that nonviolence (emerging from various traditions) indicates a mutually recognizable work of the Spirit, I am not attempting to collapse the theological differences that remain between traditions; rather, I hope to point to these common works as common works of the Spirit that can provide a sign to the churches of their unity in Christ—or at the very least, that the works of the Spirit create a non-competitive witness among presently divided churches. Such a sign does not overcome other disunions but serves as a marker to the churches that other forms of disunity must not be ignored or uncritically perpetuated.

In saying that common action is not sufficient for full ecumenism, I am ultimately suggesting that, when it comes to the question of the divided church, nonviolence may have an important but not comprehensive role. Such a modest description of nonviolence's role in ecumenical unity runs counter to proposals that emphasize the absolute nature of resistance to war for the sake of ecumenical unity, but with good reason. I am reticent to say that a common act of witness indicates unity because this tends to collapse the distinction-in-unity between the church's worship and ethics by subsuming

2. For reflections on the most recent Baptist-Catholic dialogues, see Arthur Serratelli and Paul S. Fiddes, "The Word of God in the Life of the Church: A Report of International Conversations between the Catholic Church and the Baptist World Alliance," Vatican Website, 2006–2010, http://www.vatican.va/roman_curia/pontifical_councils/chrstuni/Baptist_alliance/rc_pc_ chrstuni_ doc_20101213_ report-2006-2010_en.html.

the work of the Spirit into our creaturely response. By preserving the distinction between the church's internal life and its external witness, we are able to do justice to the specificity and integrity of the various ecclesio-logics present among the various traditions that form nonviolence in diverse ways. We are also able to say that church unity occurs in and through common witness but cannot comprise only that common witness.

As a work of the Spirit, the common witness against war presses the churches to recognize the good, specific work that the Spirit accomplishes in and through the various communions as well asthe legitimacy of other communions, insofar as the Spirit works among them. However, a difficulty emerges in regard to this proposal: If a common witness against war is an indication of the Spirit's common work, what we are to make of church communions in which this moral act is not a conclusion? As we saw with Dorothy Day, how do we regard communions that retain a divided opinion concerning resistance to war or that view resistance to war as a unique vocation or charism? Again, insofar as a unity-in-distinction exists between the church's worship and its witness, we cannot say that those communions without a strong so-called "peace witness" are somehow deficient as churches or that they lack the work of the Spirit. As we saw with Day in particular, the calling of the church to be a voice of peace in the world was understood differently by the Catholic Worker and the NCCB.

In addressing what to make of churches unpersuaded by nonviolence, naming nonviolence as a work of the Spirit can be understood in the following way. As an act that emerges from the people of God drawn together by the Holy Spirit, nonviolence serves as a sign to churches relatively unpersuaded by nonviolence that their fidelity to Christ is not in question, insofar as the gifts of the Spirit are manifold. As long as the Spirit is the one in whom all the churches are unified in both confession and witness, the work of the Spirit—present in a way that is jarring to some communions—draws churches divided on the question of war to reconsider the parameters and depths of possible witness as well as the other ways (polity, confession, and worship) in which division persists between churches called together by the same Spirit.

The nonviolence that emerges through church life is a gift to both the world and other churches. As a gift to the world, the nonviolence of the churches offers a sign of Christ's peace and a tangible witness to that peace, which is expressed in manifold ways, practices, and tactics. Insofar as war continues to impinge upon various aspects of society (as indicated in chapter 2), the churches are called to bear witness in manifold ways and to consider the moral implications of their actions—including everything from their purchases to their preaching to their tax status. In doing so, the church's gift to the world increases in complexity and depth as they meet each new iteration of war's reach with a theologically consistent witness of Christ's peace.

The nonviolence that emerges from some communions is a gift to other communions in a different way. Presented in the world as an extension of the church's internal life, nonviolence becomes a sign for churches not presently inclined toward resisting war by introducing them to new modalities of discipleship, which are fueled by the Spirit. This is not to negate the work of the Spirit within communions lacking commitments toward nonviolence but to expose them to the Spirit's work in a new way so that, in the words of the apostle Paul, God might be all in all, moving all of the churches together toward their fullness.[3]

3. 1 Cor. 15:28. Paul is specifically referring to the resurrection, but the sequencing of his language is crucial: in the same way that the Spirit attests to the resurrection of Christ, which is for the sake of the completion of God's work in the world ("that God would be all in all"),

Ecclesiology, Fullness of the Spirit, and Creaturely Life

Throughout this book, I have also considered the compatibility of these proposals. As acts of witness emerge in and through very diverse ecclesial presuppositions and configurations, they cannot be unequivocally interchanged. To say that the Holy Spirit works across confessional lines is not controversial by any means, but in what sense are these cross-confessional works of Spirit compatible, given that different ecclesial presuppositions form each one? Insofar as the Spirit's work forms the church into the image of Christ, we have asked questions in each chapter about how Christ is present, what resources are required toward the end of witness, and what practices are necessary for the church to be made fully into the image of Christ by the Spirit. Whether or not the Spirit is at work in various communions is not under debate, but there remain disputes across communions concerning whether or not each possesses equal instantiations of the Spirit.[4] To put it more sharply, if the Spirit is present more fully in one ecclesial form than in another, can we truly say that parity or compatibility exists among the various manifestations of nonviolent resistance produced by these ecclesiologies?

Returning to Bonhoeffer's formulation, the mere fact that a church *is*, through the Spirit, drives us to consider what it means that the Spirit is at work in this place and this time. As Bonhoeffer writes so powerfully in the opening chapter of *Life Together*, the measure of a church's validity is not whether it has attained all of the features

so the work of nonviolence—as a work of the Spirit—attests to Christ to other churches, so that the churches together might reach a more full maturity in their work, witness, and fidelity.

4. As Evan Kuehn points out, the "fullness of the Spirit" is often linked to "fullness of catholicity." This latter term is freighted with additional presuppositions of apostolicity and authority that determine "fullness of the Spirit," which is determined by ecumenical unity, in Evan Kuehn, "'Fullness of the Spirit' and 'Fullness of Catholicity' in Ecclesial Communion," *International Journal of Systematic Theology* 11 (2009): 271–92.

or facets that it might see as desirable, but whether it is in fact a church built in harmony and discipleship, according to what God has made it to be.[5] Christ is the center of a church that the Spirit has drawn together, not according to their prior design of "churchness," but according to the work of God; the practices of discipleship and worship, in turn, help bear out the work of the Spirit, forming the people by habit and practice into persons whose lives acknowledge that their source and unity is the Spirit who directs us to Christ.[6]

If the Spirit gives *in* and *through* diversities of communion, then it follows that a communion already possesses what it needs in terms of "fullness" because the Spirit gives according to what is needed by the body.[7] Though fullness remains to be granted in an eschatological sense, according to Bonhoeffer, that which is needed for a communion to be full is a work of the Spirit. This does not negate the gifts and lives of other communions, insofar as to be of the Spirit is to be given toward other churches, which are also founded in and through the work of the Spirit. If fullness of the Spirit is dependent upon the Spirit's work and the Spirit's fullness is dependent upon the particularities of the church as it lives before God and God's call to the world, then what draws these various formulations into conversation with one another on equal footing is not whether a church body makes use of all potential resources but whether a church is, in the end, seeking to be formed into the image of Christ by the Spirit.

This strong emphasis upon the Spirit's work would seem, ironically, to devalue the role of ecclesiology. Does this mean that the creaturely labor of the church is incidental to the Spirit's work? Far

5. Dietrich Bonhoeffer, *Life Together and Prayerbook of the Bible*, DBW 5 (Minneapolis: Fortress Press, 2005). As Bonhoeffer writes, "Christian community means community through and in Jesus Christ" (ibid., 33). This Christological community is distinguished from communities of our own design by the corporate life being "surrendered to the Holy Spirit" (ibid., 40).

6. Ibid., 40–41.

7. 1 Cor. 12:1-14.

from it. As Bonhoeffer puts it, the church's discipleship is the material way by which we enter into our union with Christ. Only as a church lives out its particular material vocation—in worship, reading of Scripture, celebration of Eucharist, formation in the virtues, and mission—does the work of the Spirit proceeds. Bonhoeffer is not speaking of an idealistic work of the Spirit that is detached from earthy realities but deeply embedded within the turns of history. Though the life of the church is of God, the church's life is lived in and through the world, amidst creaturely actions and habits.

With this acknowledgment of the Holy Spirit's work in place, the various instantiations of nonviolent resistance to war can come into contact with one another more fruitfully. For example, it may appear that Brown's support of nonviolent public policy forms is incompatible with Yoder's vision of the church as witness, particularly when we consider the distinction between the church's worship and its public ethic within Brown's own ecclesiology. But when we consider that both Yoder and Brown are working out of a framework in which the church and world are held together by Christ's work, the distance between the two is not so great as we imagine. The question Yoder and Brown must reconcile is *in what way* does Christ's holding together of church and world call for the church to participate in the world. Questions still remain concerning the way in which Christ serves as a moral example for Christians, how our own nonviolence participates in the life of God, and how to subject one church's particular confessional tradition to the critique of other traditions for the sake of common witness. While close on their common nonviolent witness, on more dogmatic issues, Brown and Yoder remain far apart, with much work to be done.

Perhaps it appears that the apocalyptic approach of Stringfellow—which supports more radical, powers-opposing acts such as burning draft offices—is incompatible with Day's approach, which emphasizes formation in virtue and development of a person's love, of treating even draft officials and their offices with charity. Such differences may seem to be particularly accentuated when we remember that Stringfellow's ecclesiology is predicated on a difference between the act of God and the church, and Day's is predicated on the church being the telos of God's activity in creation. However, when we understand that both Stringfellow and Day hold that the work of Christ supersedes any claim made by the state, their differences are reshaped in terms of what is required to make a christologically-centered witness. Day's work challenges Stringfellow to consider the ways in which the powers conscript not only our actions but also our virtues, and Stringfellow challenges Day to be less patient with structures that have become hardened toward the peaceableness of the Gospel. Ecclesiologically, Day challenges Stringfellow to reconsider—in light of God's work of redemption appears through the church—whether he should reconsider stronger associations with the institutional church; similarly, Stringfellow pushes Day to ecclesiologically consider—in light of the difference between the Church's Tradition and its actions—whether Christ's work requires embodiment in the Church to be intelligible.

Perhaps Yoder's lack of discussion concerning virtue and Day's emphasis on the formation of a person's love seem to provide incompatible forms of nonviolence: a kind of deontology on Yoder's part and a virtue-based ethic on Day's. But if we consider that, for both, the means required to follow in the pattern of Christ are related to how Christ's work implicates human life, they are not so far apart. Both Yoder's emphasis on Christ's life as that which the church is called to imitate in its life and Day's emphasis on Christ's Mystical Body calling to all people in their loves are concerned with how the church's practice follows Christ's example. In different ways, both articulate that the life of Christ implicates human existence in profound ways and that the church is intrinsic to the demonstration of that life in corporate form. *How* we are made able to follow Christ—whether in imitation or in the formation of our loves—remains an issue for discussion, framed by a common concern for Christ's normativity for human existence.

Once we recognize that the Spirit has worked through a communion different from our own, the common work of God in Christ creates a new possibility for an ecumenical witness against war that does not minimize differences among communions but creates the potential for an ecumenical nonviolence that might lead to other ecumenical discussions—and eventually, to unity among the churches. With respect to the resistance to war, the aim throughout this book has ultimately been to broaden our thinking—to draw the churches into communion with one another so that through their common witness, they might offer a full-bodied witness against war, borne from the work of the many bodies of Christ that are, in truth, the same body of Christ. It is my prayer that we might hear this hope in the words of Bonhoeffer, writing with the Second World War in view and the first one barely a memory:

> With the proclamation of peace, however, the church imparts the message of a new humanity, of the holy fellowship in Christ. Yet this fellowship is founded on the peace that Christ on the cross has brought into the world—the community of those chosen by God, of the humble who stand beneath the cross, of the watchful, the obedient, and the community of those to whom God desires to be merciful. That is the new fellowship.[8]

8. Dietrich Bonhoeffer, *Ecumenical, Academic, and Pastoral Work: 1931–1932,* DBW 11 (Minneapolis: Fortress Press, 2009), 380.

Bibliography

Ackerman, Peter and Jack DuVall. *A Force More Powerful: A Century of Nonviolent Conflict*. New York: Palgrave Macmillan, 2001.

Allman, Mark. *Who Would Jesus Kill?: War, Peace, and the Christian Tradition.* Winon, MN: St. Mary's, 2008.

Applebaum, Patricia. *Kingdom to Commune: Protestant Pacifist Culture between World War I and the Vietnam Era.* Chapel Hill: University of North Carolina Press, 2009.

———. *Against Faustus*, bk. 22, ch. 74–75, 78. In *Augustine: Political Writings.* Edited by Ernest Fortin and Douglas Kries. Indianapolis: Hackett, 1993.

———. *City of God.* Translated by Henry Bettenson. London: Penguin Books, 1984.

———. *St. Augustine: The Retractions.* Translated by Sister M. Inez Bogan, RSM. Washington D.C.: Catholic University of America Press, 1999.

Aquinas, Thomas. *Summa Theologica.* Translated by Fathers of the English Dominican Province. New York: Benzinger Brothers, 1981.

Bacevich, Andrew. *Washington Rules: The Permanent Path to War.* New York: Metropolitan Books, 2008.

Bainton, Roland H. *Christian Attitudes toward War and Peace: A Historical Survey and Critical Re-Evaluation.* Nashville: Abingdon, 1979.

Barber, Daniel Cucciello."The Particularity of Jesus and the Time of the Kingdom": Philosophy and Theology in Yoder." *Modern Theology* 23 (2007): 63–90.

Barkat, Anwar M., ed. *Conflict, Violence, and Peace: A Report of a Consultation on "Alternatives to Conflict in the Quest of Peace" in the Ecumenical Institute in Bossey in Summer, 1969* (Geneva: World Council of Churches, 1970).

Barth, Karl. *Evangelical Theology: An Introduction.* New York: Holt, Reinhart, and Winston, 1962.

Baskir, Lawrence M. *Chance and Circumstance: The Draft, the War, and the Vietnam Generation.* New York: Knopf, 1978.

Battle, Michael. *Blessed Are the Peacemakers.* Macon, GA: Mercer University Press, 2004.

Bauerschmidt, Frederick Christian. "The Politics of the Little Way: Dorothy Day Reads Therese of Lisieux." In *American Catholic Traditions: Resources for Renewal*, edited by Sandra Yocum Mize and William Portier, 77–95. Maryknoll, NY: Orbis Books, 1996.

Baxter, Michael. "'Blowing the Dynamite of the Church': Catholic Radicalism from a Catholic Radicalist Perspective." In *Dorothy Day and the Catholic Worker Movement: Centenary Essays*, edited by William J. Thorn, Phillip M. Runkel, and Sousan Mountin, 79–94. Marquette: Marquette University Press, 2001.

Bedenedetti, Charles M. *An American Ordeal: The Antiwar Movement of the Vietnam Era.* Syracuse, NY: Syracuse University Press, 1990.

Bell, Daniel M. *Just War as Christian Discipleship: Recentering the Tradition in the Church rather than the State.* Grand Rapids: Brazos, 2009.

Bender, Harold. *The Anabaptist Vision.* Scottdale, PA: Herald, 1944.

Berkhof, Hendrik. *Christ and the Powers.* Translated by John Howard Yoder. Scottdale, PA: Herald, 1962.

Berrigan, Daniel. *They Call Us Dead Men: Reflections on Life and Conscience.* New York: Macmillan, 1965.

———. To Celebrate the Death and Life of William Stringfellow." *Religion and Intellectual Life* 2 (1985): 71–74.

Benedict XV. *Ad Beatissimi Apostolorum* [Encyclical Appealing for Peace]. Vatican website. January 11, 1914. http://www.vatican.va/holy_father/benedict_xv/encyclicals/documents/hf_ben-xv_enc_01111914_ad-beatissimi-apostolorum_en.html.

Bennett, John. *Christians and the State.* New York: Charles Scribner's Sons, 1958.

Bergen, Jeremy M. *Ecclesial Repentance: The Churches Confront Their Sinful Pasts.* Edinburgh: T&T Clark, 2011.

Bethge, Eberhard. *Bonhoeffer: Exile and Martyr.* New York: Seabury, 1975.

Bezilla, Gregory. "William Stringfellow's Theology and Ethics of Eschatological Existence." MDiv Thesis, Emory University, 1998.

Biggar, Nigel. *In Defence of War.* Oxford: Oxford University Press, 2013.

———. "Specify and Distinguish! Interpreting the New Testament on 'Non-Violence.'" *Studies in Christian Ethics* 22, no. 2 (January 2009): 164–84.

Bonhoeffer, Dietrich. *Creation and Fall: A Theological Exposition of Genesis 1–3.* Edited by John W. de Gruchy. Translated by Douglas Stephen Bax. Dietrich Bonhoeffer Works 3. Minneapolis: Fortress Press, 1997.

———. *Discipleship.* Edited by John D. Godsey and Geffrey B. Kelly. Translated by Barbara Green and Reinhard Krauss. Dietrich Bonhoeffer Works 4. Minneapolis: Fortress Press, 2003.

———. *Ecumenical, Academic, and Pastoral Work: 1931–1932.* Edited by Victoria J. Barnett, Mark Brocker, Michael B. Lukens. Translated by Isabel Best, Nicholas S. Humphrey, Marion Pauck, Anne Schmidt-Lange, and Douglas W. Stott. Dietrich Bonhoeffer Works 11. Minneapolis: Fortress Press, 2012.

———. *Life Together and Prayerbook of the Bible*. Edited by Geffrey B. Kelly. Translated by Daniel W. Bloesch and James H. Burtness. Dietrich Bonhoeffer Works 5. Minneapolis: Fortress Press, 2005.

———. *Sanctorum Communio: A Theological Study of the Sociology of the Church*. Edited by Clifford J. Green. Translated by Joachim Von Soosten, Reinhard Kraus, and Nancy Lukens. Dietrich Bonhoeffer Works 1. Minneapolis: Fortress Press, 2009.

Bourne, Richard. *Seek the Peace of the City: Christian Political Criticism as Public, Realist, and Transformative*. Eugene, OR: Cascade Books, 2009.

Bretherton, Luke. *Christianity and Contemporary Politics*. Malden, MA: Wiley–Blackwell, 2010.

Brimlow, Robert. *What About Hitler? Wrestling With Jesus' Call to Nonviolence in an Evil World*. Grand Rapids: Brazos, 2006.

Brock, Peter. *Freedom from Violence: Sectarian Nonresistance from the Middle Ages to the Great War*. Toronto: University of Toronto Press, 1991.

———. *Pacifism in the United States: From the Colonial Era to the First World War*. Princeton: Princeton University Press, 1969.

Brock, Peter and Nigel Young. *Pacifism in the Twentieth Century*. Syracuse, NY: Syracuse University Press, 1999.

Brock, Rita Nakashima and Gabriella Lettini. *Soul Repair: Recovering from Moral Injury after War*. Boston: Beacon, 2012.

Brown, Robert McAfee. "An American Protestant View." *Cross Currents* 12 (1962): 232–38.

———. "The Berrigans: Signs or Models?" In *The Berrigans*, ed. William Van–Etten Casey. Avon Paperback, 1972.

———. *The Bible Speaks to You*. Philadelphia: Westminster, 1955.

———. "A Campaign on Many Fronts." *Christian Century* 82 (1965): 577–79.

———. "The Catholic Bishops and the Draft." *Christianity and Crisis* 28 (1969): 328–29.

———. "Confessions of a Political Neophyte." *Christianity and Crisis* 12 (1953): 186–91.

———. "Dead Policy, Revived Conscience." *Church and Society* 61 (1971): 15–22.

———. "Discoveries and Dangers." *Christian Century* 87 (1970): 40–45.

———. *The Ecumenical Revolution.* Garden City, NY: Doubleday, 1967.

———. "The Emerging Ecumenical Complex." *Theology Today* 20 (1964): 528–40.

———. "Eschatological Hope and Social Responsibility." *Christianity and Crisis* 13 (1953): 146–49.

———. "Further Reflections on Freedom Riding." *Christianity and Crisis* 21 (August 7, 1961): 146–47.

———. "Is Ecumenism Reversing Our Roles?." *Journal of Ecumenical Studies* 7, no. 4 (1970): 783–85.

———. *Is Faith Obsolete?* Philadelphia: Westminster, 1974.

———. "Jews, Christians, and Human Beings." *Christianity and Crisis* 22 (April 30, 1962): 62–63.

———. *Liberation Theology.* Louisville: Westminster John Knox, 1993.

———. "Military Chaplaincy as Ministry." In *Military Chaplains: From a Religious Military to a Military Religion*, ed. Harvey Cox. New York: American Report, 1973.

———. *Observer in Rome: A Protestant Report on the Vatican Council.* Garden City, NY: Doubleday, 1964.

———. "On the Steps of the Federal Building." *Social Progress* 58 (1968): 43–45.

———. *The Pseudonyms of God.* Louisville: Westminster, 1972.

———. *P.T. Forsyth: Prophet for Today.* Philadelphia: Westminster, 1952.

———. *Reflections over the Long Haul: A Memoir.* Louisville: Westminster John Knox, 2005.

———. "Reformation Then and Now—A Reformed Perspective." *Lutheran World* 14, vol. 3 (1967): 33–42.

———, ed. *Reinhold Niebuhr: Selected Essays and Addresses.* New Haven: Yale University, 1986.

———. *Religion and Violence.* 2nd ed. Philadelphia: Westminster, 1987.

———. "Revision of Selective Service." *Christianity and Crisis* 27 (1968): 322–23.

———. "The Road to Unity." *Christianity and Crisis* 21 (October 30, 1961):179.

———. *The Significance of the Church.* Philadelphia: Westminster, 1956.

———. *The Spirit of Protestantism.* Oxford: Oxford University Press, 1961.

———. "Teaching Theology in a University Setting." *Union Seminary Quarterly Review* 22 (1967): 357–65.

———. "That All May Be One." *Christianity and Crisis* 12 (1952): 59–62.

———. "Theology and the Gospel: Reflections on Theological Method." in *Theology and Church in Times of Change: Essays in Honor of John Bennett Coleman*, ed. Edward LeRoy Long and Robert T. Handy. Philadelphia: Westminster, 1970. 15–33.

———. "Theology as an Act of Gratitude." *Union Seminary Quarterly Review* 16 (1960): 83–95.

———. *Theology in a New Key: Responding to Liberation Themes.* Philadelphia: Westminster, 1978.

———. "To the Defense of Reinhold Niebuhr." *Christian Century* (January 30, 1963): 142–43.

———. "Tradition as a Protestant Problem." *Theology Today* 17 (1961): 430–54.

———. "True and False Witness: Architecture and the Church." *Theology Today* 23 (1967); 521–37.

———. "Uppsala: An Informal Report." *Journal of Ecumenical Studies* 5 (1968): 633–60.

———. "The Uses of the Past." *Theology Today* 31 (1974): 104–13.

———. "The WCC and Selective Objection." *Christianity and Crisis* 28 (1968): 195–96.

———. "What Can We Do?." *Christianity and Crisis* 30 (1971): 293–95.

———. When the Church Speaks Out." *Christianity and Crisis* 14, no. 3 (1954): 17–19.

Brown, Robert McAfee and Gustav Weigel. *An American Dialogue: A Protestant Looks at Catholicism and a Catholic Looks at Protestantism.* Garden City, NY: Doubleday, 1960.

Brown, Robert McAfee, Abraham J. Heschel, and Michael Novak. *Vietnam: Crisis of Conscience.* New York: Herder and Herder, 1967.

Burnell, Peter. "Justice in War In and Before Augustine." *Studia Patristica* 49 (2010): 107–10

Bush, Perry. *Two Kingdoms, Two Loyalties: Mennonite Pacifism in Modern America.* Baltimore: Johns Hopkins University Press, 1998.

Butler, Judith. *Frames of War: When Is Life Grievable?* London: Verso, 2009.

Buzzanco, Robert. *Masters of War: Military Dissent and Politics in the Vietnam Era.* New York: Cambridge University Press, 1996.

Byrd, James P. *Sacred Scripture, Sacred War: The Bible and the American Revolution.* New York: Oxford University Press, 2013.

Cahill, Lisa S. *Love Your Enemies.* Minneapolis: Fortress Press, 1994.

Campbell, Debra. "The Catholic Earth Mother: Dorothy Day and Women's Power in the Church." *Cross Currents* 34 (1984): 270–82.

Carmody, Denise Lardner and John T. Carmody. *The Future of Prophetic Christianity.* Maryknoll, NY: Orbis Books, 1993.

Carmody, John T. "The Baltic Security andDevelopment of Robert McAfee Brown's Ecumenical Thought." *Religion in Life* 43 (1974), 283–93.

Carnahan, Kevin. "Perturbations of the Soul and Pains of the Body: Augustine on Evil Suffered and Done in War." *Journal of Religious Ethics* 36 (2008): 269–94.

Carter, Craig. *The Pacifism of the Messianic Community: The Social Ethics of John Howard Yoder*. PhD diss., St. Michael's College, 1999.

———. *The Politics of the Cross: The Theology and Social Ethics of John Howard Yoder*. Grand Rapids: Brazos, 2001.

Carter, Stephen L. *The Violence of Peace.* New York: Beast Books, 2011.

Cassidy, Robert M. "Counterinsurgency and Military Culture: State Regulars versus Non-State Irregulars." *Defense Review* 10 (2008): 53–85.

Cavanaugh, William. "The City: Beyond Secular Parodies." In *Radical Orthodoxy: A New Theology*, ed. John Milbank, Catherine Pickstock, and Graham Ward. London: Routledge, 1998.

———. Dorothy Day and the Mystical Body of Christ in the Second World War." in *Dorothy Day and the Catholic Worker Movement: Centenary Essays*, ed. William J. Thorn, Phillip M. Runkel, and Susan Mountin, 457–64. Marquette: Marquette University Press, 2001.

———. "From One City to Two: Christian Reimagining of Political Space." *Political Theology* 7 (July 2006): 299–321.

———. "Killing in the Name of God," *New Blackfriars* 85 (September 2004): 510–26.

———. *The Myth of Religious Violence.* Oxford: Oxford University, 2009.

———. *Torture and Eucharist: Theology, Politics, and the Body of Christ.* Malden, MA:Wiley-Blackwell, 1998.

Chapman, Mark D. "William Stringfellow and the Politics of Liturgy." In *William Stringfellow in Anglo-American Perspective*, ed. Anthony Dancer, 150–62. Aldershot, UK: Ashgate Publishers, 2005.

Charles, J. Daryl. "Presumption against War or Presumption against Injustice? The Just War Tradition Reconsidered." *Journal of Church and State* 47, no. 2 (Spring 2005), 335–69.

Chatfield, Charles. "The Catholic Worker in the United States Peace Tradition." In *American Catholic Pacifism: The Influence of Dorothy Day and the Catholic Worker Movement*, ed. Anne Klejment and Nancy L. Roberts, 1–13. Westport, CN: Praeger, 1996.

Churchill, Ward. *Pacifism as Pathology*. Oakland: AK Press, 2007.

Cicovacki, Predrag, ed. *The Ethics of Nonviolence: Essays by Robert L. Holmes*. London: Bloomsbury Academic, 2013.

Clough, David L. and Brian Siltner. *Faith and Force: A Christian Debate about War*. Washington, DC: Georgetown University Press, 2007.

Coles, Robert. *Dorothy Day: A Radical Devotion*. Reading, MA: Addison-Wesley, 1989.

Cook, Martin L. "Just Peacemaking: Challenges of Humanitarian Intervention." *Journal of the Society of Christian Ethics* 23, no.1 (Spring–Summer 2003): 241–53.

Cooney, John. *The American Pope: The Life and Times of Francis Cardinal Spellman*. New York: New York Times Books, 1984.

Cortright, David. *Peace: A History of Movements and Ideas*. Cambridge: Cambridge University Press, 2008.

Coy, Patrick, "Houses of Hospitality: A Pilgrimage into Nonviolence." In *A Revolution of the Heart: Essays on the Catholic Worker*, edited by Patrick G. Coy, 239–71. Philadelphia: Temple University Press, 1988.

Crowley, Paul, ed. *Robert McAfee Brown: Spiritual and Prophetic Writings*. Maryknoll, NY: Orbis Books, 2013.

Dancer, Anthony. *An Alien in a Strange Land: Theology in the Life of William Stringfellow*. Eugene, OR: Cascade, 2010.

———, ed. *William Stringfellow in Anglo-American Perspective*. Aldershot, UK: Ashgate, 2005.

Davis, Grady Scott. *Warcraft and the Fragility of Virtue*. Moscow, ID: University of Idaho Press, 1992.

Dawson, David. "Transcendence as Embodiment: Augustine's Domestication of Gnosis." *Modern Theology* 10 (1994): 1–26.

Day, Dorothy. "Ammon Hennacy: 'Non–Church' Christian." *Catholic Worker*, February 1970.

———. "Are Our Leaders Insane?." *Catholic Worker*. April 1954.

———. "Atom Bomb and Conscription Still Issues to Be Faced." *Catholic Worker*, April 1946.

———. "The Case of Cardinal MacIntyre." *Catholic Worker*. July–August 1964.

———. "The Case of Father Duffy." *Catholic Worker*. December 1949.

———. "Catholic Worker Celebrates Third Birthday; A Restatement of C. W. Aims and Ideals." *Catholic Worker*. May 1936.

———. "Catholic Worker Ideas on Hospitality." *Catholic Worker*. May 1940.

———. "Catholic Worker Program." *Catholic Worker*. December 1933.

———. "The Church and Work." *Catholic Worker*. September 1946.

———. "Co-operative Apartment for Unemployed Women Has Its Start in Parish." *Catholic Worker*. December 1933.

———. "Day after Day." *Catholic Worker*. December 1942.

———. "Days with an End." *Catholic Worker*. April 1934.

———. *The Eleventh Virgin*. New York: Boni, 1928.

———. "Fall Appeal—November 1957." *Catholic Worker*. November 1957.

———. "Fall Appeal—October 1963." *Catholic Worker*. October 1963.

———. "Fear in Our Time." In *Peace through Reconciliation: Proceedings of the Pax Conference at Spode House,* 1–14. Eugene, OR: October 1963.

———. "Francis and Ignatius." *Catholic Worker*. September 1956.

———. *From Union Square to Rome*. Silver Spring, MD: Preservation of the Faith, 1938. Reprint, Maryknoll, NY: Orbis Books, 2006.

———. "Holy Obedience." *Ave Maria*. December 17, 1966.

———. *House of Hospitality*. London: Sheed & Ward, 1939.

———. "If Conscription Came for Women." *Catholic Worker*. January 1943.

———. "In Peace Is My Bitterness Most Bitter." In *Selected Writings,* ed. Robert Ellsberg, 115-17. Maryknoll, NY: Orbis Books, 2001. Previously published in *The Catholic Worker.* January 1967.

———. "Inventory." *Catholic Worker.* January 1951.

———. "Letter to Our Readers at the Beginning of Our Fifteenth Year." *Catholic Worker.* May 1947.

———. "Liturgy and Sociology." *Catholic Worker.* December 1935.

———. *Loaves and Fishes: The Story of the Catholic Worker Movement.* San Fransisco: Harper and Row, 1963.

———. *The Long Lonelines: The Autobiography of Dorothy Day.* With an introduction by Daniel Berrigan.New York: Harper and Row, 1952. Reprint, San Francisco: Harper, 1981.

———. "The Mystical Body and Spain." *Catholic Worker.* August 1936.

———. "On Distributism: Answer to John Cort." *Catholic Worker.* December 1948.

———. "On Pilgrimage." *Catholic Worker.* May 1948–November 1975.

———. *On Pilgrimage.* New York: Catholic Worker Books, 1948. Reprint, Grand Rapids: Eerdmans, 1999.

———. "Our Country Passes from Undeclared War to Declared War; We Continue Our Christian Pacifist Stand." *Catholic Worker.* January 1942.

———. "Our Stand." *Catholic Worker.* June 1940.

———. "Pacifism." *Catholic Worker.* May 1936.

———. "Peter's Program." *Catholic Worker.* May 1955.

———. "The Pope and Peace." *Catholic Worker.* February 1954.

———. "The Pope Is Dead. Long Live the Pope/Viva John XXIII." *Catholic Worker.* November 1958.

———. "Poverty and Precarity." *Catholic Worker.* May 1952.

———. "Poverty Is to Care and Not to Care." *Catholic Worker.* April 1953.

———. "Retreat." *Catholic Worker.* August 1959.

———. "The Scandal of the Works of Mercy." *Commonweal*, November 4, 1949.

———. *Selected Writings*. Edited by Robert Ellsberg. Maryknoll, NY: Orbis Books, 2001.

———. "Spring Mobilization." *Catholic Worker*. May 1967.

———. "Theophane Venard and Ho Chi Minh." *Catholic Worker*. May 1954.

———. *Therese: A Life of Therese of Lisieux*. Springfield, IL: Templeton, 1960. Reprint 1990.

———. "Things Worth Fighting For?" *Commonweal*. May 21, 1948.

———. "The Use of Force." *Catholic Worker*. November 1936.

———. "Wars Are Caused by Man's Loss of Faith in Man." *Catholic Worker*. September 1940.

———. "We Go on Record: CW Refuses Tax Exemption." *Catholic Worker*. May 1972.

———. "We Mourn Death of Gandhi Non Violent Revolutionary." *Catholic Worker*. February 1948.

———. "Wealth, The Humanity of Christ, Class War." *Catholic Worker*. June 1935.

———. "Where Are the Poor? They Are in Prisons, Too." *Catholic Worker*. July–August 1955.

———. "Why Do the Members of Christ Tear One Another?" *Catholic Worker*. February 1942.

Dear, John. *The God of Peace: Toward a Theology of Nonviolence*. Maryknoll, NY: Orbis Books, 1994.

———. *Put Your Sword Down: Answering the Gospel Call to Nonviolence*. Grand Rapids: Eerdmans, 2008.

DeCou, Jessica. "Relocating Barth's Theology of Culture: Beyond the 'True Words' Approach of *Church Dogmatics* IV/3." *International Journal of Systematic Theology* 15 (2013): 154–71.

Del Colle, Ralph. *Christ and the Spirit: Spirit-Christology in Trinitarian Perspective*. Oxford: Oxford University Press, 1994.

de Lubac, Henri Cardinal, SJ. *Catholicism: Christ and the Common Destiny of Man*. San Fransisco: Ignatius, 1988.

———. *Corpus Mysticum: The Eucharist and the Church in the Middle Ages*. Translated by Gemma Simmonds CJ, with Richard Prace and Christopher Stephens. Notre Dame: University of Notre Dame Press, 2006.

Dodaro, Robert. "Augustine's Use of Parallel Dialogues in His Preaching on Nonviolence." In *Ministerium Sermonis*, edited by Anthony Dupont, Mathijs Lamberigts, and Gert Partoens, 327–44. Turnhout, Bel.: Brepols, 2009.

———. "Between the Two Cities: Political Action in Augustine of Hippo." In *Augustine and Politics*, ed. John Doody, Kevin L. Hughes, and Kim Paffenroth. Lanham, MD: Lexington Books, 2005.

Doerksen, Paul G. "For and Against Milbank: A Critical Discussion of John Milbank's Construal of Ontological Peace." *Conrad Grebel Review* 18, no. 1 (Winter 2000): 48–59.

Dolet, Jean. "Un Mouvement de Spiritualitie Sacerdotale au Quebec au 20e Siecle (1931–1950): le Lacouturisme." *Societie Canadienne d'Histoire de L'Eglise Catholique* 40 (1974): 55–91.

Dreidger, Leo and Howard J. Kauffman. *The Mennonite Mosaic: Identity and Modernization*. Scottdale, PA: Herald, 1991.

Driedger, Leo and Donald Kraybill. *Mennonite Peacemaking: From Quietism to Activism*. Scottdale, PA: Herald, 1993.

Durnbaugh, Donald F. "John Howard Yoder's Role in the 'Lordship of Christ over Church and State' Conferences." *Mennonite Quarterly Review* 77 (2003): 371–86.

Dyson, R. W. *The Pilgrim City: Social and Political Ideas in the Writings of St. Augustine of Hippo*. Woodbridge, UK: Boydell, 2001.

Ebel, Jonathan H. *Faith in the Fight: Religion and the America Soldier in the Great War.* Princeton: Princeton University Press, 2007.

Egan, Eileen. "The Struggle of the Small Vehicle, Pax." In *American Catholic Pacifism: The Influence of Dorothy Day and the Catholic Worker Movement,* ed. Anne Klejment and Nancy L. Roberts, 123–52.Westport, CT: Praeger, 1996.

Elshtain Jean Bethke. *Just War against Terror: The Burden of American Power in a Violent World.* New York: Basic Books, 2003.

Enns, Fernando. *The Peace Church and the Ecumenical Community: Ecclesiology and the Ethics of Nonviolence.* Kitchener, ON: Pandora, 2007.

Flett, John. "Communion as Propaganda: Reinhard Hutter and the Missionary Witness of the 'Church as Public.'" *Scottish Journal of Theology* 62 (2009): 457–76.

———. *The Witness of God: The Trinity,* Missio Dei, *Karl Barth, and the Nature of Christian Community.* Grand Rapids: Eerdmans, 2010.

Flynn, George Q. *The Draft, 1940–1973.* Lawrence: University of Kansas Press, 1993.

———. *Roosevelt and Romanism: Catholics and American Diplomacy* 1937–1945. Westport, CT: Greenwood, 1976.

Foley, Michael S. *Confronting the War Machine: Draft Resistance During the Vietnam War.* Chapel Hill: University of North Carolina Press, 2003.

Foucault, Michel. *Discipline and Punish.* Translated by Alan Sheridan. New York: Vintage Books, 1977. Originally published as *Suveiller et Punir.* Paris: Gallimard, 1975.

———. *Security, Territory, Population: Lectures at the College de France 1977–1978.* New York: Picador, 2009.

Frary, Thomas. "The Ecclesiology of Dorothy Day." PhD diss., Marquette University, 1972.

Frei, Hans. *The Eclipse of the Biblical Narrative: A Study in Eighteenth and Nineteenth Century Hermeneutics.* New Haven: Yale University Press, 1980.

Friedland, Michael. "Breaking Silence: Churches and Opposition to the Vietnam War, 1964–1975." In vol. 3 of *The Cambridge History of Religions in America*, 1st ed, edited by Stephen J. Stein, 170–86. Cambridge: Cambridge University Press, 2012.

———. *Lift Up Your Voice Like a Trumpet: White Clergy and the Civil Rights and Antiwar Movements 1954–1973.* Chapel Hill: University of North Carolina Press, 1998.

Gaffney, Edward McGlynn, Jr. "The Challenge of Peace in an Age of Desert Storm Troopers." In *Radical Christian, Exemplary Lawyer: Honoring William Stringfellow*, edited by Andrew W. McThenia GrandRapids: Eerdmans, 1995.

Gelderloos, Peter. *How Nonviolence Protects the State.* London: South End, 2007.

Gill, Jill K. *Embattled Ecumenism: The National Council of Churches, The Vietnam War, and the Trials of the Protestant Left.* Dekalb, IL: Northern Illinois University, 2011.

Glenn, Linda. "Robert McAfee Brown: Presbyterian, Theologian, Activist." *American Presbyterian* 72 (1994): 49–59.

Gregg, Richard. *The Power of Nonviolence.* Philadelphia: J.B. Lippincott Publishing Company, 1934.

Gregory, Eric. *Politics and the Order of Love: An Augustinian Ethic of Democratic Citizenship.* Chicago: University of Chicago Press, 2008.

Griffiss, James F. "A Reluctant Anglican." In *Prophet of Justice, Prophet of Life*, edited by Robert Boak Slocum, 40–57. New York: Church, 1997.

Gros, Jeffrey and John D. Rempel, eds. *The Fragmentation of the Church and Its Unity in Peacemaking.* Grand Rapids: Eerdmans, 2001.

Gutierrez, Gustavo. "Option for the Poor." In *Systematic Theology: Perspectives from Liberation Theology*, edited by Jon Sobrino and Ignacio Ellacuria, 22–38. Maryknoll, NY: Orbis Books, 1996.

Guyot, Gilmore. *Scriptural References for the Baltimore Catechism: The Biblical Basis for Catholic Belief.* New York: Joseph F. Wagner, 1946.

Hall, Mitchell. *Because of Their Faith: CALCAV and Religious Opposition to the Vietnam War*. New York: Columbia University Press, 1990.

Hanby, Michael. "Democracy and Its Demons." In *Augustine and Politics*, edited by John Doody, Kevin L. Hughes, and Kim Paffenroth. Lanham, MD: Lexington Books, 2005.

Harink, Doug. *Paul among the Postliberals: Pauline Theology beyond Christendom and Modernity*. Grand Rapids: Brazos, 2003.

Harvey, Barry. "Accounting for Difference: Dietrich Bonhoeffer's Contribution to a Theological Critique of Culture." In *Mysteries in the Theology of Dietrich Bonhoeffer: A Copenhagen Bonhoeffer Symposium*, edited by Kristen Busch Nielsen, Ulrik Nissen, and Christiane Tietz, 81-109. Copenhagen: Vandenhoeck & Ruprecht, 2007.

———. "The Body Politic of Christ: Theology, Social Analysis, and Bonhoeffer's Arcane Discipline." *Modern Theology* 13 (1997): 319–46.

Hauerwas, Stanley. *Dispatches from the Front: Theological Engagements with the Secular.* Durham, NC: Duke University Press, 1994.

———. *The Peaceable Kingdom: A Primer in Christian Ethics.* Notre Dame: University of Notre Dame Press, 1983.

———. *War and the American Difference: Theological Reflections on Violence and National Identity.* Grand Rapids: Baker Academic, 2011.

———. *With the Grain of the Universe: The Church's Witness and Natural Theology*. Grand Rapids: Brazos, 2001.

Hauerwas, Stanley, Chris K. Huebner, Harry Huebner, Mark T. Nation, eds. *The Wisdom of the Cross: Essays in Honor of John Howard Yoder*. Grand Rapids: Eerdmans, 1999.

Hauerwas, Stanley and Samuel Wells. "Breaking Bread: Peace and War." In *The Blackwell Companion to Christian Ethics*, edited by Stanley Hauerwas and Samuel Wells, 415-27. Malden, MA: Blackwell, 2004.

Havel, Vaclav, ed. *Power of the Powerless: Citizens against the State in Central-Eastern Europe*. Armonk, NY: M.E. Sharpe, 1985.

Hays, Richard. *The Moral Vision of the New Testament*. New York: HarperOne, 1996.

———. "Narrate and Embody: A Response to Nigel Biggar 'Specify and Distinguish.'" *Studies in Christian Ethics* 22, no. 2 (January 2009): 185–98.

Healy, Nicholas. "Ecclesiology and Communion." *Perspectives in Religious Studies* 31, no. 3 (Fall 2004): 273–90.

Hector, Kevin. *Theology wqithout Metaphysics: God, Language, and the Spirit of Recognition*. Cambridge: Cambridge University Press, 2011.

Hein, David and Gardiner H. Shattuck. *The Episcopalians*. Westport, CT: Praeger, 2004.

Hershberger, Guy M. *War, Peace, and Nonresistance*. Scottdale, PA: Herald, 1946.

Heschel, Abraham Joshua. *Moral Grandeur and Spiritual Audacity*. New York: Noonday, 1996.

Hess, Cynthia. *Sites of Violence, Sites of Grace: Christian Nonviolence and the Traumatized Self*. Lanham, MD: Lexington Books, 2009.

Hixson, Walter L., ed. *The Vietnam Antiwar Movement*. New York: Garland, 2000.

Holmes, Arthur F. *War and Christian Ethics: Classic and Contemporary Readings on the Morality of War*. Grand Rapids: Baker Academic, 2005.

Homan, Gerlof D. *American Mennonites and the Great War, 1914–1918*. Scottdale, PA: Herald, 1994.

Hooper, J. Leon. "Dorothy Day's Transposition of Therese's 'Little Way.'" *Theological Studies* 63, no. 1 (2002): 68–86.

Horst, Irvin B, trans. and ed. *"Confession" and The New Birth*. Lancaster, PA: Lancaster Mennonite Historical Society, 1996.

Howes, Dustin Ells. *Toward a Credible Pacifism: Violence and the Possibilities of Politics*. Albany: State University of New York Press, 2009.

Huebner, Chris K. *A Precarious Peace: Yoderian Explorations on Theology, Knowledge, and Identity*. Scottdale: Herald, 2006.

———. "What Should Mennonites and Milbank Learn from Each Other?" *Conrad Grebel Review* 23 (Spring 2005): 9–18.

Hussain, Khurram. "Tragedy and History in Reinhold Niebuhr's Thought." *American Journal of Theology and Philosophy* 31 (2010): 147–59.

John XXIII. *Mater et Magistra* [Encyclical on Christianity and Social Progress]. Vatican Website. May 15, 1961. http://www.vatican.va/holy_father/john_xxiii/encyclicals/documents/hf_j-xxiii_enc_15051961_mater_en.html.

———. *Pacem in Terris* [Encyclical on Establishing Universal Peace in Truth, Justice, Charity, and Liberty]. April 11, 1963. New York: Abingdon, 1963.

Johnson, James Turner. "Can a Pacifist Have a Conversation with Augustine? A Response to Alain Epp Weaver." *Journal of Religious Ethics* 29, no.1 (Spring 2001): 87–93.

———. *Just War Tradition and the Restraint of War*. Princeton: Princeton University Press, 1981.

Johnston, Marshall Ron. "Bombast, Blasphemy, and the Bastard Gospel: William Stringfellow and American Exceptionalism." Unpublished PhD diss., Baylor University, 2007.

Jones, Paul Daffyd. *The Humanity of Christ*. Edinburgh: T&T Clark, 2008.

Justin Martyr, *First Apology*. In *St. Justin Martyr: The First and Second Apologies*, translated by Leslie William Barnard. Mahwah, NJ: Paulist, 1997.

Kalantzis, George. *Caesar and the Lamb: Early Christian Attitudes on War and Military Service.* Eugene, OR: Cascade Books, 2012.

Kantorowicz, Ernest. *The King's Two Bodies: A Study in Medieval Political Theology*. Princeton: Princeton University Publishing, 1957.

Keenan, James. *The Works of Mercy: The Heart of Catholicism.* Lanham, MD: Sheed & Ward, 2008.

Keim, Albert and Grant Stoltzfus. *The Politics of Conscience: The Historic Peace Churches and America at War, 1917–1955*. Scottdale, PA: Herald, 1988.

Kent, Peter C. "The War Aims of the Papacy." In *FDR, The Vatican, and The Roman Catholic Church in America, 1933–1945*, edited by David B. Woolner and Richard G. Kurial, 163–79. New York: Palgrave MacMillan, 2003.

Kent, Stephen A. *From Slogans to Mantras: Social Protest and Religious Conversion in the Late Vietnam War Era.* Syracuse, NY: Syracuse University Press, 2001.

Kerr, Nathan R. *Christ, History, and Apocalyptic: The Politics of Christian Mission.* Eugene, OR: Cascade Books, 2009.

Kinghorn, Warren. "Combat Trauma and Moral Fragmentation: A Theological Account of Moral Injury." *Journal of the Society of Christian Ethics* 32 (2012): 57–74.

Klejment, Anne. "The Radical Origins of Catholic Pacifism: Dorothy Day and the Lyrical Left During World War I." In *American Catholic Pacifism: The Influence of Dorothy Day and the Catholic Worker Movement*, edited by Anne Klejment and Nancy L. Roberts, 15–32. Westport, CN: Praeger, 1996

Kosek, Joseph. *Acts of Conscience: Christian Nonviolence and Modern American Democracy*. New York: Columbia University Press, 2009.

Kuehn, Evan. "'Fullness of the Spirit' and 'Fullness of Catholicity' in Ecclesial Communion." *International Journal of Systematic Theology* 11 (2009): 271–92.

Kurlansky, Mark. *Nonviolence: The History of a Dangerous Idea.* New York: Modern Library, 2006.

Lang, Anthony. "Authority and the Problem of Non-State Actors." In *Ethics, Authority and War: Non-State Actors and the Just War Tradition,* edited by Eric Heinze and Brent Steele, 1-15. New York: Palgrave-Macmillan, 2009.

Langan, John. "The Elements of St. Augustine's Just War Theory." *Journal of Religious Ethics* 12, no.1 (1984): 19–38.

Lawrence, Joel. *Bonhoeffer: A Guide for the Perplexed.* London: T&T Clark, 2011.

Lee, Gregory W. "Republics and Their Loves: Rereading *City of God* 19." *Modern Theology* 27 (2011): 553–81.

Lewy, Guenter. *Peace and Revolution: The Moral Crisis of American Pacifism.* Grand Rapids: Eerdmans, 1988.

Lovin, Robin. *Reinhold Niebhur and Christian Realism.* Cambridge: Cambridge University Press, 1995.

Lucas, George R., Jr. "'New Rules for New Wars' in International Law and Just War Doctrine for Irregular War." *Case Western Reserve Journal for International Law* (2011): 677–705.

Macquarrie, John. *The Concept of Peace.* New York: Harper and Row, 1973.

Maguire, Daniel C. *The Horrors We Bless: Rethinking the Just-War Legacy.* Minneapolis: Fortress Press, 2007.

Marion, Jean-Luc. "Resting, Moving, Loving: The Access to the Self according to Saint Augustine." *Journal of Religion* 91 (2011): 24–42.

Markus, R. A. "St. Augustine's Views on the 'Just War.'" In *The Church and War*, edited by W.J. Sheils. Studies in Church History 20. London: Basil Blackwell, 1983.

Markwell, Bernard Kent. *The Anglican Life: Radical Social Reformers in the Church of England and the Protestant Episcopal Church, 1846–1954.* Brooklyn: Carlson, 1991.

Marsh, Charles. *Reclaiming Dietrich Bonhoeffer: The Promise of His Theology*. New York: Oxford University Press, 1994.

Marsh, James L. and Anna Brown, eds. *Faith, Resistance, and the Future: Daniel Berrigan's Challenge to Catholic Social Thought*. New York: Fordham University Press, 2013.

Martens, Paul. *The Heterodox Yoder*. Eugene, OR: Cascade Books, 2011.

Martin, David A. *Pacifism: A Historical and Sociological Study*. New York: Schoken Books, 1966.

Mathewes, Charles. *A Theology of Public Life*. Cambridge: Cambridge University Press, 2007.

Mattox, John Mark. *Saint Augustine and the Theory of Just War*. London: Continuum, 2006.

McBrien, Richard. *The Church: The Evolution of Catholicism*. New York: HarperOne, 2008.

McBride, Jennifer. *The Church for the World: A Theology of Public Witness*. Oxford: Oxford University Press, 2012.

McGreevy, John. *Catholicism and American Freedom*. New York: W.W. Norton, 2003.

McNeal, Patricia. *Harder than War: Catholic Peacemaking in Twentieth-Century America*. New Brunswick, NJ: Rutgers University Press, 1992.

McThenia, Andrew W. "How This Celebration Began." Introduction to *Radical Christian and Exemplary Lawyer*, edited by Andrew W. McThenia. Grand Rapids: Eerdmans, 1995.

McThenia Andrew W., ed. *Radical Christian and Exemplary Lawyer: Honoring William Stringfellow*. Grand Rapids: Eerdmans, 1995.

Merriman, Brigid O'Shea. *Searching for Christ: The Spirituality of Dorothy Day*. Notre Dame: University of Notre Dame Press, 1994.

Mersch, Emile. *The Whole Christ*. Translated by John R. Kelly. Milwaukee: Bruce, 1938.

Milbank, John. *Theology and Social Theory*. Malden, MA: Wiley–Blackwell, 1993.

———. *The Word Made Strange: Theory, Language, Culture*. Oxford: Blackwell, 1997.

Miller, Orie. "Aggressive Peace Work." *Gospel Herald* 18 (1926): 858–59.

———. "Our Peace Policy." *Mennonite Quarterly Review* 3 (1929): 26–32.

Miller,Richard B. *Interpretations of Conflict: Ethics, Pacifism, and the Just-War Tradition*. Chicago: The University of Chicago Press, 1991.

Miller, William. "Dorothy Day." In *Saints Are Now: Eight Portraits of Modern Sanctity*, edited by John J. Delaney, 17-39. Garden City, NY: Doubleday, 1981.

———. *Dorothy Day: A Biography*. San Francisco: Harper and Row, 1982.

———. *A Harsh and Dreadful Love: Dorothy Day and the Catholic Worker Movement*. New York: Liveright, 1973.

Moskos, Charles C. and John Whiteclay Chambers, eds. *The New Conscientious Objection: From Sacred to Secular Resistance*. Oxford: Oxford University Press, 1993.

Murray, Harry. *Neglect Not Hospitality: The Catholic Worker and the Homeless*. Philadelphia: Temple University Press, 1990.

Murray, John Courtney. *Religious Liberty: Catholic Struggles with Pluralism*. Louisville: Westminster John Knox, 1993.

Musto, Ronald G. *The Catholic Peace Tradition*. Maryknoll, NY: Orbis Books, 1986.

Nation, Mark Thiessen. *John Howard Yoder: Mennonite Patience, Evangelical Witness, Catholic Convictions*. Grand Rapids: Eerdmans, 2005.

———, ed. *Karl Barth and the Problem of War, and Other Essays on Barth*. By John Howard Yoder. Eugene, OR: Cascade, 2003.

———. "The Vocation of the Church of Jesus the Criminal." In *William Stringfellow in Anglo-American Perspective*, edited by Anthony Dancer, 117-32. Aldershot, UK: Ashgate, 2005.

Nation, Mark Theissen, Anthony G. Siegrist, and Daniel Umbel. *Bonhoeffer the Assassin? Challenging the Myth, Recovering His Call to Peacemaking.* Grand Rapids: Baker Books, 2013.

Neuhaus, Richard John. “The War, the Churches, and Civil Religion.” *Annals of the American Academy of Political and Social Science* 387 (January 1970): 135–42

Newbigin, Leslie. *The Gospel in a Pluralist Society.* Grand Rapids: Eerdmans, 1989.

Niebuhr, Reinhold. *Beyond Tragedy.* New York: Charles Scribner’s Sons, 1938.

———. “A Critique of Pacifism.” In *Love and Justice: Selections from the Shorter Writings of Reinhold Niebuhr*, edited by D.B. Robertson, 241-47. Louisville: Westminster John Knox, 1957.

———. *Faith and History: Comparison of Christian and Modern Views of History.* New York: Charles Scribner’s Sons, 1949.

———. *An Interpretation of Christian Ethics.* Louisville: Westminster John Knox, 2013.

———. *Moral Man and Immoral Society: A Study in Ethics and Politics.* New York: Charles Scribner’s Sons, 1935.

———. *Nature and Destiny of Man.* 2 vols. Louisville: Westminster John Knox, 1996.

———. “Why the Christian Church is Not Pacifist.” In *The Essential Reinhold Niebuhr: Selected Essays and Addresses*, edited by Robert McAfee Brown, 102-22. New Haven: Yale University, 1986.

Nolan, Hugh Joseph, ed. *Pastoral Letters of the United States Catholic Bishops, Vol. 3: 1962–1974.* Washington, DC: National Catholic Council of Bishops, 1998.

Nugent, John C. *The Politics of Yahweh: John Howard Yoder, the Old Testament, and the People of God.* Eugene, OR: Cascade Books, 2011.

O'Connor, June. "Dorothy Day's Christian Conversion." *Journal of Religious Ethics* 18 (1990): 159–80.

O'Donovan, Oliver. *The Desire of Nations: Recovering the Roots of Political Theology*. Cambridge: Cambridge University Press, 1995.

———. *The Just War Revisited.* Cambridge: Cambridge University Press, 2003.

———. *Objects of Common Love: Moral Reflection and the Shaping of Community.* Grand Rapids: Eerdmans, 2002.

Ollenburger, Ben C. and Gayle Gerber Koontz, eds. *A Mind Patient and Untamed: Assessing John Howard Yoder's Contribution to Theology, Ethics, and Peacemaking*. Telford, PA: Cascadia, 2003.

Overholt, Thomas W. "Seeing Is Believing: The Social Setting of Prophetic Acts of Power." *Journal for the Study of the Old Testament* 23 (1982): 3–31.

Parrent, Allan M. "On War, Peace, and the Use of Force." In *The Crisis in Moral Teaching in the Episcopal Church*, edited by Timothy Sedgwick and Philip Turner, 94-113. Harrisburg, PA: Morehouse, 1992.

Pelton, Robert S. ed. *The Church as the Body of Christ.* Notre Dame: University of Notre Dame Press, 1963.

Peters, Ben. "Nature and Grace in the Theology of John Hugo." In *God, Grace, and Creation,* edited by Philip J. Rossi, 59–79.Annual Publication of the College Theology Society 55.Maryknoll, NY: Orbis Books, 2010.

Peterson, Andrew. *Sword of the Spirit, Shield of Faith: Religion in American War and Diplomacy.* New York: Random House, 2012.

Piehl, Mel. *Breaking Bread: The Catholic Worker and the Origin of Catholic Radicalism in America.* Philadelphia: Temple University Press, 1982.

———. "The Politics of Free Obedience." In *A Revolution of the Heart: Essays on the Catholic Worker*, edited by Patrick G. Coy, 177–216. Philadelphia: Temple University Press, 1982.

Pierce, Nathaniel W. and Paul L. Ward. *The Voice of Conscience: A Loud and Unusual Noise?* Charlestown, MA: Charles River, 1989.

Pius X. *Une Fois Encore* [Encyclical on the Separation of Church and State]. Vatican Website. June 1, 1907. http://www.vatican.va/holy_father/pius_x/encyclicals/documents/hf_p-x_enc_06011907_une-fois-encore_en.html.

Pius XI. *Nova Impendent* [Encyclical on the Economic Crisis]. Vatican Website.February 10, 1931. http://www.vatican.va/holy_father/pius_xi/encyclicals/documents/hf_p-xi_enc_02101931_nova-impendet_en.html.

Pius XII. *Mystici Corporis Christi* [Encyclical on the Mystical Body of Christ]. Vatican Website. June 29, 1943. http://www.vatican.va/holy_father/pius_xii/encyclicals/documents/hf_p-xii_enc_29061943_mystici-corporis-christi_en.html.

———. *Optatissima Pax* [Encyclical on Prescribing Public Prayers for Social and World Peace]. Vatican Website. December 18, 1947. http://www.vatican.va/holy_father/pius_xii/encyclicals/documents/hf_p-xii_enc_18121947_optatissima-pax_en.html.

———. *Summi Maeroris* [Encyclical on Public Prayers for Peace]. Vatican Website. July 19, 1950. http://www.vatican.va/holy_father/pius_xii/encyclicals/documents/hf_p-xii_enc_19071950_summi-maeroris_en.html.

Porter, Matthew and Myles Werntz. "On 'Seeing' Nonviolence in 1983: Nonviolence and Ecclesiology in Hauerwas and Yoder." *Conrad Grebel Review* (2011): 32–45.

Prather, Scott. *Christ, Power, and Mammon: Karl Barth and John Howard Yoder in Dialogue.* Edinburgh: T&T Clark, 2013.

Prusak, Bernard P. *The Church Unfinished: Ecclesiology through the Centuries.* Mahaw, NJ: Paulist, 2004.

Radner, Ephraim. *A Brutal Unity: The Spiritual Politics of the Christian Church.* Waco, TX: Baylor University Press, 2012.

———. *The End of the Church: A Pneumatology of Christian Division in the West.* Grand Rapids: Eerdmans, 1998.

———. *Hope among the Fragments: The Broken Church and Its Engagement of Scripture.* Grand Rapids: Brazos, 2004.

Ramsey, Paul. *The Just War*. New York: Scribner's, 1969.

Ramsey, Paul and Stanley Hauerwas. *Speak Up for Just War or Pacifism: A Critique of the United Methodist Bishops' Pastoral Letter "In Defense of Creation."* State College, PA: Penn State Press, 1988.

Rasmussen, Arne. "'The Curious Fact That . . . the Lord Always Puts Us on the Just Side': Reinhold Niebuhr, America and Christian Realism." *Studia Theologica* 66 (2012): 41–61.

Rhodes, Joel P. *The Voice of Violence: Performative Violence as Protest in the Vietnam Era.* Westport, CN: Praeger, 2001.

Riegle, Rosalie G. *Dorothy Day: Portraits by Those Who Knew Her.* Maryknoll, NY: Orbis Books, 2003.

Rose, Gideon. *How Wars End: Why We Always Fight the Last Battle.* New York: Simon & Schuster, 2010.

Rowland, Christopher. "William Stringfellow's Apocalpytic Hermeneutics." In *William Stringfellow in Anglo-American Perspective*, edited by Anthony Dancer, 138–52. Aldershot, UK: Ashgate, 2005.

Saint Joseph Baltimore Catechism. Baltimore, MD: Catholic Book Publishing Corp., 1995.

Schlabach, Gerald. "Is Milbank Niebuhrian Despite Himself?" *Conrad Grebel Review* 23, no. 2 (Spring 2005): 33–40.

———. "Just Policing and the Reevalution of War in a Less Divided Church." In *Just Policing, Not War: An Alternative Response to World Violence*, edited by Gerald Schlabach, 3–24. Collegeville, MN: Liturgical, 2007.

———. "Just Policing: How War Could Cease to Be a Church-Dividing Issue." *Journal of Ecumenical Studies* 41, no. 3–4 (Summer–Fall 2004): 409–30.

Serratelli, Arthur and Paul S. Fiddes. "The Word of God in the Life of the Church: A Report of International Conversations between the Catholic

Church and the Baptist World Alliance." Vatican Website. 2006–2010. http://www.vatican.va/roman_curia/pontifical_councils/chrstuni/Bapstist%20alliance/rc_pc_chrstuni_doc_20101213_report-2006-2010_en.html.

Shank, David A. and John Howard Yoder. "Biblicism and the Church." *Concern* 2 (1955): 67–101. Reprinted in *The Roots of Concern: Writings on Anabaptist Renewal 1952–1957*, edited by Virgil Vogt, 67-101. Eugene, OR: Cascade Books, 2009.

Sharp, Gene. *Nonviolent Action: A Research Guide*. New York: Garland, 1997.

———. *The Politics of Nonviolent Action*. Boston: Porter Sargent, 1974.

Shay, Jonathan. *Achilles in Vietnam: Combat Trauma and the Undoing of Character*. New York: Simon & Schuster, 1995.

Sicius, Francis J. "Prophecy Faces Tradition: The Pacifist Debate during World War II." In *American Catholic Pacifism: The Influence of Dorothy Day and the Catholic Worker Movement*, edited by Anne Klejment and Nancy L. Roberts, 66–76. Westport, CN: Praeger, 1996.

Simpson, Gary M. *War, Peace, and God*. Minneapolis: Fortress Press, 2007.

Sittser, Gerald. *A Cautious Patriotism: The American Churches and the Second World War*. Chapel Hill: University of North Carolina Press, 2010.

Slocum, Robert Boak, ed. *Prophet of Justice, Prophet of Life: Essays on William Stringfellow*. New York: Church, 1997.

Smith, J. Warren. "Augustine and the Limits of Preemptive and Preventitive War." *Journal of Religious Ethics* 35, no.1 (March 2007): 141–62.

Smith, Ruth L. "Reinhold Niebuhr and History: The Elusive Liberal Critique." *Horizons* 15 (Fall 1988): 283–98.

SNCC. "Student Nonviolent Coordinating Committee Position Paper: On Vietnam." Position statement made available by The Sixties Project, 1993. http://www2.iath.virginia.edu/sixties/HTML_docs/Resources/Primary/Manifestos/SNCC_VN.html.

Stackhouse, John G. *Making the Best of It: Following Christ in the Real World.* Oxford: Oxford University Press, 2008.

Stanley, Brian. *The World Missionary Conference, Edinburgh 1910.*Grand Rapids: Eerdmans, 2009.

Stassen, Glen, ed. *Just Peacemaking: Ten Practices for Abolishing War.* Cleveland: Pilgrim, 1998.

———. "The Unity, Realism and Obligatoriness of Just Peacemaking." *Journal of the Society of Christian Ethics* 23, no. 1 (Spring–Summer 2003): 171–94.

Statnick, Roger A. "Dorothy Day's Religious Conversion: A Study in Biographical Theology." PhD diss., University of Notre Dame, 1983.

Stayer, James M. *Anabaptists and the Sword.* Lawrence, KS: Coronado, 1973.

Stevenson, William R., Jr. *Christian Love and Just War: Moral Paradox and Political Life in St. Augustine and His Modern Interpreters.* Macon, GA: Mercer University Press, 1987.

Stone, Ronald H. *Politics and Faith: Reinhold Niebuhr and Paul Tillich at Union Seminary in New York.* Macon, GA: Mercer University Press, 2012.

Stout, Harry. *Upon the Altar of the Nation: A Moral History of the American Civil War.* New York: Penguin Books, 2007.

Stringfellow, William. "An American Tragedy." *Christian Living*, January 1967.

———. "The Bishops at O'Hare: Mischief and a Mighty Curse." *Christianity and Crisis* 34, no. 15 (September 16, 1974): 195–96.

———. The Case against Christendom and The Case against Pierre Berton." In *The Restless Church: A Response to the Comfortable Pew*, edited by William Kilbourn, 11–25. Philadelphia: J.P. Lippincott, 1966.

———. "The Christian Lawyer as Churchman." *Christian Scholar* 40 (1957): 211–13.

———. "The Church in the City." *Theology Today* 20, no. 2 (July 1963): 145–51.

———. *Instead of Death.* New York: Seabury, 1963.

———. *Conscience and Obedience*. Waco, TX: Word Books, 1977.

———. *Count It All Joy: Reflections on Faith, Doubt and Temptation Seen through the Letter of James*. Grand Rapids: Eerdmans, 1967.

———. "The Demonic in American Society." *Christianity and Crisis* 29, no. 16 (September 29, 1969): 244–48.

———. *Dissenter in a Great Society*. New York: Holt, Reinhart, and Winston, 1966.

———. "Do We Need a New Barmen Declaration?" *Christianity and Crisis* 33, no. 22 (December 24, 1973): 275.

———. "Ecumenicity and Entomology: New Church Problem." *Christian Century* 81, no. 41 (October 7, 1964): 1239–41.

———. *An Ethic for Christians and Other Aliens in a Strange Land*. Waco, TX: Word Books, 1973.

———. The Ethics of Violence." *Cross Beat* (March 1966): 3–6.

———. "Evangelism and Conversion." *International Journal of Religious Education* 40, no. 3 (November 1963): 6–7, 22.

———. *Free in Obedience*. New York: Seabury, 1967.

———. "God, Guilt and Goldwater." *Christian Century* 81, n0. 36 (September 2, 1964): 1079–183

———. The Great Society as a Myth." *Dialog* 5, no. 4 (Autumn 1966): 252–57.

———. "Harlem, Rebellion and Resurrection." *Christian Century* 87, no. 45 (November 11, 1970): 1345–48.

———. *Imposters of God: Inquiries into Favorite Idols*. Washington, DC: Witness Books, 1969.

———. "Jesus the Criminal." *Christianity and Crisis* 30, no. 10 (June 8, 1970): 119–122.

———. "The Law, the Church, and the Needs of Society." *Proceedings of the Thirty-Second Annual Convention of the Canon Law Society of America* (1970): 45–52.

———. The Life of Worship and the Legal Profession. New York: New York National Council, 1955.

———. "Liturgy as Political Event." *Christian Century* 82, no. 51 (December 22, 1965): 1573–75.

———. "The Mission of the Church in the Decadent Society." *The Episcopal Theological School Journal* 8 (1962): 3–8.

———. "Must the Stones Cry Out?" *Christianity and Crisis* 32, no. 18 (October 30, 1972): 233–38.

———. *My People Is My Enemy: An Autobiographical Polemic.* New York: Holt, Reinhart, and Winston, 1964.

———. "Open Letter to Jimmy Carter." *Sojourners*, October 1976, 7–8.

———. "An Open Letter to the Presiding Bishop." *The Witness* 63 (January 1980): 10–11.

———. "Politics on Block Island." *Sojourners*, January 1978, 17–18.

———. *A Private and Public Faith.* Grand Rapids: Eerdmans, 1962.

———. *A Second Birthday.* Garden City, NY: Doubleday, 1970.

———. "The Secret of Christian Unity." *Christian Century* 78, no. 37 (September 13, 1961): 1073–76.

———. *A Simplicity of Faith: My Experience in Mourning.* Nashville: Abingdon, 1982.

———. "The State, the Church and the Reality of Conscience." *IDOC Internazionale* 31 (September 11, 1971): 19–26.

———. "Technocracy and the Human Witness." *Sojourners,* November 1976.

———. "Too Little, Too Late, and too Lily–White." *The Christian Scholar* 45, no. 1 (Spring 1962): 78–80.

———. "The Unity of the Church as the Witness of the Church." *Anglican Theological Review* 46 (October 1964): 394–400.

———. The Violence of Despair." *Notre Dame Lawyer* 40 (1965): 527–33.

———. "Watergate and Romans 13." *Christianity and Crisis* 33, no. 10 (June 11, 1973): 110–12.

———. "Why Is Novak So Uptight?" *Christianity and Crisis* 30, no. 19 (November 30, 1970): 259.

———. "The Witness of a Remnant." *The Witness* 72 (1989): 21, 23.

Stringfellow, William and Anthony Towne. *The Bishop Pike Affair: Scandals of Conscience and Heresy, Relevance and Solemnity in the Contemporary Church.* New York: Harper and Row, 1967.

———. *The Death and Life of Bishop Pike.* Garden City, NY: Doubleday, 1976.

———. *Suspect Tenderness: The Ethics of the Berrigan Witness.* New York: Holt, Reinhart and Winston, 1971.

Swift, Louis. *The Early Fathers on War and Military Service.* Wilmington, DE: Michael Glazier, 1983.

Sykes, Stephen. *Power and Christian Theology*. London: Continuum, 2006.

Tanner, Kathryn. *Theories of Culture: A New Agenda for Theology.* Minneapolis: Fortress Press, 1997.

Tillard, J.–M.–R. *Flesh of the Church, Flesh of Christ: At the Source of the Ecclesiology of Communion.* Translated by Madeliene Beaumont. Collegeville, MN: Liturgical, 2001.

Toews, Paul. Review of *Nevertheless: A Meditation on the Varieties and Shortcomings of Religious Pacifism,* by John Howard Yoder. *Direction* 1 (1972): 134–35.

Toole, David. *Waiting for Godot in Sarajevo: Theological Reflections on Nihilism, Tragedy, and Apocalypse.* Boulder, CO: Westview, 1998.

Turse, Nick. *The Complex: How the Military Invades Our Everyday Life.* New York: Metropolitan Books, 2008.

United States Conference of Catholic Bishops. *The Challenge of Peace: God's Promise and Our Response, A Pastoral Letter on War and Peace.* United States Conference of Catholic Bishops Website. May 3, 1983. http://www.usccb.org/upload/challenge–peace–gods–promise–our–response–1983.pdf.

Valliere, Paul. "The Spirituality of War." *Union Seminary Quarterly Review* 38 (1983): 5–14.

Vatican Council II. *Gaudium et Spes* [Dogmatic Constitution on the Church in the Modern World]. July 12, 1965. Vatican website. http://www.vatican.va/archive/hist_councils/ii_vatican_council/documents/vat-ii_cons_19651207_gaudium-et-spes_en.html.

Volf, Miroslav. *Exclusion and Embrace: A Theological Exploration of Identity, Otherness, and Reconciliation.* Nashville: Abingdon, 1996.

Von Harnack, Adolf. *Militia Christi: The Christian Religion and the Military in the First Three Centuries.* Translated by David M. Gracie. Philadelphia: Fortress Press, 1981.

Warner, Michael. *Changing Witness: Catholic Bishops and Public Policy, 1917–1994.* Grand Rapids: Eerdmans, 1995.

Watts, Craig M. "Church Unity and the Necessity of Nonviolence." *Journal of Ecumenical Studies* 39 (2002): 368–75.

Weaver, Alain Epp. "On Exile: Yoder, Said, and a Theology of Return." *Cross Currents* 52 (2003): 439–61.

———. "Unjust Lies, Just Wars? A Christian Pacifist Conversation with Augustine." *Journal of Religious Ethics* 29, no.1 (Spring 2001): 51–78.

Weaver, J. Denny. "Forgiveness and (Non)Violence: the Atonement Connections, *Mennonite Quarterly Review* 83 (2009): 319–347.

———. "The John Howard Yoder Legacy: Wither the Second Generation?." *Mennonite Quarterly Review* 77 (2003): 451–71.

———. "Violence in Christian Theology." *Crosscurrents* 51 (2001): 150–76.

Weigel, George. Tranquillitas Ordinis: *The Present Failure and Future Promise of American Catholic Thought on War and Peace.* Oxford: Oxford University Press, 1987.

Werntz, Myles. "War in Christ's World: Bonhoeffer and Just Peacemaking on War and Christology." *Dialog: A Journal of Theology* 50 (2011): 90–96.

Williams, Rowan. *On Christian Theology.* Malden, MA: Blackwell, 2000.

Wink, Walter. *Engaging the Powers: Discernment and Resistance in a World of Domination*. Philadelphia: Fortress Press, 1992.

———. "Stringfellow on the Powers." In *Radical Christian, Exemplary Lawyer: Honoring William Stringfellow*, edited by Andrew W. McThenia, 17-31. GrandRapids: Eerdmans, 1995.

———. "William Stringfellow: Theologian of the Next Millennium, A Review Essay." *Cross Currents* 45, no. 2 (Summer 1995): 205–16.

Winright, Tobias. Just Cause and Preemptive Strikes in the War on Terrorism." *Journal of the Society of Christian Ethics* 26, no. 2 (Fall–Winter 2006): 157–81.

———. "The Liturgy as a Basis for Catholic Identity, Just War Theory, and the Presumption Against War." In *Catholic Identity and the Laity*, edited by Tim Muldoon, 134–51. Annual Publication of the College Theology Society 54. Maryknoll, NY: Orbis Books, 2009.

———. "Two Rival Versions of Just War Theory and the Presumption Against Harm in Policing." *Annual of the Society of Christian Ethics* 18 (1998): 221–39.

Wylie–Kellerman, Bill, ed. *A Keeper of the Word: Selected Writings of William Stringfellow*. Grand Rapids: Eerdmans, 1994.

Yoder, John Howard. *Anabaptism and Reformation in Switzerland: An Historical and Theological Analysis of the Dialgoues between Anabaptists and Reformers*. Edited by C. Arnold Snyder. Translated by David Stassen and C. Arnold Snyder. Kitchener, ON: Pandora, 2003.

———. "The Anabaptist Dissent: The Logic of the Place of the Disciple in Society." In *The Roots of Concern: Writings on Anabaptist Renewal 1952–1957*, edited by Virgil Vogt, 29–44. Eugene, OR: Cascade Books, 2009.

———. "Anabaptist Vision and Mennonite Reality." In *Consultation on Anabaptist–Mennonite Theology*, 1–46. Fresno, CA: Council of Mennonite Seminaries, 1970.

———. "Another Option to a Just War." *This Day*, July 1968.

———. "Armaments and Eschatology." *Studies in Christian Ethics* 1, no. 1 (1988): 43–61.

———. *As You Go: The Old Mission in a New Day.* Focal Pamphlet 5. Scottdale, PA: Herald, 1961.

———. "Binding and Loosing." In *The Royal Priesthood*, edited by Michael G. Cartwright. Grand Rapids: Eerdmans, 1994. Originally published in *Concern* 14 (1967): 2–32.

———. *Body Politics: Five Practices of the Christian Community Before the Watching World.* Scottdale, PA: Herald, 1984.

———. "Caesar and the Meidung." *Mennonite Quarterly Review* 23 (1949): 76–98.

———. "Capital Punishment and the Bible." *Christianity Today,* February 1960.

———. *Christian Attitudes to War, Peace, and Revolution.* Elkhart, IN: Mennonite Co-op Bookstore, 1983

———. *Christian Witness to the State.* Scottdale, PA: Herald, 1992.

———. "The Constantinian Sources of Western Social Ethics." In *The Priestly Kingdom: Social Ethics as Gospel,* 135-50. Notre Dame: University of Notre Dame Press, 1984.

———. "Der Statt im Neuen Testament." *Der Mennonit,* December 1957.

———. "Developing a Christian Attitude toward War." *Journal of the Methodists for Church*

Renewal (April 1966): 8–12.

———. "Discipleship as Missionary Strategy." *Christian Ministry,* January–March 1955.

———. *Discipleship as Political Responsibility.* Scottdale, PA: Herald, 1964. Reprint 2000.

———. *The Ecumenical Movement and the Faithful Church.* Scottdale, PA: Mennonite Publishing House, 1958.

———. "The Free Church Ecumenical Style." *Quaker Religious Thought* 10/11 (1968): 29–38.

———. "The Hermeneutics of Peoplehood." In *The Priestly Kingdom: Social Ethics as Gospel*, 15-45. Notre Dame: University of Notre Dame Press, 1984.

———. "A Historic Free Church View." In *Christian Unity in North America: A Symposium,* edited by J. Robert Neslon, 87–97. St. Louis: Bethany, 1958.

———. *The Jewish-Christian Schism Revisited*, ed. Michael G. Cartwright and Peter Ochs. Grand Rapids: Eerdmans, 2003.

———. *Karl Barth and the Problem of War.* Nashville: Abingdon, 1970.

———. "The Lordship of Christ and the Power Struggle." In *The Lordship of Christ: Proceedings of the Seventh Mennonite World Conference, August 1–7, 1962, Kitchener, Ontario*, 507–512. Elkhart, IN: Mennonite Publishing House, 1962.

———. "The Nature of the Unity We Seek." In *The Royal Priesthood*, edited by Michael G. Cartwright. Grand Rapids: Eerdmans, 1994. Originally published in *Religion in Life* 26 (1957): 215–22.

———. *Nevertheless: A Meditation on the Varieties and Shortcomings of Religious Pacifism*. Scottdale, PA: Herald, 1971.

———. "The New Testament View of Ministry." *Gospel Herald*, February 8, 1955.

———. *Nonviolence: A Brief History*. Edited by Paul Martens, Matthew Porter, and Myles Werntz. Waco, TX: Baylor University Press, 2009.

———. *The Original Revolution: Essays in Christian Pacifism*. Scottdale, PA: Herald, 1971.

———. "The Otherness of the Church." In *The Royal Priesthood*, edited by Michael G. Cartwright. Grand Rapids: Eerdmans, 1994. Originally published in *Concern* 8 (1960): 19–29.

———. Papers. Mennonite Church USA Archives. Goshen, IN.

———. "The Peace Testimony and Conscientious Objection." *Gospel Herald*, January 21, 1958.

———. "A People in the World: Theological Interpretation." In *Concept of the Believers' Church,* edited by James Leo Garrett, 250–83. Scottdale, PA: Herald, 1969.

———. "The Place of Peace Witness in Missions." *Gospel Herald*, January 3, 1961.

———. *The Politics of Jesus*. Grand Rapids: Eerdmans, 1972.

———. *The Politics of Jesus*. 2nd ed. Grand Rapids: Eerdmans, 1994.

———. *Preface to Theology*. Edited by Stanley Hauerwas and Alex Sider. Grand Rapids: Brazos, 2002.

———. "Reinhold Niebuhr and Christian Pacifism." *Mennonite Quarterly Review* 29 (1955): 101–17.

———. *Revolutionary Christianity: The 1966 South American Lectures*. Edited by Paul Martens, Mark Thiessen Nation, Matthew Porter, and Myles Werntz. Eugene, OR: Cascade, 2012.

———. *The Royal Priesthood: Essays Ecclesiastical and Ecumenical.* Edited by Michael G. Cartwright. Grand Rapids: Eerdmans, 1994. Reprint Scottdalle, PA: Herald, 1998.

———, trans. *The Schleitheim Confession*. Scottdale, PA: Herald, 1977.

———. *A Theology of Mission: A Believers Church Perspective*. Edited by Gayle Gerber Koontz and Andy Alexis-Baker. Downers Grove, IL: IVP Academic, 2014.

———. "The Theology of the Church's Mission." *Mennonite Life*, January 1966.

———. "The Things That Are Ceasar's." Pts. 1–3. *Christian Living*, July–Septemter 1960.

———. "Vietnam: A Just War?" *His*, April 1968.

———. "Vietnam: Another Option." *His*, May 1968.

———. *The War of the Lamb: The Ethics of Nonviolence and Peacemaking*. Edited by Glenn Stassen, Mark Theissen Nation, and Matt Hamsher. Grand Rapids: Brazos, 2009.

———. "The Way of Peace in a World of War." *Gospel Herald*, July 18, 1961.

———. "The Way of the Peacemaker." In *Peacemakers in a Broken World*, edited by John A. Lapp, 111–25. Scottdale, PA: Herald Press, 1969.

———. "What Are Our Concerns?" In *The Roots of Concern: Writings on Anabaptist Renewal 1952–1957*, edited by Virgil Vogt, 164–76. Eugene, OR: Cascade Books, 2009.

———. "When the State Is God." *Gospel Herald*, February 16, 1954.

———. "Why Should We Speak to Government?" *The Mennonite*, January 25, 1966.

Yoder, Thomas R. Neufeld. "Ecclesiology and Policing: Who Calls the Shots?" *Conrad Grebel Review* 26, no.2 (2008): 91–101.

Young, Nigel. *Pacifism in the Twentieth Century*. Syracuse, NY: Syracuse University Press, 1999.

Zahn, Gordon. *Another Part of the War: The Camp Simon Story*. Amherst, MA: University of Massachusetts, 1979.

———. *War, Conscience and Dissent*. New York: Hawthorn Books, 1967.

Zimmerman, Earl. *Practicing the Politics of Jesus: The Origin and Significance of John Howard Yoder's Social Ethics*. Telford, PA: Cascadia, 2007.

Zwick, Mark and Louise. *The Catholic Worker Movement: Intellectual and Spiritual Origins*. Mahwah, NJ: Paulist, 2005.

Index